Julien Duvivier

Manchester University Press

DIANA HOLMES AND ROBERT INGRAM *series editors*
DUDLEY ANDREW *series consultant*

FRENCH FILM DIRECTORS

Chantal Akerman MARION SCHMID
Auteurism from Assayas to Ozon: Five Directors KATE INCE
Jean-Jacques Beineix PHIL POWRIE
Luc Besson SUSAN HAYWARD
Bertrand Blier SUE HARRIS
Catherine Breillat DOUGLAS KEESEY
Robert Bresson KEITH READER
Laurent Cantet MARTIN O'SHAUGHNESSY
Leos Carax GARIN DOWD AND FERGUS DALY
Marcel Carné JONATHAN DRISKELL
Claude Chabrol GUY AUSTIN
Henri-Georges Clouzot CHRISTOPHER LLOYD
Jean Cocteau JAMES S. WILLIAMS
Jacques Demy DARREN WALDRON
Claire Denis MARTINE BEUGNET
Marguerite Duras RENATE GÜNTHER
Jean Epstein CHRISTOPHE WALL-ROMANA
Georges Franju KATE INCE
Jean-Luc Godard DOUGLAS MORREY
Mathieu Kassovitz WILL HIGBEE
Diane Kurys CARRIE TARR
Patrice Leconte LISA DOWNING
Louis Malle HUGO FREY
Chris Marker SARAH COOPER
Georges Méliès ELIZABETH EZRA
Negotiating the Auteur JULIA DOBSON
François Ozon ANDREW ASIBONG
Marcel Pagnol BRETT BOWLES
Maurice Pialat MARJA WAREHIME
Jean Renoir MARTIN O'SHAUGHNESSY
Alain Resnais EMMA WILSON
Jacques Rivette DOUGLAS MORREY AND ALISON SMITH
Alain Robbe-Grillet JOHN PHILLIPS
Eric Rohmer DEREK SCHILLING
Coline Serreau BRIGITTE ROLLET
Bertrand Tavernier LYNN ANTHONY HIGGINS
André Téchiné BILL MARSHALL
François Truffaut DIANA HOLMES AND ROBERT INGRAM
Agnès Varda ALISON SMITH
Jean Vigo MICHAEL TEMPLE

Julien Duvivier

BEN MCCANN

Manchester University Press

Copyright © Ben McCann 2017

The right of Ben McCann to be identified as the author of this work has been asserted
by him in accordance with the Copyright, Designs and Patents Act 1988.

Published by Manchester University Press
Altrincham Street, Manchester M1 7JA, UK
www.manchesteruniversitypress.co.uk

British Library Cataloguing-in-Publication Data is available

ISBN 978 0 7190 9114 8 *hardback*
ISBN 978 1 5261 3955 9 *paperback*

First published by Manchester University Press in hardback 2017

This edition first published 2019

The publisher has no responsibility for the persistence or accuracy of URLs for any external or third-party internet websites referred to in this book, and does not guarantee that any content on such websites is, or will remain, accurate or appropriate.

Typeset by Out of House Publishing

To my children: Monty, Cleo, and Marlowe

Contents

LIST OF PLATES	*page* viii
SERIES EDITORS' FOREWORD	x
ACKNOWLEDGEMENTS	xii
Introduction: we need to talk about Julien	1
1 **The 'impure' auteur**	8
2 **Duvivier's silent films**	26
3 **Sound, image, Gabin: Duvivier and the 1930s**	54
4 **'Piloting with concentration': Julien goes to Hollywood**	110
5 **1946–56: darkness and light**	142
6 **Late style**	186
Conclusion	225
FILMOGRAPHY	230
SELECT BIBLIOGRAPHY	248
INDEX	249

List of plates

All plates appear between pages 101 and 109.

1. A man at work: Duvivier on the set of *Anna Karenina* (1948), courtesy of Photofest — page 101
2. Confronting the spectator: Camille Bert in the opening shot of *Haceldama ou le prix du sang* (1919), courtesy of La Cinémathèque Française — 101
3. Piloting with concentration: Duvivier prepares to shoot *Au bonheur des dames* (1930), courtesy of Getty Images — 102
4. The grasping woman: a father–daughter relationship turns sour in *David Golder* (1930), courtesy of Getty Images — 102
5. Creating a myth: Jean Gabin in *Pépé le Moko* (1937), courtesy of Christophel Collection — 103
6. Frenchie goes to Hollywood: Gabin (left) in *The Impostor* (1944), courtesy of Alamy — 104
7. There's no fool like an old fool: Gabin's tenderness meets Danièle Delorme's duplicity in *Voici le temps des assassins* (1956), courtesy of Christophel Collection — 104
8. Star quality, Hollywood style: Henry Fonda and Ginger Rogers in *Tales of Manhattan* (1942), courtesy of Alamy — 105
9. The uncanny on show: Edgar Barrier and a set of masks in *Flesh and Fantasy* (1943), courtesy of Photofest — 105
10. The quintessential Duvivier image: a bloodied Michel Simon at the mercy of the crowd in *Panique* (1946), courtesy of Alamy — 106
11. Authorial tussles: Orson Welles comes between producer Alexander Korda, star Vivien Leigh, and director Duvivier on the set of *Anna Karenina* (1948), courtesy of Christophel Collection — 106

12	A lighter touch: Fernandel and a broken egg in *L'Homme à l'imperméable* (1957), courtesy of Getty Images	**107**
13	The group fractured by guilt and suspicion: Bernard Blier, Noël Roquevert, Serge Reggiani, and Danielle Darrieux in *Marie-Octobre* (1959), courtesy of Alamy	**107**
14	Juju the Terrible and BB: Duvivier directs Bardot in *La Femme et le pantin* (1959), courtesy of Alamy	**108**
15	When an old master met a new waver: Duvivier prepares Jean-Pierre Léaud for filming in *Boulevard* (1960), courtesy of Alamy	**109**
16	The model professional: adept, efficient, versatile, courtesy of Wikimedia	**109**

Series editors' foreword

To an anglophone audience, the combination of the words 'French' and 'cinema' evokes a particular kind of film: elegant and wordy, sexy but serious – an image as dependent upon national stereotypes as is that of the crudely commercial Hollywood blockbuster, which is not to say that either image is without foundation. Over the past two decades, this generalised sense of a significant relationship between French identity and film has been explored in scholarly books and articles, and has entered the curriculum at university level and, in Britain, at A-level. The study of film as art-form and (to a lesser extent) as industry, has become a popular and widespread element of French Studies, and French cinema has acquired an important place within Film Studies. Meanwhile, the growth in multi-screen and 'art-house' cinemas, together with the development of the video industry, has led to the greater availability of foreign-language films to an English-speaking audience. Responding to these developments, this series is designed for students and teachers seeking information and accessible but rigorous critical study of French cinema, and for the enthusiastic filmgoer who wants to know more.

The adoption of a director-based approach raises questions about auteurism. A series that categorises films not according to period or to genre (for example), but to the person who directed them, runs the risk of espousing a romantic view of film as the product of solitary inspiration. On this model, the critic's role might seem to be that of discovering continuities, revealing a necessarily coherent set of themes and motifs which correspond to the particular genius of the individual. This is not our aim: the auteur perspective on film, itself most clearly articulated in France in the early 1950s, will be interrogated in certain volumes of the series, and, throughout, the director will be treated as one highly significant element in a complex process of film production and reception which includes socio-economic and political determinants, the work of a large and highly skilled team of artists and technicians, the mechanisms of production and distribution, and the complex and multiply determined responses of spectators.

The work of some of the directors in the series is already well known outside France, that of others is less so – the aim is both to provide informative and original English-language studies of established figures, and to extend the range of French directors known to anglophone students of cinema. We intend the series to contribute to the promotion of the formal and informal study of French films, and to the pleasure of those who watch them.

DIANA HOLMES
ROBERT INGRAM

Acknowledgements

I would like to thank Diana Holmes and Robert Ingram for initially commissioning this book, and Matthew Frost and Paul Clarke at Manchester University Press for their immense patience and assistance; Hazel Bird for her fine copy-editing; the staff and librarians at the BFI Library (London), the Bibliothèque du Film, the Bibliothèque des Littératures Policières, the Bibliothèque du Cinéma François Truffaut, the Bibliothèque Nationale de France, Institut National Audiovisuel, the Cinémathèque de France (Paris), the Centre National de la Cinématographie (Bois d'Arcy), the Cinémathèque Française Archives (St. Cyr), and the Margaret Herrick Library (Los Angeles); Getty Images, Alamy, Photofest, and the Christophel Collection; my colleagues at the University of Adelaide Peter Pugsley, John Walsh, and John West-Sooby for their advice and good humour, and Colin Crisp for his suggestions. Most of all, I am indebted to my family, both in England and Australia, who have had to live with the wonderful world of Julien Duvivier for an awfully long time. My final special thanks go, of course, to Jacqueline, Monty, Cleo, and Marlowe: my very own *belle équipe*.

Introduction: we need to talk about Julien

> When the French cinema dies, it might do worse than find his [Duvivier's] name written across its retina.
> (Alistair Cooke 1971: 125)
>
> No one speaks of Julien Duvivier without apologising.
> (Dudley Andrew 1997: 283)

Once upon a time, Julien Duvivier (1896–1967) was considered one of the world's great film directors. He was beloved by Orson Welles, Rouben Mamoulian, Frank Capra, and John Ford, while Ingmar Bergman once admitted that, of all the careers that he would have liked to have had, it would be Duvivier's. The English novelist Graham Greene, in a much-quoted article from 1938, rated Duvivier and Fritz Lang as 'the two greatest fiction directors still at work' (1972: 195). Jean Renoir's 1967 obituary tribute, 'Duvivier, ce professionel', focused on Duvivier's love of 'l'ouvrage bien fait' ('work well done') as his signature legacy. His frequent scriptwriter Maurice Bessy said he had the best career of any French director, primarily because he never stopped working (1977: 49).

Indeed, over the course of a five-decade career, Duvivier zigzagged between multiple genres. He turned his hand to, among others, literary adaptations (*Poil de carotte* [1932], *Pot-Bouille* [1957]), biblical epic (*Golgotha* [1935]), the 'sketch' film (*Un Carnet de bal* [1937], *Tales of Manhattan* [1942]), comedy (the Don Camillo series [1952, 1953]), the 'Hollywood' film (*The Great Waltz* [1938]), *film noir* (*Voici le temps des assassins* [1956]), poetic realism (*Pépé le Moko* [1937]), and the propaganda film (*Untel père et fils* [1945]). Such fluidity and range make the case for Duvivier as a director of exemplary adaptability and proficiency. Like his Hollywood contemporaries Raoul Walsh, Michael Curtiz, and William Wyler, Duvivier could seemingly turn his hand to anything, imbuing each of his assignments with startling visuals or deft narrative turns while all the while serving the film's source material as efficiently as possible. Duvivier never left anything to chance – lighting, editing, framing, and camera movement were all impeccably planned. From the silent period right through to the late 1960s, Duvivier often joined forces with the same group of actors and technicians, returning to them over a series of consecutive projects. He worked with some of French cinema's most acclaimed screenwriters, including Henri Jeanson, Charles Spaak, and René Barjavel, and collaborated with some of French cinema's abiding stars, such as Harry Baur, Fernandel, and Jean Gabin. For a period in the 1930s, he was French cinema's most respected and exportable director, and prizes quickly followed. *La Fin du jour* (1939), for instance, won Best Foreign Film at the National Board of Review Awards, came second in the New York Film Critics Circle Awards, and won the Best Screenplay Award at the Venice Biennale.

Nowadays, Duvivier's stylistic qualities are discussed in terms of their intricacy, eclecticism, and modernity. Eight of his films were shown in newly restored versions at the Festival Lumière in Lyon in October 2015. As I write this, Criterion Collection (2015) is preparing a November 2015 release of a four-disc DVD box set of his 1930s films; its website notes Duvivier's 'formidable innate understanding of the cinematic medium'. And yet this was not always the case. For a director synonymous with the technical beauty, narrative fluidity, and poise of French 'classical' cinema exemplified by *La Fin du jour*, a strange phenomenon occurred from about 1947 to the late 1990s: slowly, but very surely, Julien Duvivier and most of his films were all but erased from film history. This, I think, was due to a number of reasons, some trivial, some important: Duvivier's spiky personality, the perceived uneven quality of his canon, his penchant for literary adaptations, his unwillingness to 'explain' his craft, the difficulty in tracking down his films (some are lost forever, and many others have never been released on VHS or DVD), the overemphasis on *La Belle équipe* (1936) and *Pépé le Moko*, and his critical marginalisation at the hands of *Cahiers du cinéma* and *Positif*. Even today, when we think of the key directors of the French pre-war era, Duvivier is often the one omitted from a list usually headed by Jean Renoir, René Clair, Jacques Feyder, and Marcel Carné. The language used to describe Duvivier was, and often remains, shrill and highly patronising. Jacques Rivette once wrote that Jean Gabin could be considered 'comme un metteur en scène presque davantage que Duvivier' ('almost more of a director than Duvivier') (1957: 26). Jean-Luc Godard included Duvivier in a long list of directors he accused of desecrating French cinema with their 'fausse technique' ('false technique'): 'vos mouvements d'appareil sont laids parce que votre sujet est mauvais, vos acteurs jouent mal parce que vos dialogues sont nuls, en un mot, vous ne savez pas faire de cinéma parce que vous ne savez plus ce que c'est' (1998: 194).[1] Internet sites and film festival retrospectives still now use words such as 'plodder', 'journeyman', 'Jack of all trades', 'workaholic', and 'hack' to describe him. For Dudley Andrew, 'so many of his fifty-odd films are embarrassing to watch' (1997: 283); David Thomson describes Duvivier's style as 'spruce but seldom original or interesting' (1975: 156).[2] Slowly, but very surely, an enduring discourse took root. It is high time to rehabilitate Duvivier.

So, the purpose of this book, the first ever full-length English-language study of Duvivier, is to argue that Duvivier not only was a consummate technician and an assiduous craftsman but also created a scrupulous moral universe. Duvivier's world is frequently cruel and pessimistic, harrowing and misanthropic. He reflected in 1946, while filming *Panique* (1946), perhaps his darkest film, that he was perpetually drawn to the murkier side of human nature: 'Je sais bien qu'il est plus aisé de réaliser des films poétiques, doux, charmants avec de belle photographie, mais ma nature me pousse vers des thèmes âpres, noirs, amers' (Duvivier 1946: 10).[3] Again and again, he returned to the same core themes: pessimism, misanthropy, the

---

1 'Your camera movements are ugly because your subjects are bad, your casts act badly because your dialogue is worthless; in a word, you don't know how to create cinema because you no longer even know what it is.'
2 In a rare attempt to balance the argument, Michael Atkinson calls Duvivier a 'demi-auteur'; one of the many 'overlooked and under-remembered artistes who helped build cinema history and often did so with hypnotic brio, and yet remain unpantheonised' (2009).
3 'I know it is much easier to make films that are poetic, sweet, charming, and beautifully photographed, but my nature pushes me towards harsh, dark and bitter material.'

cruelty of the crowd, fatalism, defective memory, masquerading, exile, and the (im)possibility of escape.

Another objective is to fit Duvivier's work within broader political and social conditions. Duvivier always considered his most obviously 'political' work to be anything but. In 1957, he told Charles Ford and René Jeanne (1957) that '*La Belle Equipe* n'avait pourtant aucun caractère politique. Ou bien, alors, tous les films qui mettraient en scène des ouvriers seraient des œuvres de gauche?'[4] Duvivier's cinema, unlike Jean Renoir's or André Cayatte's, rarely grappled with politics or wider debates about history and nation. Yet, occasionally, his films offered up contested ideological readings. While Duvivier was politically agnostic through a very conflictual period of French history, I will show how his films engaged with significant historical developments, such as pre-war anti-Semitism, class and race in America, the climate of reprisal in post-Occupation France, and the emergence of 1950s youth culture. Given that Duvivier has often been accused of misogyny, I shall also look at his take on gender politics and demonstrate the problematic status of women in his work, either as a pre-war threat to homosocial bonds or a post-war symbol of social disunity. The twin endings of *La Belle équipe* epitomise such tensions: one features a 'happy' ending, in which order is restored, the *femme fatale* banished, and male camaraderie and collective endeavour championed; the bleaker ending sees one man murder another while the divisive woman looks on. The fact that Duvivier pushed for the darker finale, against the wishes of worried producers who preferred the restorative, trouble-free conclusion, is a useful yardstick for us to measure Duvivier's ethical stance.

How these themes were then presented on a stylistic level is another component of the book. Duvivier's visual style can sometimes seem invisible: this is a filmmaker who tended to reject the ostentatious and the obvious. Yet Duvivier's 'touch' is often highly noticeable, most conspicuously in the use of expressive close-ups and double exposures, highly fluid camera movements, strong central performances by established stars and new actors, and the nuanced incorporation of music, costume, and production design. Duvivier rarely left anything to chance – lighting, editing, framing, and camera movement

---

4 '*La Belle équipe* has no political character whatsoever; unless every film that treats the working class must be considered leftist.'

all cohere to 'become' the meaning of his films. He favoured characters on the periphery of society, often trapped in down-at-heel settings, at the mercy of a *femme fatale* who threatened to tear asunder the male group. These narrative patterns were then coded in the *mise en scène*; Duvivier's theatre of cruelty often took place in the city, in dark, claustrophobic spaces, with walls and roofs pressing in on characters and diagonal shafts of light casting ominous shadows. As Sam Rohdie (2015) notes, '[t]he design of scenes is like the narratives, which are enclosures from which there is no way out, no relief, liberation, no alternatives – only limits, like the burdens and memories of the past from which his characters seek a respite in vain'.

My final aim is to reveal how Duvivier is all about opposites: misanthropic versus good-hearted, cruel versus sentimental, auteur versus *metteur en scène*, commerce versus art, French versus 'international', Hollywood versus artisanal, 'maniaque de la précision' versus 'rêveur'. Like his two conflicting writers in *La Fête à Henriette* (1952), Duvivier was a jumble of contradictions; it is this productive conflict that forms the warp and weft of his remarkable career.

Although I am sensitive to the risks of carving up Duvivier's work into neat periods, the book will follow a chronological format that uses key moments of technological, historical, and cultural change as staging posts in Duvivier's career. Chapter 1 will look in more detail at the Duvivier 'touch', his formal and thematic preoccupations, and will give an overview of the way his reputation has shifted over time and of his early life. Chapter 2 will focus on the twenty films he made during the silent period. Chapter 3 is set in the 1930s and will show how Duvivier transitioned into the era of the talkies, helped to establish the properties of the 'classic French cinema', and began injecting bleaker, more muted tones into his work. Chapter 4 takes us to America, where Duvivier worked from 1940 to 1945, and tells of Duvivier's interfacing with Hollywood and the various artistic and professional compromises he was obliged to make. Duvivier returned to post-Occupation France in 1945, and Chapter 5 recounts the difficulties he faced on his return. It will examine in close detail a set of films that oscillated in tone from breezy comedy to *noir*-drenched paranoia, and make the case for a director of dynamic variability. Chapter 6 charts the final years of Duvivier's career, arguing that he developed a compelling 'late style' that implanted his later work with a startling modernity.

A final brief word about the book's approach. Duvivier made sixty-eight films, which means that an in-depth discussion of all of them will be impossible, given the limitations of the book series to which I am contributing. There have already been many discussions of Duvivier's work, his technique, and his importance as a figure in French cinema in book chapters, journal articles, and online essays, but they have tended to focus, broadly speaking, on films he made with Jean Gabin, such as *La Belle équipe* and *Pépé le Moko*. In this book, some films will be analysed in detail based on their historical importance or aesthetic significance within Duvivier's career. More familiar works, such as the two aforementioned, plus the likes of *La Bandera* (1935), *Un Carnet de bal*, the Don Camillo series, and *Pot-Bouille*, will also be discussed, but we also need to look closely at the less well-known Duvivier films to see how they are equally representative of his artistic prowess and how they showcase his exemplary technical and narrative control. I have watched fifty-seven of his sixty-eight films (i.e. 84 percent) during the course of writing this book. Those films that I have not seen, but refer to in passing, are marked with an asterisk (*). Information about these asterisked films has been gleaned from print and online plot summaries and *dossiers de presse*.

References to Duvivier's films throughout the book are as complete as possible. Many reviews, particularly of his early films and those from his time in America, were consulted at the extensive electronic database at the Bibliothèque du Film at the Cinémathèque Française in Paris. The scanning of these reviews has often resulted in the omission and deletion of page numbers and dates of publication.

All translations from French to English are my own unless stated otherwise.

References

Andrew, D. (1997), 'Julien Duvivier', in *International Dictionary of Films and Filmmakers*, vol. 2, 3rd edn, ed. Laurie Collier Hillstrom, Detroit, St. James Press, pp. 281–3.

Criterion Collection (2015), 'Eclipse Series 44: Julien Duvivier in the 1930s', available at www.criterion.com/boxsets/1136-eclipse-series-44-julien-duvivier-in-the-thirties, accessed 6 September 2016.

Atkinson, M. (2009), 'Time Regained', *Moving Image Source*, available at www.movingimagesource.us/articles/time-regained-20090504, accessed 6 October 2015.

Bessy, M. (1977), *Les Passagers du souvenir*, Paris, Editions Albin Michel.

Cooke, A. (1971), *Alistair Cooke at the Movies*, London, Penguin.

Duvivier, J. (1946), 'Julien Duvivier fête ses 30 ans de cinéma: Interview with Marcel Idzkowski', *Cinémonde*, 639, 29 October, pp. 10–11.

Ford, C. and R. Jeanne (1957), 'Entretiens radiophoniques avec Julien Duvivier', 8 episodes broadcast weekly on Radio France from 15 April to 3 June 1957, available at http://www.franceculture.fr/emissions/la-nuit-revee-de/voix-nue-julien-duvivier-12-partie-1-et-25-1ere-diffusion-16-et-17011995, accessed 6 September 2016.

Godard, (1998), J.-L. 'Le Jeune cinéma a gagné', *Arts*, 719, 22–28 April, p. 5.

Greene, G. (1972), *The Pleasure-Dome: The Collected Film Criticism, 1935–40*, ed. John Russell Taylor, London, Secker and Warburg.

Renoir, J. (1967), 'Duvivier, ce professionnel', *Le Figaro littéraire*, 6 November.

Rivette, J. (1957), 'Six personnages en quête d'auteur', *Cahiers du cinéma*, 71, May, pp. 16–29.

Rohdie, S. (2015), 'Love unto Death', *Screening the Past*, 39, available at www.screeningthepast.com/issue-39, accessed 6 October 2015.

Thomson, D. (1975), *A Biographical Dictionary of the Cinema*, 1st edn, London, Secker & Warburg.

1

The 'impure' auteur

Je ne suis qu'un artisan consciencieux.[1]
(Duvivier, in Leprohon 1968: 203)

Ferdinand: Je dirais c'est comme *Pépé le Moko*.
Marianne: Qui?
Ferdinand: *Pépé le Moko*.
Marianne: Qui est-ce?
Ferdinand: Décidément, tu ne connais rien![2]
Pierrot le Fou (Jean-Luc Godard, 1965)

Accounts of Duvivier's life usually go along the following lines. He was a talented director in the early days of sound cinema who luckily managed to marshal around him teams of actors and technicians to create a set of films that tapped into a particular mindset of 1930s pre-war France. Duvivier was then invited to Hollywood, where he churned out a series of forgettable B-movies before returning to France in the mid-1940s to a much-changed landscape. By this time, his *noir* sensibilities and penchant for literary adaptation were deemed out of sync with the need for cinematic renewal championed by the critics of *Cahiers du cinéma*, and so he spent the rest of his career as a director for hire, trudging across Europe making

---

[1] 'I'm really just a conscientious craftsman.'
[2] FERDINAND: Just like *Pépé le Moko*.
MARIANNE: Who?
FERDINAND: *Pépé le Moko*.
MARIANNE: Who's that?
FERDINAND: Wow, you really don't know much!

nondescript versions of pot-boiler French fiction and irking everyone in the process, from Vivien Leigh to Brigitte Bardot to Jacques Rivette.

There are fragments of truths here, but the reality is far more complex, and needs unpacking. Much of this book will examine the key themes and recurring visual patterns and formal properties of Duvivier's films and identify a particular worldview that emanates from the silent films right through to *Diaboliquement vôtre* (1967). In short, the book will answer the following question: what makes a Duvivier film a Duvivier film?

Beginnings

Very little is known about Duvivier's early life, not least because of his extreme reticence to talk about his past. We do know that he was born in Lille, in northern France, on 8 October 1896 and grew up in the Catholic area of the city. Later, he was sent over the border to Froyennes, in Belgium, for a strict Jesuit education. His father was a travelling salesman who ran a photographic development lab at the back of the house; his mother was pianist at the Lille Conservatoire and inculcated into Duvivier an early love of poetry. His friend Maurice Bessy – a film journalist who later worked with Duvivier as a screenwriter – traced the root of Duvivier's future shyness and prickliness back to this *petit bourgeois* upbringing, where meals were eaten in silence and any show of intimacy discouraged.

Exempted from fighting in the First World War, Duvivier and his father left Lille in late 1914 to escape the invading German army and headed to Paris. It was here that Duvivier's passion for the theatre was developed. He joined the Théâtre de l'Odéon (his first role was in March 1915, in Frédéric Soulié's *La Closerie des genêts*). Much has been made of Duvivier's stage fright – it appears that in November 1915, during a matinee performance of a Molière play for war-wounded soldiers, Duvivier forgot his lines and suffered a mild panic attack, causing the stage curtains to be prematurely lowered. The incident is often recounted in recollections of Duvivier's early career (there is a similar scene in *La Fin du jour* [1939] when Michel Simon's ageing actor forgets his lines and is whistled off the set: for Simon, read Duvivier), but it did not finish off his theatrical career, as many claimed. He returned to the stage in the summer of 1916 in the Belgian comedy *Le Mariage de Mademoiselle Beulemans* (which Duvivier later adapted for the screen in 1927).

Unlike Marcel Carné or René Clair, who entered the film industry as journalists and theoreticians, Duvivier set foot in the profession almost by chance. In late 1915, he met André Antoine. A key figure in the Duvivier story, Antoine was the pioneering theatre director of the Théâtre-Libre (1888–97) and the Théâtre-Antoine (1897–1906) and had integrated naturalist practices across the company's output. After seeing Duvivier on stage, Antoine offered Duvivier work as his assistant at the newly formed Société Cinématographique des Auteurs et Gens de Lettres (SCAGL), the *film d'art* branch of Pathé, whose remit was to produce high-level literary adaptations designed to entice a more elite audience to the cinema. Duvivier assisted Antoine on several SCAGL productions – *Les Frères corses* (1917), *Le Coupable* (1917), *Les Travailleurs de la mer* (1918), *La Terre* (1921, an early film version of a Zola novel), and *L'Arlésienne* (1922) – which all stayed true to Antoine's aesthetic preoccupations.

As a theatre director now turning to film, Antoine believed that cinema's key objective was 'to convince the spectator of the verisimilitude of the spaces and actions represented on the screen' (Abel 1988: 105). Influenced as much by nineteenth-century traditions of Impressionist painting and literary naturalism as by the technical possibilities of film, Antoine formulated a set of filmic practices that would assist in creating and maintaining this *verism*. He formed a cohort of actors who would work from film to film; used multiple camera set-ups and movements to create a set of dynamic, fluid visual compositions; and, most importantly, insisted, wherever possible, on filming on location. The new-found portability of lighting and recording equipment and the accessibility of natural surroundings led to an upsurge in 'pictorialist-naturalist' films, including *L'Homme du large* (1920), *L'Appel du sang* (1920), *Jocelyn* (1922), and *La Brière* (1925), in which directors such as Marcel L'Herbier, Louis Mercanton, Léon Poirier, and Jacques de Baroncelli, as well as Antoine's aforementioned output, each placed non-professional actors within real landscapes and offered up stories within the social realism field advocated by Antoine. Writing about Antoine's theories of film while he worked for SCAGL, Susan Hayward notes his vital influence on French realist cinema: 'location shooting [...] multi-camera point of view [...] an editing style that would involve the spectator in the narrative [...] the importance of the scenario [...] and the need for professional writers who would transpose the literary classics' (2005: 86). Hayward might just as easily be describing Duvivier here.

Indeed, these diverse working practices would soon be adopted by Duvivier, most notably in the juxtaposition of location and studio shooting. Across his career, we see constant examples of sequences shot on location, whether in the teeming mass of Les Halles in *Voici le temps des assassins* (1956), the nocturnal streets of pre-wall Berlin in *La Grande vie* (1960), or the Moroccan desert of *Les Cinq gentlemen maudits* (1931). All of these spaces might just as well have been meticulously reconstructed in a Joinville studio, as Marcel Carné and Alexandre Trauner, the great director–designer team of 1930s and 1940s French cinema, frequently did. But Duvivier was convinced that Antoine's approach was more cinematic. He absorbed his mentor's revolutionary approach to film realism in all areas – acting, subject matter, narrative technique, and style – and returned to it again and again over his career.

Duvivier's next step was to graduate to full-blown director – at the end of the war, he found himself in Marseille, where he was invited by Gaston Haon, from the Army's Cinema Service, to come with him to Bordeaux to direct a feature film for his recently established film company. This would eventually lead, in 1919, to Duvivier's debut feature, *Haceldama ou le prix du sang*, and the start of an extraordinarily fruitful period of work. As we shall see, *Haceldama* was an accomplished piece of work for a first-time director, and it foreshadowed a number of the director's future preoccupations with style and form.

Restoring a reputation

Duvivier has long been airbrushed out of French cinema for three reasons. Firstly, a critical consensus that dates back to at least the mid-1950s has marginalised him to the point of obliteration. For these critics, Duvivier was a journeyman director, without a signature style or personal approach, bereft of invention, and reliant upon the scripts of others. In short, he was not Jean Renoir, or Robert Bresson, or Jean Cocteau. Even before *Cahiers du cinéma* had published François Truffaut's infamous 1954 article/assassination, 'Une certaine tendance du cinéma français' (Truffaut 1954), in which the world of the auteur and the *metteur en scène* were forever separated, critics were in the habit of condemning Duvivier as representative of the old guard of film-making. Jean-Pierre Vivet (1951) lambasted him in a review of *Sous le ciel de Paris* ('[Il] me fait penser à ces octogénaires qui pour se mettre au goût du jour vont danser le be-bop [...] seulement M. Duvivier n'a plus ses jambes'[3]), while Michel Dorsday singled him out in his 1952 *Cahiers* review of Christian-Jacque's *Adorables créatures*, entitled 'Le cinéma est mort'. Dorsday (1952: 55) criticised Duvivier, as well as Jacques Becker and Jean Delannoy, for creating cinema that was 'mort sous la qualité, l'impeccable, le parfait'.[4] Reviewing Duvivier's *Marianne de ma jeunesse* (1955), Truffaut (1955: 5) ranked the film among those 'qui naissent démodés' and 'arrivent, dans le cinéma français, avec quinze ans de retard'.[5] Because his 'personality' did not shine through, Duvivier was regarded as a mere *metteur en scène*, a 'stager'. Duvivier has been trapped in this echo chamber for six decades.

Secondly, Duvivier was regarded as undiscerning; he made too many films, and was unable to discriminate between the assignments he was offered. Maurice Bessy (1977: 49) described Duvivier's favoured working method as follows: 'créer pour lui, c'était tenter. C'était aussi se tromper pour mieux réussir ensuite'.[6] Such working practices – efficient, fast, adept – are highly sought after in today's film culture, but French critics have sometimes viewed Duvivier's resourcefulness with suspicion. At a time when Duvivier was regularly acclaimed in domestic critical circles, Roger Leenhardt (1935: 332), critic for *L'Esprit*, reproached him for making too many films between 1933 and 1935:

> La production d'un cinéaste n'est valable que si une unité de ton, de style, d'atmosphère [...] exprime une direction de pensée, une vision personnelle du monde. Aussi, quoi qu'il en soit de leurs réalisations, attendons-nous toujours beaucoup d'un Clair, d'un Feyder, d'un

---

3 'He makes me think of those men in their eighties who dance to bebop in a bid to stay trendy [...] The only thing is, Mr. Duvivier's legs have gone.'
4 'dead under the weight of its impeccable, perfect quality'.
5 'which are born out of date', 'arrived in French cinema fifteen years too late'.
6 'For him, to create was to attempt something. It was also to make a mistake, so as to be more successful next time.'

> Renoir ou d'un Chenal – rien d'un Duvivier. Et nous trouvons par-
> faitement ridicule la mousse faite autour de ce 'probe artisan', de ce
> 'bon ouvrier du cinéma français'![^7]

For Leenhardt, it was considered improper to work so quickly, to produce so many films. Because Duvivier was so prolific, no discernible style, thematic consistency, or personal commitment could emerge from his work. Yet, in the space of eighteen months in 1956–7, Duvivier directed Jean Gabin in a *noir*, Fernandel in a comedy-thriller, and Danielle Darrieux in a Zola adaptation. Nowadays, such narrative swerves – whether in the work of Richard Linklater, Takashi Miike, or François Ozon – are hailed as hallmarks of a director's boldness and versatility. One can easily imagine the response in *Cahiers* had Howard Hawks or Billy Wilder – exact contemporaries of Duvivier – glided between such divergent stories. Perhaps this incessant give and flex in Duvivier's mid-1950s period, and the fluid flitting from genre to genre, have made him a victim of his own eclecticism. Once a hack, always a hack.

Thirdly, Duvivier's significance as a director has been diminished due to his unsavoury reputation among his colleagues. While personal behaviour and idiosyncrasies should not be used to 'explain' a director's particular style, in the case of Duvivier, it is clear that his on-set conduct has come to influence how he has been remembered. In interview after interview with actors, screenwriters, and technicians, Duvivier comes across as tyrannical, unlikeable, mean-spirited, and in constant conflict with those who worked with him. Charles Spaak, screenwriter of *La Belle équipe* (1936) and *Panique* (1946), said that working with him was like doing military training (Lagouche 2011). Jean Gabin christened him 'Juju the Terrible' (Leprohon 1968: 249). When the esteemed writer Jean Aurenche, who worked with Duvivier on the Brigitte Bardot vehicle *La Femme et le pantin* (1959), was asked what was it like working with him, he responded simply: 'Je le déteste' ('I hate him') (1975: 17). Actors were frequently the target of Duvivier's

---

7 'The production of a cineaste has value so long as a unity of tone, style, and atmosphere [...] convey a particular way of thinking, a personal vision of the world. Consequently, whatever their films turn out to be, we always expect a great deal from a Clair, a Feyder, a Renoir or a Chenal, and nothing from a Duvivier. And we find all the froth written about this "honest craftsmen", this "fine workman in the French cinema", perfectly ridiculous.'

ire. Bardot, George Sanders, Jean-Claude Brialy, Pierre-Richard Willm, Danielle Darrieux, and Robert Le Vigan all recount Duvivier's dictatorial demeanour; his implacable, inscrutable air; and his seeming willingness to pick a fight at the slightest provocation.

But does all of this mean Duvivier was a bad filmmaker? Just because he did not convey the easy conviviality of a Renoir, a Chabrol, or a Guédiguian, he should not be dismissed as defective or second rate. I argue that he should rather be seen as the model professional: adapting to specific narrative and visual conditions and studio requirements, positioning himself at the apex of a hierarchy of talent and specialist expertise, and inculcating his visual 'touch' into successive assignments. Being the 'best' director is not just about artistic and thematic consistency. Being a director is also about responding to particular scripts in ways that would impress producers and could be made quickly and within budget, something that Duvivier scrupulously guaranteed. Duvivier's guiding principles were not about setting trends or delivering messages but simply keeping on working, and the sheer longevity of his career is testament to this reliability. Yes, he was a perfectionist, and obstinate, but he made nearly seventy films. Jean-Pierre Melville was an equally authoritarian figure but shot only thirteen films over a quarter of a century.

For every uncomfortable recollection by a disgruntled colleague, an industry figure queued up to praise Duvivier. For many, he was the most technically astute of French directors. Henri Jeanson (1937: 3) noted that the most noticeable aspect of his style was 'la technique, avant toute chose' ('technique above all else'). Henri Alekan, the great cinematographer who worked with Duvivier on *Anna Karenina* (1948), recalled his precision: 'On pouvait savoir à l'avance, simplement à la lecture du script, où on allait placer la caméra, quel objectif on devait mettre pour tel angle' (Niogret 2010: 56).[8] For Michel Romanoff, his assistant on ten films, 'c'était un homme qui savait tout faire [...] Il pouvait corriger un décor [...] Si le directeur de la photo était défaillant, il prenait sa place et c'était parfait' (Niogret 2010: 93–4).[9] Actors too redressed the balance, recalling Duvivier's ability to get the

8 'We knew in advance, simply by reading the script, where we were going to put the camera, what lens we should use for a certain angle.'
9 'He was a man who could do anything [...] He could correct a set [...] If the director of photography was unable to work, he would replace him, and he would do so perfectly.'

best from them with only a few words of direction. Danièle Delorme (in Niogret 2010: 73) said: 'C'est un des metteurs les plus directifs que j'ai eu'; Louis Jouvet (1967) added that he was one of the rare directors 'qui vous donne envie de tourner la scène suivante'.[10]

Since the late 1990s, attempts have been made to repair Duvivier's reputation. To celebrate the centenary of his birth, a roundtable was convened at Florence in November 1996 where he was dubbed a 'cinéaste complet' ('complete filmmaker') (Garnier 1996). Lenny Borger's 1998 article in *Sight and Sound* kickstarted a rediscovery of Duvivier's films; this came at the same time as Ginette Vincendeau's (1998) detailed account of *Pépé le Moko* (1937) was published by the British Film Institute. Three books on Duvivier were then released – Yves Desrichard's *Julien Duvivier: Cinquante ans de noirs destins* (2001), Eric Bonnefille's two-volume *Julien Duvivier: Le Mal aimant du cinéma français* (2002a, 2002b), and Hubert Niogret's *Julien Duvivier: 50 ans de cinéma* (2010), the last of these to mark a two-month-long Duvivier retrospective at the Cinémathèque Française in Paris. While examining the extensive *dossiers de presse* on Duvivier's work in various Paris archives, I detected an explicit shift in his critical reputation, from cool detachment to a warmer acceptance. Though it would be a stretch to argue that Duvivier has been restored to the lofty position he commanded in the late 1930s, we have at least reached a point where his legacy and his diverse output are being re-evaluated. In this regard, it is time to lay our cards on the table. Duvivier is an auteur.

Adaptateur or *auteur*?

Duvivier himself would not agree. He consistently maintained that a film's style was dictated by its subject and not its director. In 1934, he famously outlined his approach to film-making:

> Trop de gens s'imaginent que le cinéma est un art d'amateur, qu'on a la vocation et que la foi suffit pour faire naître des chefs-d'œuvre. Au cinéma, la révélation brutale d'une personnalité inexpérimentée n'existe pas. Le génie, c'est un mot, le cinéma c'est un métier, un rude métier que l'on acquiert. Personnellement, plus je travaille, plus je

---

10 'He was one of the most hands-on directors I ever worked with'; 'who made you want to film the next scene'.

> m'aperçois que j'apprends et que je ne sais rien proportionnellement aux infinies possibilités cinématographiques [...] Rien chez moi ne se crée sans effort.[11]

The principal reason given to deny Duvivier the status of auteur is that he is a perennial adapter, turning more than fifty pieces of literature (novels, plays, short stories) into films. In this sense, by merely staging the works of others in ways that are 'theatrical' and visually lacklustre, we might term Duvivier an 'impure' auteur. He may be in charge of the budget, the *découpage*, and the choice of actors, but he is compromised when it comes to directing his own screenplays and layering them with a robust visual style or personal touch. Moreover, if we follow Leenhardt's earlier perspective, Duvivier's lack of a quality-control filter means that his body of work can never claim auteur status because it is so dispersed (in tone, in genre, in look) and so it is hard to detect thematic continuities in it.

Duvivier's 'impurity' may also stem from the fact that he not only adapted texts but also collaborated with screenwriters on those adaptations. Many directors, such as Duvivier, Marcel Carné, Claude Autant-Lara, Christian-Jaque, Henri Decoin, and Henri Verneuil, were seen not so much as part of a *cinéma d'auteur* or a *politique des auteurs* as a *politique des tandems*, which was in vogue in French cinema from the 1930s to the 1960s. In the twenty-one films Duvivier made from 1946 to 1967, he worked three times with Charles Spaak, six times with René Barjavel, and six times with Henri Jeanson. Yet these partnerships with different writers allowed a different Duvivier to emerge each time. For example, the films he made with Spaak were bleak and often brutal. At the end of *La Belle équipe*, Jean (Jean Gabin) describes to the gendarme who has come to arrest him the worker's collective they had established earlier: 'C'était une belle idée: trop belle pour marcher.'[12] That one line sums up Duvivier and Spaak's

---

11 'Too many people imagine that the cinema is an amateur's art, that one has a calling and that faith is all one needs to create a masterpiece. The sudden revelation of an inexperienced personality in filmmaking is a myth. Genius is just a word; filmmaking is a craft, a tough craft that must be learned. Personally, the more I work, the more I realise how little I know in proportion to the infinite possibilities of cinematic expression [...] For me, to create things takes effort' (in Borger 1998: 30).
12 'It was a lovely idea, but too lovely to ever really work.'

worldview. The partnership with Jeanson ran from pre-war (*Pépé le Moko, Un Carnet de bal* [1937]) to post-*Panique* comedies (*La Fête à Henriette* [1952]) and the *drame psychologique* (*Marie-Octobre* [1959]). Jeanson brought an acerbic wit to Duvivier's work (in *Marie-Octobre*, amid recriminations about past treachery, one character tells another 'Nous n'allons tout de même pas te dresser un Arc de Triomphe en margarine'[13]). These partnerships amplify and embellish Duvivier's authorial status.

And so, Duvivier *is* an auteur. In this sense, I am following Niogret (2010: 8–9), who also argues for Duvivier's auteur status: 'Si être un auteur de films, c'est exprimer sa personnalité et les thématiques qui le préoccupent, à travers la mise en scène [...] Julien Duvivier est un auteur de films'.[14] Duvivier's films are consistently visually articulate and assiduously cast, designed, shot, and produced. Even though he might be working from scripts by Spaak and Jeanson, we are still watching 'a Julien Duvivier film'. Duvivier is still guiding his writers with the dialogue, the framing devices, the voiceovers, the characterisation, and so on. He is both 'author' and 'technician'. Duvivier is also spoken of as a highly technical and efficient director who always prepared a detailed *découpage* in which shots, camera angles, and actors' movements would be precisely calibrated. Sets would only be built that were required for the shooting of the scene, guaranteeing an on-budget and on-schedule production. Leenhardt's indiscriminateness suddenly becomes Duvivier's prolificness.

A further measure of Duvivier's authorial status comes from the complete control he exerted on set. He was the master builder. Review after review praises him for knowing how to make a film, and usually contains phrases such as 'Il connaît son métier' or 'C'est un film bien construit'.[15] A 1981 retrospective of his career defined Duvivier's notion of *mise en scène* as 'comment réussir une séquence' ('how to successfully pull off a sequence') (Simsolo 1981: 100). While this A + B = C 'art' of Duvivier's films might at first glance appear piecemeal, unadventurous even (linking together individual sequences in the hope of forming a balanced whole), Duvivier's skill was to present such sequences in highly formal and technical terms.

13 'We won't be building you an Arc de Triomphe out of margarine.'
14 'If being an auteur is about expressing one's personality and thematic preoccupations through *mise en scène* [...] then Julien Duvivier is an auteur.'
15 'He knows how to do his job'; 'It's a well put-together film.'

His visual brio frequently mixed together realism, fantasy, impressionism, and expressionism to create worlds that were nightmarish and claustrophobic, or tender and romantic.

Another feature of Duvivier's films is the 'paroxystic moment'. His films contain frequent examples of 'paroxysms', or sudden explosions of verbal or physical violence. This bringing of a scene to a violent conclusion from a tense build-up can be traced back to Duvivier's theatrical apprenticeship under André Antoine and to an understanding that a slow accretion of details before an outburst of violence is infinitely more dramatically satisfying. Such eruptive tonal changes happen quickly, and often without warning. In *Chair de poule* (1963), Daniel (Robert Hossein) throws a pan of boiling oil into an attacker's face; in *Voici le temps des assassins*, Catherine (Danièle Delorme) is ripped apart by a dog; and, in an extraordinary scene in *Pépé le Moko*, the treacherous Régis (Charpin) is executed to the accompanying hectic sounds of an accidentally triggered pianola. It was at that very moment, wrote the English novelist and film critic Graham Greene, that Duvivier 'admirably rais[ed] the thriller to a poetic level' (1972: 145).

Auteur theory can be critiqued because it privileges a few directors over the many and creates false and misleading dichotomies that suggest that some directors are not worthy of analysis. This book will attempt to point towards the lesson drawn from Duvivier's career – that monolithic blocks established by the *politique des auteurs* in the 1950s need to be demolished, or at the very least picked apart. Duvivier straddles the avant-garde and the popular, the commercial and the art-house, the adapter and the auteur. As this book will show, Duvivier continually succeeds at this balancing act.

Themes and patterns

Cutting across Duvivier's films are the following key themes and narrative patterns, which I shall discuss in more detail over the course of the book.

Men's stories ...

Duvivier (1959: 14) had a lifelong penchant for what he called 'histoires d'hommes' ('men's stories'). Several films feature a set of conflicts, clashes, or combat – between men and women (*Voici le temps des assassins*), men and other men (*La Bandera* [1935]), and men and authority (*The Impostor* [1944]). His films are frequently homosocial and ultra-masculine, and often revolve around troubled father–son relationships, whether real or symbolic. In Duvivier's world, men prefer each other's company. This is exemplified by *La Belle équipe*, with one character remarking that 'un bon copain, ça vaut mieux que toutes les femmes du monde'.[16] Mateship is often configured as a way of reasserting male values.

... but not women's stories

Charges of misogyny have frequently been levelled at Duvivier. Burch and Sellier (1996: 226) call him a 'vieil expert en misogynie' ('a long-standing expert in misogyny') due to the frequent central conflict in his films between the 'good' male and a 'dangerous' female figure. Viviane Romance's *sale garce* (evil bitch) in *La Belle équipe* has become even more hostile in *Panique*. Here, Romance double-crosses Michel Simon by planting a clue in his room that shows him to be a murderer who is then lured to a violent, mob-chased death. Indeed, *Panique* demonstrated the resurgence of *film noir* in the post-war period, this time as an exemplar of the viciously misogynistic *réalisme noir*, which appeared to scapegoat women for war-time collaboration. In *Pépé le Moko*, the women attached to Pépé's gang are brutalised, and Inès, Pépé's lover, leads him to his death. Even the rich Gaby is subjugated to an older man. *Maria Chapdelaine* (1934), *Un Carnet de bal*, *Lydia* (1941), *Anna Karenina*, *Au royaume des cieux* (1949), and *La Grande vie* all feature women as the major protagonists, but Duvivier is more interested in how the male(s) interact with them than in critiquing the gendered distribution of agency and empowerment.

'Black realism'

Duvivier has often been described as a 'cinéaste de la noirceur' ('a bleak filmmaker'). Critics refer to the sadistic treatment of his characters, as if they were 'des mouches prisonnières sous un verre retourné' ('flies trapped beneath a glass') (Simsolo 1981: 103). *Panique*

---

16 'a good bloke is worth more than all the women in the world'.

begins with a tramp lying across a public bench while his dog scavenges through dustbins. It ends with a song whose ironic lyrics echo around the town square: 'l'amour, c'est la beauté du monde' ('love is the beauty of the world'). In between, our 'hero', Michel Simon, has been hounded to his death by a crowd baying for blood. Happiness, solidarity, friendship, and love are all illusions.[17] Duvivier is drawn to marginalised characters who are often suicidal (Anna Karenina, *Poil de carotte* [1932]). In *Pépé le Moko*, Jean Gabin kills himself; he becomes a sacrificial lamb to be punished for believing in freedom and love. Pessimism, despair, existential nihilism, deception, and duplicity course through these works.

The outsider coming in

Many of Duvivier's films feature the arrival of an outsider into a world heavily regulated by strict gender, spatial, or social frameworks and systems. (Albert Lapierre entering the Brussels brasserie in *Le Mariage de Mademoiselle Beulemans* [1927], or Dita Parlo's Denise making her way tentatively to her uncle's store in *Au bonheur des dames* [1930], or Gaby entering the Algiers Casbah in *Pépé le Moko* and falling in love). Often, the role of the Duvivier outsider is to overturn the routines and practices of the social order. Within these worlds, a theatre of cruelty slowly unravels. It often takes place in the city but can also be staged in retirement homes, hilltop garages, or isolated country estates.

The group

Duvivier often establishes idealised micro-communities that gradually fall apart as inherently good people (often men) are brought down by the machinations of others (usually women) or by their own inherent weaknesses and internal conflicts. *Les Cinq gentlemen maudits*, *Le Paquebot Tenacity* (1934), *La Fin du jour*, and *Marie-Octobre* all present at the outset coherent groups gradually riven by suspicion, doubt, and jealousy. Often, the film's claustrophobic *mise en scène* will collude in that destruction (the African bush in *The Impostor*, the old people's home in *La Fin du jour*, or the drawing room in *Marie-Octobre*).

---

17 Unsurprisingly, it was Duvivier himself who wrote these lyrics.

Style and technique

The following list offers examples of Duvivier's intrinsic norms that recur from film to film.

Setting

A strongly evoked sense of space is a recurring element of Duvivier's films. Leprohon (1968: 209) refers to Duvivier's innate ability to form 'une atmosphère qui colle à l'intrigue' ('an atmosphere that clings to the plot'). This sensitivity to ambience and place can be detected in works as diverse as *Au bonheur des dames*, *The Impostor*, *The Great Waltz* (1938) and *Pot-Bouille* (1957); more specifically, rivers, lakes, and seas play important roles in *Haceldama*, *La Belle équipe*, *Black Jack* (1950), *Sous le ciel de Paris* (1951), and *La Chambre ardente* (1962). The opening shots of *Pépé le Moko* cut from an Algiers police station (shot at studios in Joinville, in south-east Paris) to documentary footage of the Casbah. Duvivier's skill in gluing together 'interior and exterior settings, open and constrained spaces, uniformly lit or mysterious, involving slow editing and fast, level camera and highly variable angles' would become a hallmark of his career (Crisp 2002: xxiii). The effect of this juxtaposition in *Pépé le Moko* underpins key themes: the impossibility of escape and the exotic or impenetrable allure of the colonial space. Time and again, Duvivier plays on contrasting locations – often early in a film – to showcase technical dexterity and his adeptness at cross-cutting, but also to paraphrase what will later become the film's central core concerns. Like the Casbah, the Salvation Army soup kitchen (*La Charrette fantôme* [1939]), a retirement home for ageing actors (*La Fin du jour*), a girls' boarding school (*Au royaume des cieux*), and a mansion deep in the Black Forest (*La Chambre ardente*) are all imprisoning spaces that offer glimpses of escape but ultimately lead to madness and death. Often, Duvivier intercuts documentary footage of a real space with its studio-built equivalent; the resulting strangeness adds to the dreamlike nature of the film. Sam Rohdie (2015) notes that Duvivier's films brim with 'communal dances, funfairs, merry-go-rounds, the cancan, opera, concerts, parades, festivities, audiences, scenes of crowds turning round and round'. The circular nature of these trajectories suggests both freedom and escape *and* enclosure from which there is no way out. The scene in which Monsieur Hire is buffeted to and fro in his dodgem car in *Panique* is a beautiful metaphor for that film's cruelty.

'Colour'

Here is Jean Fayard (1935) reviewing *La Bandera*: 'Ce reportage sur la légion [...] sent la vérité à tous les instants.'[18] Duvivier's films are full of 'colour'. Authentic sights and sounds, real places shot on location, and documentary inserts all layer his films with truthfulness and 'being there-ness'. Duvivier spent his career looking for ways to inculcate an 'atmosphere' into each film. Even the minor films towards the end of his career are frequently saturated with a specific look, style, visual pattern, and mood. Alistair Cooke also applauded the director's 'sensible realism' in *La Bandera* and concluded that he was one of the few directors to 'loo[k] generously at beautiful scenery without bursting into sobs' (1971: 125). The use of 'colour' was no short cut; it was part of the detached eye Duvivier brought to his films. André Lang (1935) describes the Duvivier 'touch' as the ability 'de disparaître résolument derrière l'œuvre' ('to resolutely disappear behind his work'). Paradoxically, Duvivier seeks an *invisibility* of style, often at the very moment that his films feel most visible (in the case of *La Bandera*, in the heart – and heat – of the Saharan desert). As far as Duvivier is concerned, it is the subject of the film that imposes a particular visual style on the director, and not the other way round. Local colour underpins and mirrors the central themes of *La Bandera*; Duvivier never bends it to reflect his own worldview.

Cinematography

The magical aspects of these 'voyages of discovery' are reinforced through a series of woozy camera effects, canted angles, and poetic lighting. When characters feel 'out of place', their discomfort or wonder is mirrored in the cinematography. This happens, for instance, to Dita Parlo in *Au bonheur des dames*, as she moves, almost hypnotically, through Paris. Other examples include the Dutch tilts in *Un Carnet de bal*, the flashbacks sequences to Algeria in *Diaboliquement vôtre*, and the icy compositions of *La Chambre ardente*. In *David Golder* (1930), a crucial conversation about Golder's roots as a poor Jewish immigrant

18 'This report on the [Spanish Foreign] Legion [...] feels true to life all the time.'

is filmed as off-screen noise, while Duvivier's camera stays motionless on a butler pouring wine. Duvivier fluctuates between ensemble shots, close-ups, medium close-ups, and long shots, and often includes the *pano-travelling*, a long, unbroken shot that was his signature gesture. *La Belle équipe* includes a shot of Jean Gabin coming down the stairs of his apartment building that lasts for almost two minutes. Such complex negotiation of décor is not just technically astute; it also reinforces one of Duvivier's key preoccupations: how individuals interact with their environment.

Song and music

Duvivier transitioned from silent films to the sound film tradition with ease, and he pushed the limits of early sound technique. Songs in particular were deployed as an inventive way of showcasing a film's sonic texture, enhancing the deeply atmospheric stories he was telling and often encapsulating the film's message.[19] Duvivier's incorporation of song into *La Tête d'un homme* (1932) and *Pépé le Moko* contributes to the unhinging of the main characters, 'infecting' them and sending them to their doom amid kinetic camerawork (Andrew 1995: 252). Songs could be used in other ways – playfully (Maurice Chevalier singing to a character played by Maurice Chevalier in *L'Homme du jour* [1936]), poetically (Maurice Jaubert's 'Valse grise' ['Grey Waltz'] in *Un Carnet de bal* and Jacques Ibert's oneiric score for *Marianne de ma jeunesse* create moods of romantic despair as much as any other element of the *mise en scène*), or proleptically (the lyrics of the opening lines of the song performed by Germaine Montero during the credits of *Voici le temps des assassins* tell us all we need to know about that film's tone: 'Voici le temps des assassins, du poison, de la corde').[20]

And so, Duvivier is ripe for rediscovery. Admittedly, there are box-office and critical flops among the abiding masterpieces, but, over the course of a seventy-film career, this is to be expected. Quite beautifully, Noël Herpe (2010) describes Duvivier's cinema as 'entre chien et loup' – a kind of twilight style that bridges the silent and the talkie, naturalism and expressionism, realism and the *fantastique*.

---

19 Six of the fifteen films Duvivier made in France that feature songs contain lyrics written by him.
20 'It's the time for assassins, for poison, for rope.'

For Duvivier, dialectical style is everything. Sift away the impurities and the gold begins to shine. And so it is *Haceldama*, and the start of Duvivier's career, to which we now turn.

References

Abel, R. (1988), *French Cinema: The First Wave, 1915–1929*, Princeton, Princeton University Press.

Andrew, D. (1995), *Mists of Regret: Culture and Sensibility in Classic French Film*, Princeton, Princeton University Press.

Aurenche, J. (1975), 'Le diable au corps à corps: Entretien avec Claude Gauteur et Stéphane Lévy-Klein', *Positif*, 168, pp. 12–20.

Bessy, M. (1977), *Les Passagers du souvenir*, Paris, Editions Albin Michel.

Bonnefille, E. (2002a), *Julien Duvivier: Le Mal aimant du cinéma français*, vol. 1, Paris, Harmattan.

Bonnefille, E. (2002b), *Julien Duvivier: Le Mal aimant du cinéma français*, vol. 2, Paris, Harmattan.

Borger, L. (1998), 'Genius Is Just a Word', *Sight and Sound*, September, pp. 28–31.

Burch N. and G. Sellier (1996), *La drôle de guerre des sexes du cinéma français (1930–1956)*, Paris, Nathan.

Cooke, A. (1971), *Alistair Cooke at the Movies*, London, Penguin.

Crisp, C. (2002), *Genre, Myth, and Convention in the French Cinema, 1929–1939*, Bloomington, Indiana University Press.

Desrichard, Y. (2001), *Julien Duvivier: Cinquante ans de noirs destins*, Paris, BiFi/Durante.

Dorsday, M. (1952), '*Adorables créatures*', *Cahiers du cinéma*, 16, October, pp. 55–8.

Duvivier, J. (1959), 'J'ai la chance de n'avoir pas de mémoire', Interview with Julien Duvivier by Pierre des Vallières and Hervé Le Boterf, *Cinémonde*, 1310, 15 September, pp. 14–16.

Fayard, J. (1935), '*La Bandera*', *Candide*, 26 September, np.

Garnier, P. (1996), 'La fête à Duvivier de Florence à Paris', *Libération*, 11 November, available at http://next.liberation.fr/culture/1996/11/14/la-fete-a-duvivier-de-florence-a-paris-a-l-occasion-de-plusieurs-retrospectives-et-publications-reev_188577, accessed 12 March 2015.

Greene, G. (1972), The *Pleasure-Dome: The Collected Film Criticism, 1935–40*, ed. John Russell Taylor, London: Secker and Warburg.

Hayward, S. (2005), *French National Cinema*, 2nd edition, London and New York, Routledge.

Herpe, N. (2010), 'Qui êtes-vous Julien Duvivier?', available at https://www.canal-u.tv/video/cinematheque_francaise/qui_etes_vous_julien_duvivier_conference_de_noel_herpe.5778#l_1, accessed 12 March 2015.

Jeanson, H. (1937), 'Julien Duvivier: d'Antoine au Carnet de bal', *Pour vous*, 441, 29 April, p. 3.
Jouvet, L. (1967), 'Julien Duvivier', *Paris-Presse*, 31 October, np.
Lagouche, P. (2011), 'Julien Duvivier: jeunesse et genèse', *La Voix du nord*, 16 November, available at http://www.lavoixdunord.fr/region/julien-duvivier-jeunesse-et-genese-ia5364b0n1109465, accessed 6 September 2016.
Lang, A. (1935), '*La Bandera*', *Pour vous*, 357, 19 September, p. 6.
Leenhardt, R. (1935), '*Encore Le Mouchard et La Bandera*', *Esprit*, November, pp. 331–2.
Leprohon, P. (1968), *Julien Duvivier*, Paris, Avant-Scène/Collection Anthologie du Cinéma.
Niogret, H. (2010), *Julien Duvivier: 50 ans de cinéma*, Paris, Bazaar and Co.
Rohdie, S. (2015), 'Love unto Death', *Screening the Past*, 39, available at http://www.screeningthepast.com/issue-39, accessed 6 October 2015.
Simsolo, N. (1981), 'A propos de Julien Duvivier ou *Comment réussir une séquence*', *Image et Son*, 366, pp. 99–104.
Truffaut, F. (1954), 'Une certaine tendance du cinéma français', *Cahiers du cinéma*, 31 January, pp. 15–28.
Truffaut, F. (1955), 'Le vieillissement de films', *Arts*, 535, 28 September–4 October, p. 5.
Vincendeau, G. (1998), *Pépé Le Moko*, London, BFI.
Vivet, J.-P. (1951), '*Sous le ciel de Paris*', *France-Observateur*, 18 April, np.

2

Duvivier's silent films

> Zola, vous pouvez tressaillir! Non plus d'angoisse, mais d'aise, et
> même d'orgueil: vous avez été respecté et compris.[1]
> (Anonymous review of *Au Bonheur des dames* in *Cinémagazine*,
> May 1930)

In Bernard Favre's 2005 documentary *Julien Duvivier: Cinéaste des désillusions*, the American critic Lenny Borger states that, in order to understand and appreciate Duvivier's entire fifty-year catalogue, we first need to watch his silent films: 'Duvivier savait construire une histoire [et] savait construire l'ambiance tout de suite'.[2] Duvivier was undoubtedly the most prolific of the new generation of French directors who emerged in the early 1920s, making far more silent films than Jacques Feyder, René Clair, or Jean Renoir. Genres were chosen insouciantly, from religious film to broad comedy, from proto-*noir* to bourgeois melodrama. What remains today are twenty-one silent films shot over eleven years, from *Haceldama ou le prix du sang* (1919) to *Au bonheur des dames* (1930), that introduce the visual, narrative, and thematic patterns that would become the hallmarks of Duvivier's career.

Such choices reveal much about the genres that were most in vogue in French cinema in the late silent period, and may, on the surface, appear unfocused, confused, even dilettantish, with Duvivier shuttling

---

1 'Zola, you can tremble! No longer with anxiety but with ease and even with pride: you have been respected and understood.'
2 'Duvivier knew how to construct a narrative [and] knew how to create an atmosphere from the off.'

from genre to genre, register to register, but lacking an internal harmony. Yet, despite this diversity, there is a startling modernity depicted in many of his silent films, not just in their subject matter but also in the way they are shot, composed, and framed. He never claimed to be a member of the avant-garde or to belong to the same school as Louis Delluc, Germaine Dulac, Marie Epstein, Abel Gance, or Marcel L'Herbier. Rather, he applied many of the techniques that those directors pioneered and in turn layered them onto his various subjects. Throughout the 1920s, Duvivier deployed a raft of techniques: montage, rapid cuts, superimpositions, camera tricks, deep focus, a mobile camera, and an extensive use of close-ups. Here is a director already developing a singular style, a visual brio and formally daring approach to narrative. By cutting across genre so comfortably, Duvivier was establishing the eclecticism that would typify his career. He also, in these early stages, revealed himself as the master adapter. Working from texts as distinctive as those by Germaine Acremant, Henri Bordeaux, Ludovic Halévy, and Émile Zola, Duvivier amplified his source material each time and fashioned it into something specific to his view of the world. This flitting tendency suggests an artist eager to test himself in the world of cinema, importing specific technical or visual innovations into each assignment and matching story with style and tone. Behind this assortment of stories and styles is one particular thematic consistency – dramatic conflict. Its repetition begins to underpin this book's central premise: Duvivier's status as an auteur.

From *Haceldama* to *L'Homme à l'Hispano:* a style is born

Grandiosely announced in the opening credits as 'la grande scène dramatique en quatre parties de M. Julien Duvivier',[3] *Haceldama ou le prix du sang* (1919) was shot on location in the Corrèze, in southwest France. With its use of establishing and long shots, its harsh depiction of the landscape, its recourse to melodrama, and its Americanised character names (Landry Smith, Bill Stanley, Minnie, Kate Lockwood), the film resembles one of Frank Borzage's or William S. Hart's early westerns. It begins with an intertitle – a

---

3 'dramatic action on a grand scale in four parts by Julien Duvivier'.

convention frequently used by Duvivier during this period – from the Apostle of St. John: 'Et alors Judas se rendit dans un lieu qu'on a surnommé depuis: Haceldama, c'est à dire, "Prix du Sang", et il se pendit.'[4] In a dry, rugged terrain, we see a man hanging from a tree, wearing a black hooded gown, followed by a cut to a hand holding a bloody knife. The story is complex: Jean Didier (Jean Lorette) seeks to avenge the death of his father at the hands of Landry Smith (Séverin Mars). Smith lives with his ward (Minnie [Suzy Lilé]) and his servant (Kate Lockwood [Yvonne Brionne]). Complications ensue when Kate asks Bill Stanley (Camille Bert) to kill Smith; Jean eventually discovers that Smith is his real father. Duvivier wrote *Haceldama* himself, and, as one might expect from his theatrical background, he weaves together the melodramatic and naturalistic moments within a highly prescribed and complex four-part structure.

Far from the fiasco the film is often made out to be (Borger described it 'as one of the most dismally unpromising debuts in film history' [1998: 30]), *Haceldama* is remarkably ambitious for a first film. As one would expect following an apprenticeship with André Antoine, Duvivier films everything as authentically as possible. He inserts multiple location shots of ravines and long pans across the landscape. Standard silent visual effects are also adopted. At the start, via an iris-out shot, Smith is shown looking directly at the audience and smiling. Other characters are presented in close-up, or as part of a tableau, while Duvivier also rapidly cuts between close-ups of faces and extreme long shots that trace the movements of a man riding a horse on the horizon. In a scene reminiscent of the famous ending of Edwin S. Porter's *The Great Train Robbery* (1903), when we first see Bill, the Mexican cowboy on the trail of Smith, he draws his gun and fires it point blank at the audience.

Other optical tricks are used. Duvivier suggests that characters are recalling the past or hallucinating in the present, by having them appear and disappear at will or change from one character to another in the space of a shot. Many of his silent films infuse their realist settings with such uncanny incursions, using the camera's optical capabilities to create tension, unease, and a sense of the *fantastique* seeping into the 'realistic' stories. Such tactics fit squarely into the

---

4 'And then Judas went to a place named Haceldama, "Blood Money", and hanged himself.'

tradition of 'cinema of attractions', where films draw attention to themselves by displaying their visibility and rupture a self-enclosed fictional world for a chance to solicit the attention of the spectator (see Gunning 1990).

Both Desrichard (2001: 12) and Bonnefille (2002: 18) describe *Haceldama* as a 'brouillon' ('first draft'), yet the ease with which Duvivier handles film grammar – especially the use of cross-cutting and close-ups – already suggests a confident director. Duvivier expertly choreographs the scene in which John and Bill fight in a bar, editing and framing the action to make it easy to follow. In a later scene in which the two men fight again, this time atop a galloping horse, the rhythm, pacing, and overall command of the filmic space appear effortless. The final moments of *Haceldama* introduce a key Duvivier motif: Landry takes his leave of the two lovers; takes a long, slow walk down a country lane; and leaves in a boat. This idea of leaving the world behind, of fleeing and starting anew, recurs again and again in Duvivier's work. The boat that leaves without Pépé at the end of *Pépé le Moko* (1937) is but one version of this escapist myth. We encounter it again in *David Golder* (1930), *Le Paquebot Tenacity* (1934), and *Black Jack* (1950).

If *Haceldama* marked the beginnings of a proto-Duvivier style, then the director's next two films – *Les Roquevillard** (1921–2) and *L'Ouragan sur la montagne** (1922), shot over the course of nine months – saw the emergence of a more rounded visual and narrative approach that could deal with more commercial material.[5] Before that, in October 1921, Duvivier first headed to London to provide a snapshot of the British film industry for the journal *Hebdo Film*. Duvivier particularly admired the professionalisation of London's film studios; here, 'le cinéma était une industrie, et non point un jouet d'enfant, ou un passe-temps de dilettante' (Duvivier 1921b: 19).[6] French releases were noticeably absent from London's screens (Duvivier 1921a: 29), and Duvivier urged his domestic industry to

---

5 Duvivier's initial follow-up to *Haceldama* was *La Réincarnation de Serge Renaudier*, shot in Bordeaux in 1920. Unfortunately, the film negative was entirely destroyed in a fire at the Burdigala Studios, and no copy survived. Duvivier also shot *Le Logis de l'horreur* (1922), but it was never exhibited. Its whereabouts are unknown.

6 'cinema is an industry, and not a child's toy, or the hobby of an amateur'.

adopt a comparable commercial model: '[C]hoisissons des sujets universels, simples, et qui aient pour mobiles les sentiments qui sont à la base du cœur humain' (1921b: 4).[7] This promotion of a coexistence between commercial and personal would later come to define Duvivier's career.

At the same time as his trip to London, Duvivier wrote two screenplays (*Crépuscule d'épouvante* and *L'Agonie des aigles*, for Henri Etiévant and Dominique Bernard-Deschamps respectively) for Gaumont studios and founded the Société Régionale de Cinématographie (SRC). *Les Roquevillard*, adapted from Henry Bordeaux's highly successful 1906 novel, was the first film Duvivier made under the auspices of the SRC, and, like *Haceldama*, was primarily shot on location, this time in Chambéry and Annecy (with interiors filmed at Epinay, in Paris). If *Haceldama* is a 'mythic' Western, then *Les Roquevillard* is a bourgeois family drama, focusing on the repercussions for a family of respectable lawyers whose son has fled to Italy with the wife of the town's notary. When the son returns in disgrace, Roquevillard *père* must defend his son's – and the family's – honour.

Critics admired Duvivier for his skill at bringing the story to life, often noting how Bordeaux's original novel did not lend itself easily to adaptation. For *L'Echo de Paris* (Tournier 1922: 5), Duvivier 'a si bien extériorisé la vie intérieure des personnages du livre qu'on a l'impression de les voir sur l'écran non seulement agir, mais penser'.[8] Duvivier's ease with the practices of literary adaptation is showcased from the outset of his career: his naturalness in transposing word to image, his fluid visual style (which paraphrases the original text), and his ability to give prominence to a character's interior state of mind or thought processes would all become recognisable traits in his adaptations. Techniques that would become common components of his work were used for the first time in *Les Roquevillard*, namely the use of aerial shots to establish location and import an Antoine-like *verism* into the film (here, of the Savoie countryside) and the inclusion of *surimpressions* ('double exposures') of the family ancestors who utter words of advice to Roquevillard as he is summing up at the end of the

---

7 'Let's choose universal and simple subjects, whose motives are those feelings that can be found at the heart of all of us.'
8 'has externalised the inner lives of the characters of the novel so well that one gets the impression that they are not just acting but thinking'.

trial. This use of *surimpression* became one of Duvivier's trademark practices in the silent period as a means of eschewing conventional editing rhythms. Like Jean Epstein's *Cœur fidèle* (1924) and Rene Clair's *Entr'acte* (1924), *Les Roquevillard* often uses the technique to convey hallucinatory, dream-like images and interior psychological states. Such devices, along with distorting lenses, the uses of gauzes, and slow lap dissolves, were all part of early experimental French cinema's attempts to challenge audience expectations and nudge film towards the surreal. As we shall see, Duvivier's later sound films (*La Charrette fantôme* [1939], *Flesh and Fantasy* [1943]) would also deploy *surimpressions* to layer their narratives with a distinctive oneiric quality.

L'Ouragan sur la montagne was filmed in Munich in early 1922 and marked the first Franco-German co-production since the end of the war. Switching genres again, Duvivier turned to a murder mystery set in an isolated Alpine hotel. With its tales of stolen pearls, a murdered *maître d'*, and an assassin who takes on the identity of a police inspector, *L'Ouragan sur la montagne* is part locked-room mystery and part *policier*, and it looks ahead to Duvivier's future forays into those genres. The idea that a criminal might easily assume the role of a detective, duping everyone else in the process, also anticipates core thematic concerns that play on notions of deception, imposture, and fluidity of identity (such as *Le Reflet de Claude Mercœur* [1923], *The Impostor* [1944], and *Diaboliquement vôtre* [1967]). Critics such as Auguste Nardy (1922) once again applauded Duvivier for his editing and cutting: 'Pas de longueurs; pas de scènes inutiles: du mouvement et du rythme accéléré qui convient au parfait développement du film.'[9] Already, Duvivier's first three films had demonstrated a remarkable eclecticism: western, literary adaptation, and *policier*.

Other filmic practices that would become commonplace in Duvivier's work were established at this time. *L'Ouragan sur la montagne* marked the first time he worked with the actor Gaston Jacquet. They would collaborate together regularly throughout the 1920s, and Jacquet would make a final appearance in *Pot-Bouille* (1957). This reteaming anticipates Duvivier's later long-term partnerships with actors such as Harry Baur and Jean Gabin and underlines the

9 'No excessively lengthy sections; no unnecessary scenes: just movement and accelerated rhythm which perfectly suits the film's development.'

importance Duvivier placed on enduring alliances and teamwork. *Le Reflet de Claude Mercœur*, starring Jacquet, remains one of Duvivier's most intriguing films from the silent period. It was another adaptation (this time of a Frédéric Boutet short story) in which Jacquet plays two identical characters: one a politician, the other his exact double. The politician – the Claude Mercœur of the title – takes up an offer from his double, a mysterious man named Berjean, to replace him at certain functions and events, thus freeing up Mercœur for more important engagements. The complicating action occurs when Mercœur's fiancée, Gilberte, is kept in the dark about the plan and begins to fall in love with Berjean. The film ends with Berjean dead and disfigured (to hide the fact he was Mercœur's double) and Gilberte returning, reluctantly, to Mercœur.

The 'double' has long been a common trope in literature – from Edgar Allan Poe's short story 'William Wilson' (1839) to *The Double* by José Saramago (2002) – and film has frequently mined both the potential of the double in terms both fraught (*Lost Highway* [1997], *Dead Ringers* [1988]) and comic (*Dave,* [1993], *Adaptation* [2002]). In *Multiplicity* (1996), a workaholic Michael Keaton clones himself to spend more time with his family. It is in this lighter territory that *Le Reflet de Claude Mercœur* initially positions itself. Mercœur works too hard and has little time for his fiancée, and the proposal of a 'double' is enthusiastically accepted. And yet, on accepting Berjean's Faustian pact, complications quickly ensue. Offering up the sensation of both wonder and terror at the emergence of an exact replica of an original, Duvivier creates an uneasy atmosphere.

From the off, Duvivier envelops his story in an eerie atmosphere. We first see Mercœur at a lavish party given in his honour, isolated and unhappy, as Duvivier cuts between fireworks and fountains to a solemn Mercœur, standing apart from the other guests. When the two doubles first meet each other, it is on a deserted street. They are both dressed in black, casting large shadows against high white walls. It is a striking tableau, reminiscent of the oppressive cityscapes in Louis Feuillade's *Fantômas* (1913–14) and *Les Vampires* (1915–16), which deploy shadows and high-angled shots to create atmospheres of disquiet and the dream-like. By using double exposure to ensure both men are in the frame at the same time, Duvivier incorporates a theme that emerges periodically in his work – namely, the emergence of something strange or unusual ('insolite' is a term often used to describe Duvivier's fantasy and *noir* films) from within the confines of the everyday. André Antoine's influence can also be felt, both through the importing of real Paris places (*hôtels particuliers* and boulevards) and the incorporation of a flashback in which Duvivier jumps back a year to when Berjean first saw Mercœur in the newspaper, recognised that they are identical, and began to dress like him. A final point to note is that the concept of doubles links Duvivier's film to German Expressionist cinema. Doppelgängers were a common feature of Expressionism (*The Cabinet of Doctor Caligari* [1920], *The Student of Prague* [1926]) and their presence allowed the exploration of diverse themes (immortality, whore/Madonna complex, and schizophrenia) to be presented in visually radical ways (mirrors, chiaroscuro lighting, stylised décor). *Le Reflet de Claude Mercœur* faithfully replicates this *mise en scène* and can thus be read as an example of the integration of Expressionist imagery into French cinema and the way the former's narrative patterns could be refracted in a new context. The tense triangular relationship between the 'two' Claude Mercœurs and Gilberte also plays out a narrative of doubling, identity crisis, and Oedipal plotting that looks ahead at future Duvivier films, both dramatic (*The Impostor*, with Jean Gabin playing a man who assumes the identity of another) and light-hearted (*La Fête à Henriette* [1952], with two scriptwriters playing split versions of the same personality).

Taking advantage of a delay in the filming of *Credo ou la tragédie de Lourdes* (to be discussed later in this chapter), Duvivier wrote and shot *Cœurs farouches** (1923) in less than two weeks. Filmed in the south of France, the film is a bitter tale: one night, four brothers who live and work in the mountains are visited by a young woman, Marthe (Desdemona Mazza). Gradually, each of the men falls in love with her. When Marthe is found beaten and abandoned at the side of the road, she refuses to give up the names of the brother who attacked her and the brother she loves. The film is notable for the way it once again augurs future Duvivier projects, such as the portrayal of a close-knit working community in *La Belle équipe* (1936), which will be similarly destabilised (though here, innocently) by the arrival of a woman or the suspense of *Marie-Octobre* (1959) and *La Chambre ardente* (1962), in which numerous false aspersions of guilt and concealment are cast before the final truth is revealed. Its rural setting is also relevant here, for most of Duvivier's films were set in urban spaces. Those films that do contain scenes set in the countryside usually offer up bucolic spaces of beauty and simplicity to ironically counterpoint the trials of the city left behind. The setting of *Cœurs farouches*, with its vast landscapes and abundant natural light, reveres the rural space but also inflects it with emotional turmoil and criminal behaviour: the film ends with one brother dead, another leaving with Marthe, and two who remain behind broken-hearted. It is a sour, brutal film that demonstrates the ways in which Duvivier's narrative concerns could play out against numerous backdrops. Around this time, Duvivier also directed *L'Œuvre immortelle** (1924), the story of a doctor in love with a young woman whose mother he was in love with years earlier. Searching for a cure for tuberculosis, the doctor dies the very day that he discovers the antidote. Filmed outside Brussels, the film was a great success in Belgium (it starred two famous Belgian actors of the time, Suzanne Christy and Jimmy O'Kelly) but was never released in France. *L'Abbé Constantin** (1925) was another adaptation, this time of Ludovic Halévy's novel that recounts the love affair between an orphan and a rich American woman who has taken up residence in a nearby country house.

Duvivier took a detour into non-fiction with *La Machine à refaire la vie* (1924), a clip-based documentary, co-directed with Henry Lepage, about the early days of cinema. Via a judicious selection of films, scenes, and extracts, Duvivier offers a chronology of the cinema at once nostalgic and didactic up to the mid-1920s to demonstrate how it had evolved into France's 'septième art' ('seventh art'). Duvivier's film essay lists inventions (Etienne-Jules Marey's chronophotographic gun, the phenakistoscope, the zoetrope), first films (*L'Arroseur arrosé* [1895]), key developmental stages in narrative cinema (*L'Assassinat du duc de Guise* [1908], Feuillade, Griffith, Linder, Sjöström, *The Cabient of Dr. Caligari* [1920]), and technical advancements (make-up, editing, camera movement, *surimpressions*). Duvivier would make two more sonorised versions of the documentary in 1933 and 1943, both times detailing new developments and innovations (the arrival of sound, Dreyer's *Jeanne d'Arc* [1928]) before moving on to a discussion of Feyder's *La Kermesse héroïque* (1935) and his very own *La Fin du jour* (1939).[10] The silent version of *La Machine à refaire la vie* was

---

10 The 1943 version is the only surviving version of the film, viewable in the Institut National Audiovisuel archives in Paris.

shown as part of a three-hour conference in more than a hundred cities in 1926 and 1927; Duvivier himself provided the live commentary during the projection of the film. This is a documentary that serves multiple purposes – historical, pedagogical, economic, and above all propagandistic. Part of Duvivier's narrative laments the downturn in the French domestic film industry in the aftermath of the First World War. Before 1914, Paris had been the epicentre of cinema; now, post-Chaplin and Griffith, its influence had waned (but, with the new potential of Abel Gance and Marcel L'Herbier, was on the upturn again). *Comœdia* was one of many that applauded Duvivier's project: 'il faut conclure [...] que notre production nationale reconquiert peu à peu la place perdue du fait de la guerre et qu'elle s'imposera bientôt au premier rang' (Anon. 1924a: 2).[11]

This first part of Duvivier's silent career culminated in *L'Homme à l'Hispano* (1926), an adaptation of Pierre Frondaie's popular novel. Duvivier was not involved in writing the screenplay (René Hervil, the original director, retained the writing credit) and so his work here is revealing for the way in which his directing style for the first time responds to pre-existing character trajectories and narrative choices. *L'Homme à l'Hispano* is another example of Duvivier serving material that is not his own in ways that are still visually and formally radical. The film fits squarely into a genre Richard Abel has termed the 'modern studio spectacular', in which stylish sets, costumes, and furnishings plus a narrative focus on the trials and tribulations of the Parisian *nouveau riche* produced 'a picturesque image of contemporary France according to American stereotypes' (1984: 205).

Georges Dewalter (Georges Galli) is financially ruined and prepares to leave France, exiled for Senegal. Destiny, one of Duvivier's favoured narrative devices, duly intervenes. The ship bound for Africa is confined to port for a week, and, while walking the streets, Dewalter meets Deleone (Anthony Gildès), who invites him to Biarritz and loans him his car – the titular Hispano. Lady Oswill (Huguette Duflos) falls in love with Dewalter, mistakenly believing him rich on account of his car. This misunderstanding sets in motion a passionate imbroglio that ends with Dewalter's suicide and an emotionally distraught

---

11 'one has to conclude [...] that little by little our national industry is winning back the position it lost because of the war, and that it will soon re-establish itself as number one.'

Lady Oswill. The crux of the film is encapsulated in Deleone's plea to Dewalter: 'Partez, si vous êtes un homme; l'amour c'est une maladie'.[12] It is not just love that is harmful; money is also something that tarnishes and warps. When Dewalter runs out of money, he believes Oswill will now despise him for having lied to her. There are a series of long, slow pans down dining tables and through ornately decorated rooms that serve to remind Dewalter what he will miss out on. This lifestyle is one of conspicuous consumption that Dewalter does not wish to abandon. Like Duvivier's later *David Golder*, *L'Homme à l'Hispano* offers a scathing depiction of a hypocritical, small-minded upper class. Only Savill's notary offers some sort of counter-balance to his greedy and grasping employer. When Savill orders him to give Dewalter two hundred thousand francs to disappear, the notary replies: 'il y a des âmes qui ne sont pas à vendre'.[13]

Desrichard has argued that, because Duvivier did not write the screenplay, *L'Homme à l'Hispano* is one of his more impersonal works: 'il est évident qu'il est ailleurs' ('it's obvious his mind is elsewhere') (2001: 20). However, the film exemplifies the way Duvivier was prepared on each assignment to serve the material as faithfully as possible. The film remains a fascinating time capsule, with its location shots of the Ritz Hotel and the Place Vendôme in Paris and the main promenade, hotels, and beaches of Biarritz complete with several slow-motion shots of people splashing in water. This is Duvivier as ethnographer, capturing the leisured class in much the same way as Marcel Carné would in his Parisian working-class documentary *Nogent, Eldorado du dimanche* (1929). Duvivier's 'work for hire' on *L'Homme à l'Hispano* is an opportunity to inject a visually astute aesthetic into late French silent cinema, in the same way as did Carné, Georges Lacombe, and Jean Dréville.

Duvivier interleaves a series of double exposures to heighten the romantic mood and suggest a growing intimacy between Dewalter and Lady Oswill. In one scene, as a violinist plays at a nightclub, Duvivier emphasises characters' yearning by overlaying the shot of the violinist with images of lakes, rivers, and woods. As their hands move slowly over the table and eventually touch, her breathing becomes more pronounced, and more rural scenes are overlaid on

12 'If you are a man, then leave. Love is an addiction.'
13 'some people are not for sale'.

the violinist. Shortly afterwards, when Dewalter returns to his hotel, he stands on his balcony, recalling the evening's events. Oswill's superimposed face appears on screen and there is a rapid cut to her room. 'Je suis seule, venez' ('I am alone. Come to me'), reads the intertitle, as she telephones Dewalter. He is ecstatic, stealing to her room, where they embrace passionately.

By late 1926, Duvivier had firmly established himself as a director of importance in France and was recognised as such in various trade papers and film journals. Jean-Louis Croze (1926: 3) acclaimed in *Comœdia* that Duvivier had achieved 'une des réalisations les plus grandioses, les plus vraies que les *metteurs en scène* aient jamais tentée et réussie'.[14] The French film industry had by now anointed Duvivier as one of the standard-bearers of a new kind of narrative film that could be regarded as the equivalent of the German or American industry. An embryonic Duvivier style had thus begun to emerge over the course of a dozen films: technically adept, dramatically astute, thematically constant, visually rich. He was working with the same team from film to film, which assisted in the development of a consistent visual approach, something that showed no signs of slowing in the final years of silent film in France.

Experimenting with form

For a director frequently branded humourless, it is worth remembering that Duvivier had great critical and commercial success over his career writing and directing comedy. We shall come to *L'Homme du jour* (1936), the Don Camillo series (1952, 1953), and *L'Homme à l'imperméable* (1957) in due course, but Duvivier's first foray into a comic tone, *Le Mariage de Mademoiselle Beulemans* (1927), reveals a playfulness and a lightness of touch that is often overlooked by critics. Shot on location in Brussels, it is adapted from a play by the Belgian duo Frantz Fonson and Fernand Wicheler. Duvivier deals in a different register, a sort of domestic chamber piece far removed from the expansive 'excitement' of *Haceldama* and *L'Homme à l'Hispano*. Delpierre (Jean Dehelly) is a young Frenchman who comes to Brussels

14 'one of the most spectacular, most authentic achievements ever attempted and brought off by a director'.

to learn the brewing trade. He soon falls in love with Suzanne, the daughter of the Beulemans, one of the city's most important brewers. This light satire pokes fun at the petty-mindedness of the Belgian middle class (the Beulemans' maid brushes fly droppings from sugar cubes). There is an enduring craft-like quality to the film, exemplified by the use of decorative handwritten intertitles and by the opening scene of the film, which shows the pages of a guidebook of Belgium overlaid with documentary images of Bruges, Anvers, Ghent, paintings by Rubens, and the statue of the Manneken Pis. Duvivier directs the larger scenes with gusto. One of the most notable is the *concours de la pipe*, in which a group of men see who can keep their pipes lit the longest by frantically puffing on them. The scene is one of bluff machismo and masculine competitiveness, and it indicates how Duvivier could occasionally trade in moments of light-heartedness.

On the surface, Duvivier's next film continues the parodic playfulness of *L'Ouragan sur la montagne* and the comic set-pieces of *Le Mariage de Mademoiselle Beulemans*. *Le Mystère de la Tour Eiffel** (1927) parodies Louis Feuillade serials such as *Barrabas* (1920) with its episodically structured tale of a masked gang, money, crime, and kidnapping. When Philibert de Puyfontaine (1927: 7) visited the set in June, he described the film in *La Critique cinématographique* as 'une mystérieuse histoire, où les gens ne sont jamais ceux que l'on croit, et où ceux que l'on reconnaît ne sont jamais ceux que l'on a vus'.[15] Once again, Duvivier was drawn back to a favoured theme – the deceptiveness of appearances. He had already explored similar territory in *L'Ouragan sur la montagne* and once again bolted a *policier* plot onto its central story of doubles and confused identity. *Le Mystère de la Tour Eiffel* featured the music-hall star Tramel. He played the Mironton brothers, who pose as Siamese twins; these two 'doubles' nod to *Le Reflet de Claude Mercœur* and allow a mixture of the vaudevillian and the melodramatic to emerge. Tramel was praised for his work, with reviews appreciative of his physical humour, his gestures and mannerisms, and his ability to hold the attention of the audience. The film also contained several strange scenes, including an invisible ray that destroys everything and a manic chase across the top of the Eiffel Tower. Paul Souillac (1927) in *Le Cinéopse* praised Duvivier and

---

15 'a mysterious story, where people are never who you think they are, and those you recognise are never the same ones that you've already seen'.

his assistant, future director André Berthomieu, for their 'technique savante, avisée et habile' ('shrewd, astute and skilful technique'). Souillac concluded that the film was a triumph for French cinema and a template for other directors: 'Peu de prétention [...], mais de l'originalité, de la fantaisie, du goût, du mystère et du comique.'[16]

Duvivier's work rate showed no sign of decline. *Le Tourbillon de Paris* (1928) was conceived as a star vehicle for the German actress Lil Dagover, with whom French audiences were familiar from *The Cabinet of Dr. Caligari*. Duvivier again turned to literature as his source material, adapting Germaine Acremant's novel *La Sarrazine* to tell the story of a once-famous opera singer Amisicia Negeste (Dagover), who now lives as a recluse in a remote mountain chalet. Encouraged to return to Paris – the 'maelstrom' of the title – she regains her status as an opera singer but finally renounces fame and fortune and retreats to a Scottish castle with her aristocratic husband. This tension between duty as a wife and desire for independence, and the discrepancy between familial stability and the temptations of an urban, cosmopolitan *demi-monde*, is explored several times by Duvivier in this silent period. Formally, the film marks a great leap forwards in his style, and hints at the complexity and technical dexterity that would cohere even more fully in his 'poetic realist' work of the 1930s and his forays into Hollywood a decade or so later.

Dagover's performance is highly impressive. In her portrayal of an artist with deep psychological scars, she excels at exteriorising Amisicia's fraught mental state. Once back in Paris, she dresses in furs and jewels and imagines in her mind's eye the Moulin Rouge, the Eiffel Tower, and the Opera. She refuses to return to Scotland, so fascinated is she by the bright neon lights advertising the city's music halls, clubs, restaurants, and *dancings*. Duvivier shows how she has re-entered Parisian high society by having her sing Fauré's 'Les Berceaux' to a crowd of rapt onlookers. As in previous films, he uses visual shorthand to heighten the psychological realism. While Amisicia sings, Duvivier inserts a double exposure of a ship leaving a harbour while a woman is left behind rocking a cradle. Later on, he superimposes the image of a toad onto the face of an unscrupulous character. In a striking scene, Amisicia's husband, back

16 'Very little flashiness [...], just originality, fantasy, flavour, mystery and comedy.'

in Scotland, turns on the radio as she is about to begin her comeback performance. While on stage, she is stricken with stage fright and starts screaming. The crowd becomes restless, and Duvivier uses a crash-zoom into the face of someone in the crowd whistling and jeering. Looking out into the auditorium, Amisicia sees only contorted, grimaced close-ups of faces laughing at her, while superimposed onto the stage are crashing waves. The curtain is lowered, then raised again, and she finally starts to sing, to great acclaim. Might we read this therapeutic closing scene as corrective to Duvivier's own harrowing experiences on stage fifteen years earlier? Is Dagover's performance a cathartic moment not just for her character but also for her director? What follows is a masterful use of editing and camera technique: rapid cuts between audience and singer, a mobile camera craning up and over the audience, and cutting backwards and forwards from the Paris stage to the Scottish castle as the husband listens to the radio. The deployment of a mobile camera to capture the fleeting impressions of urban life and the sensations of movement would coalesce in *Au bonheur des dames* and Duvivier's early sound work. Here, one sees the sketching out of a desired visual and formal framework in which the hostile reactions of the crowd create a strong psychological reaction in both Amisicia and the viewer. As A. Tenevain (1928), in *Le Cinéopse*, put it, *Le Tourbillon de Paris* was 'un drame cinégraphique d'une exceptionnelle valeur [...] un de ces films français qui, enfin, sont dignes de notre patrimoine intellectuel'.[17] Like the later antagonistic crowds in *Golgotha* (1935) and *Panique* (1946), in which the collective forcefully turns against the individual, the silent grimacing faces in *Le Tourbillon de Paris* suggest a common thread in Duvivier's work: conflict, aggression, and the isolation of the individual. Here, finally, Amisicia sings, and is redeemed. Future Duvivier protagonists would not be so lucky.

1929: towards a new aesthetic

The last year of silent film in France was another busy one for Duvivier. He began with the mystical drama *La Divine croisière* (1929),

---

17 'a cinematic drama of exceptional merit [...] one of those French films which are finally worthy of our intellectual heritage'.

which, after the city-based melodramas and religious films of the late 1920s, showed the guile with which Duvivier could cut across genre. The plot combines several of Duvivier's preferred themes – nature, the clash between the exploiter and the exploited, the power of collective action. When the dilapidated ship the *Cordillière* is ordered back into commission by Ferjac (its greedy owner), its crewmembers, fearing for their lives while out on treacherous seas, mutiny. With radio contact lost, the families back on the mainland start to come to terms with the loss of the *Cordillière*. Simone (Suzanne Christy), daughter of the missing captain (Jean Murat), has a vision that her father and his crew are still alive. She charters a boat, heads out onto the high seas, and begins her search.

Duvivier intercuts between the claustrophobia of the *Cordillière* – the rousing mateship, excessive drinking, and physical exertions – and the community left behind, who ritualistically paint frescos on the walls of the church in a bid to bring the men back safely. After weeks of no news of the *Cordillière*, the townsfolk head off up the hill to Ferjac's castle demanding retribution. Angry women barge into the middle of a dinner party, and Duvivier uses a series of extreme close-ups on the women's faces to capture their sorrow. By shuttling between two different tones, from Duvivier's typical 'men's stories' in which strong, swarthy men are confined to a life of drinking and dangerous labour to the quasi-religious backdrop of prayers and rituals, Duvivier incorporates dynamic cross-cutting into *La Divine croisière*. When one woman sets fire to Ferjac's house in a final show of anger, Duvivier suggests that violence and retribution simmer beneath the surface of even the most devout communities. It would not be the first time that Duvivier would show how primal forces could be unleashed by women to disturb the calmness and order of a community. To mark the release of *La Divine croisière*, *La Cinématographie française* (Anon. 1929) published a full-page article congratulating this 'superproduction française' ('French superproduction') that further bolstered the 'légende moderne de Julien Duvivier' ('modern legend of Julien Duvivier').

Maman Colibri (1929) is an important film in the Duvivier canon because it marked the first time that the director would work on location in Algeria, developing a fascination with the exoticism, atmosphere, and pictorial beauty of a landscape that he would return to several times in the 1930s. *Maman Colibri* tells the story of a rich Parisian socialite Irène (Maria Jacobini) who abandons her husband

and children to begin an affair with De Chambry, a much younger Spahi officer (Frank Lederer), and leave with him for Africa. Once there, she realises that the officer no longer loves her and returns, chastened, to her husband. As with his previous films (*L'Homme à l'Hispano*, *Le Tourbillon de Paris*), Duvivier creates a character seduced by the trappings of wealth and glamour, prepared to risk domestic stability for the sake of immediate sexual gratification. This time, mother and wife Irène is invited to a masked ball where she meets De Chambry. The immediacy of the connection between the two is signalled by the use of rapid alternating extreme close-ups of the couple, while the age difference hints at Oedipal fantasy.

When De Chambry is recalled to Africa, we, like Irène, go with him. This narrative turn is the pretext to introduce a long-standing Duvivier fascination: the lure of the exotic colonial space and its spectacle, landscape, culture, and customs. In a move that foreshadows later films such as *La Bandera* (1935), *Pépé le Moko* and *The Impostor*, Duvivier bombards us with picture-postcard images of the continent – we see real palm trees, deserts, streams, sand, sun, and camel trains. Richard Abel reminds us that exotic narratives of romance and adventure from the late-silent period 'offered an acceptable escape from the economic and ideological problems wracking post-war French society' (1984: 151); here, Duvivier transplants a tale of marital breakdown that could easily have taken place within the Paris *demi-monde* to a far-flung setting. At the end of the affair, Irène's return to France marks a return to her senses. It is as if 'a magical African aura has worn off' (Slavin 2001: 31). After weeks in the African heat, she returns to a wintry Paris. In the film's final scene, she is dressed in black, puts on her coat with a resigned look while her husband looks on sternly, and makes to leave. Yet the older son begs the father not to banish the mother. The father changes his mind, relents, and Irène stays. The closing image of *Maman Colibri* sees Irène looking at her granddaughter in a crib. Normally, within melodrama's moralising paradigms, the errant mother has to be punished, yet here, for Duvivier, the stability of the family unit can only be guaranteed by the return of the mother and her reintegration into a heavily gender-defined maternal role.

Duvivier's final silent film was *Au bonheur des dames*, an adaptation of Emile Zola's 1883 novel. Zola was one of the most adapted authors in 1920s French cinema, with eleven of his novels forming the basis of films between 1919 and 1929, including André Antoine's *La Terre* in 1921. In 1928 and 1929, two of four Zola adaptations were taken from his Rougon-Macquart series: *L'Argent* (1928), directed by Marcel L'Herbier, and Duvivier's *Au bonheur des dames*, a year later (though not released until 1930). Duvivier's is perhaps his most famous silent film, and it boasts a series of exhilarating technical and stylistic accomplishments. It takes as its central theme progress. From the outset, via an epigraphic intertitle, Duvivier primes the spectator to the social and historical relevance of Zola's work: 'Le grand magasin contre la petite boutique [...] Problème toujours d'actualité. Lutte cruelle, inégale, qui engendre les deuils et les ruines, et dont seul est responsable celui qui règle la marche du monde: le progrès.'[18] Both visually and technically, Duvivier updates Zola's perspective on modernity, change, and progress in the late nineteenth century for a late 1920s audience. The critical reception for *Au bonheur des dames* was full of admiration for Duvivier: Jean-Paul Coutisson (1930: 6) was not alone when he wrote in *Comœdia* of a film 'qui fait honneur à la production française et qui démontre clairement toute la valeur de son metteur en scène Julien Duvivier'.[19]

Au bonheur des dames is a film of movement, of propulsion, of people ricocheting around Paris. In its justly celebrated opening sequence, we see a train pulling into Saint-Lazare station (the way it is shot, with a camera attached to the tender, would be replicated by Jean Renoir in another Zola adaptation, *La Bête humaine*, in 1938), disgorging Dita Parlo's Denise into the seething crowds of Paris. What follows is a pure Eisensteinian montage of dizzyingly swift cuts, swooping pans, documentary inserts, sound effects, and cross-cutting.[20] Duvivier captures the wide-eyed wonder of Parlo's extraordinary face in a series of still close-ups that alternate with the rapid sense impressions of the city unspooling before her and us. As Denise walks from Saint-Lazare to her uncle's shop, Duvivier uses a series of hidden cameras (again foreshadowing a Renoir technique,

18 'The big department store versus the little shop. [...] The problem still exists today. A cruel, unfair struggle that ends in death and destruction, and to blame, the thing that regulates the ticking of the world: progress.'

19 'which does justice to French film production and quite clearly shows the great worth of its director Julien Duvivier'.

20 This rapidity is constant. Charles O'Brien notes that the film contains over a thousand shots, with an average shot length of 5 seconds (2009: 117).

this time in *Boudu sauvé des eaux* [1932]) to capture the teeming metropolis and the seeming non-stop wave of passers-by that threatens to engulf Denise. This virtuoso three-and-a-half-minute scene is, it seems to me, the culmination of Duvivier's silent work, pushing camera movement and montage almost to the point of abstraction. The visual overload of these opening moments places the film in the company of a group of documentary films that stage similarly frenetic depictions of the urban space, such as Alberto Cavalcanti's *Rien que les heures* (1926), Walter Ruttman's *Berlin: Symphony of a Metropolis* (1927), André Sauvage's *Etudes sur Paris* (1928), and Dziga Vertov's *Man with a Movie Camera* (1929). It is only at the end of this relentless opening, when we enter Au Vieil Elbeuf, the musty little shop owned by Baudu, Denise's uncle, that the frenetic pace slows, and Duvivier's camerawork and editing become more restrained. After so much briskness comes calmness, and Zola's story begins to emerge.

Throughout *Au bonheur des dames*, female desire is writ large on the urban space, usually confirmed by Parlo's ecstatic smile. As Denise moves through the streets at the start, a plane drops small slips of paper that float onto the street: 'TOUT ... ce que vous désirez ... Au Bonheur des dames.'[21] The name of the department store pervades the film. We see it in illuminated lights, on flags, on publicity leaflets and posters, on balloons and sandwich boards, and, in the film's final shot, written in the sky by the smoke trails of a passing plane. Duvivier plays on this double irony throughout – does the 'Bonheur' represent true happiness or just a warped sense of progress in which customers have become enslaved consumers worshipping at the gates of a false temple? Denise has come to Paris to find work at her uncle's store but is quickly seduced by the prospect of crossing the street to work at Octave Mouret's vast 'Ladies' Paradise'. For Duvivier, the store has become a shrine for consumerism and conspicuous consumption. He employs a series of establishing and low-angle shots to suggest that the 'Bonheur', and the mostly feminine crowds that pour in and out of its front doors, represents a new kind of religion.

The interiors of the 'Bonheur' were filmed inside the Galeries Lafayette in Paris, at that point the largest department store in the

21 'EVERYTHING ... you desire ... Au Bonheur des Dames.'

world.[22] Brian Nelson (1995) has noted how the Second Empire department stores described by Zola relied upon intricate 'mechanisms of seduction', such as advertising, free entry into the store, and a deliberate spatial disorder that encouraged shoppers to browse, wander, and purchase on impulse. Most notable was the 'seduction of the eye through an almost orgiastic display of visual pleasures enticingly encased in their wrappings and sealed by the surrounding womb of warmth and light' (xi). Duvivier's supple camerawork captures these alluring wonders once inside the store, and, through a series of pans, zooms, and close-ups, replicates Denise's conveyor-belt-like eyes as she moves through the 'Bonheur', staring at clothing, glasses, cups, and shiny appliances. Later on, Octave Mouret looks out over the streets of Paris and gestures that his expansion plans will make him even more powerful. This equation between power and commerce runs through the film and remains true to Zola's original attitudes towards spatial domination, commodification, and modern business practices. Of the alterations Duvivier makes to Zola's original, one of the most significant is his altering of Denise's employment. Zola's sales assistant has now become Duvivier's dress model. Margaret C. Flinn (2014: 130–1) reads the scene where Denise is forced to undress in front of the other models and male employees as one of 'cruelty extending to violation', itself a typical Duvivier gesture. However, equally relevant is the notion that Denise's ascent to the apex of the 'Bonheur' is contingent on her ease with self-display and exhibitionism; the more she models, the faster she climbs. From her initial humiliation, a vital form of empowerment emerges: if, as the opening intertitles inform us, the theme of *Au bonheur des dames* is 'Progress', then it applies as much to Denise's rise as it does the fall of her uncle's boutique.

Au bonheur des dames is a splendidly modern film that uses various cinematic innovations, such as matte shots for the external shots of the Bonheur, and a slow-motion diving sequence. There are scenes of parallel montage, such as when Baudu's head is framed underneath a set of sledgehammers that destroy the surrounding neighbourhood – including his own shop – to make way for the expansion of the Bonheur. At the same time, Duvivier also cross-cuts between this destruction of the *quartier* and an idyllic lakeside party, strengthening the equation between leisure, commerce, and urban progress.

22 The interior set dressing was done by Christian-Jaque, a future director.

Despite its silent origins, it seems as though Duvivier is attempting to 'film' noise: we can almost hear the traffic and the urban thrum at the start of the film, as Parlo battles down the street, and, later, the clank of cranes and machinery as 'progress' takes control. Richard Abel describes the film's tone as 'pathetic and nostalgic' (1984: 217) and it is easy to see why. The death of the uncle at the hands of a delivery truck, the shabbiness of Au Vieil Elbeuf, and the eventual destruction of the *quartier* all suggest unease at the pace of economic and architectural progress and the growing gap between old and new France.

Au bonheur des dames would be Duvivier's twenty-first, and last, silent film. When it was released in Paris in March 1930, the film was not a commercial success, and it was subsequently re-released in a sound version six months later (this would not be the last time that producers would interfere with Duvivier's artistic vision). The sound version of the film is vastly inferior, with random, unconnected sounds shoehorned into the soundtrack. A month later, Duvivier would begin shooting his first sound film, *David Golder*, at Paris' Epinay studios. Like René Clair's *Sous les toits de Paris*, shot in the same backlot earlier in 1929, Duvivier's first talkie would prove to be highly influential, revealing to an industry still undecided about the artistic and technical merits of sound a new, radical direction for French cinema to take.

Duvivier and religion

Before we move into the 1930s and examine in more detail some of the more familiar work in the Duvivier canon, I would like to dwell on a trio of films, shot at different points in the decade, that dealt with a religious subject matter: *Credo ou la tragédie de Lourdes* (1924, henceforth, *Credo*), *L'Agonie de Jérusalem* (1927), and *La Vie miraculeuse de Thérèse Martin* (1929). As we have seen, Duvivier traded in diverse genres throughout his first ten years as a filmmaker, but in these three we can trace a continuity of themes and preoccupations. Critics have sometimes labelled Duvivier a Catholic filmmaker, by virtue of his strict Jesuit upbringing, early fascination with the accoutrements of the Catholic faith, and profound sense of hope and spiritual inspiration that can be detected in the likes of *Le Tourbillon de Paris* and *La Divine croisière*.

Credo is based on a real-life event: in 1922, a young Reims girl was cured at Lourdes; her father converted to Catholicism that same day. In Duvivier's version, the girl is the daughter of a renowned doctor (Henry Krauss) who is struck seriously ill. Conflict arises when the young woman's fiancé takes her to Lourdes to be cured, against the wishes of the atheist father. Coming directly after the baroque imagery of *Le Reflet de Claude Mercœur*, Duvivier offers a more restrained, sober film-making style. There are numerous fixed establishing shots, and he relies far more than in his other silent films on multiple intertitles to advance the story. The most novel aspect of *Credo* was its series of remarkable documentary shots of Lourdes. In a 1923 interview with *Mon ciné*, Duvivier recalled that he had to obtain special permission to film in Lourdes (it was the first film ever to be shot there) and used a hidden camera to allow his actors to mingle freely with the crowds amid the pilgrimages and procession. The hidden camera technique allowed Duvivier to capture the town's singular atmosphere. Duvivier described the production as 'un documentaire excessivement curieux' ('an extremely curious documentary'), and, seen now, this direct engagement with the rituals of Lourdes remains the film's strongest point.

The reviews for *Credo* were mixed. *L'Eveil provençal* loved it, applauding Duvivier as being part of a new wave of directors who are 'entreprenants' and can 'allier le sens de la propagande avec l'habileté technique' (Anon. 1924b).[23] *Cinémagazine* (Anon. 1925: 200), like many others, instead denounced its 'conception faible' ('weak conception') and 'technique fort inégale' ('highly uneven technique').

In *L'Agonie de Jérusalem*, Gaston Jacquet plays Marc Verdier, a devout Catholic living on the outskirts of Jerusalem with his brother and paralysed wife. Their son Jean-Louis is studying law in Paris, where he is also a member of an anarchist organisation. While in Paris, Verdier discovers his son has been badly injured in a riot and has gone blind. Jean-Louis returns to Jerusalem with his father and visits the city's holy sites in a bid to regain his sight. While at Gethsemane, his sight returns. For Duvivier, *L'Agonie de Jérusalem* was the chance to extend themes previously presented in *Credo*; as he did at Lourdes in the first film, Duvivier shot on location in Jerusalem for two weeks in places visited by Jesus during his ministry in the Holy

23 'resourceful', 'link together propaganda and technical skill'.

Land: Bethlehem, Nazareth, Galilee, Gesthsemane, and the slopes of the Mount of Olives. The film is once again notable for its adroit grasp of cinematic grammar: the iris-in onto a thicket of trees on the Mount to pinpoint the villa where the Verdiers live; a rapid series of dolly shots to imply characters moving from one side of the frame to the other; the filming of the cruiser's wash dissolving into a train track as Verdier makes his week-long trip from Jerusalem to Paris; the camera out of focus after Jean-Louis has been hit across the head; the misfocusing then refocusing of the trees in Gethsemane to indicate that Jean-Louis has regained his sight. These are all audacious choices by Duvivier and reinforce the sense that he was undertaking a drawn-out apprenticeship in the 1920s in which film's technical and visual potential were gradually being explored and mastered. In a piece for *Comœdia*, Duvivier (1926: 3) described *L'Agonie de Jérusalem* as a 'drame de la famille' ('family drama') and a 'drame de conscience' ('drama of conscience') – in other words, two genres embedded in the same film. The first half, with its parallel narratives set in Jerusalem and Paris, is melodrama tinged with social comment (Jean-Louis wishes to sabotage an electrification project planned for Palestine). Then, with the return to the Holy Land, the film shifts to a religious register as Jean-Louis is taken on his pilgrimage. Duvivier stages a series of tableaux to illustrate scenes from the Bible and has Jean-Louis tend to a badly injured man in a Pieta-style pose. In the final scenes, Jean-Louis asks for forgiveness and mercy from his weeping parents, and the film concludes with the family reunited.

The most commercially successful of these three films was *La Vie miraculeuse de Thérèse Martin*, an account of the life of the Carmelite Saint Thérèse of Lisieux. Thérèse was a late nineteenth-century Discalced Carmelite nun who died from tuberculosis and was subsequently canonised in 1925; her autobiography – *Histoire d'une âme* – formed the basis of Duvivier's adaptation. The film's register is made explicit in the opening intertitle: 'Premier film d'art Chretien: un mystère cinématographique de Julien Duvivier'.[24] The film follows Thérèse as she leaves her home in Lisieux and is admitted to the austere world of the Carmelites. The Devil appears to her twice – before she takes the veil (tempting her as she doubts herself) and as she lies ill towards the end of her life.

---

24 'The first film of Christian art: a cinematic mystery, by Julien Duvivier'.

The first portion of the film is one long, complex flashback – in 1843, a man (André Marnay) walks across a snowy mountain and arrives at a monastery. We then cut to 1858 and to a woman being shown into a church. The intertitle finally allows us to make sense of these disjointed opening scenes: 'Par une étrange prédestination, une même scène se jouait, à 15 ans de distance, au Monastère du St-Bernard, et à l'Hôtel-Dieu d'Alençon'.[25] Both wish to enter the church, but are refused. Duvivier places two mirrors in the frame – one labelled 1843 on the left, the other labelled 1858 on the right – to allow both characters (eventually revealed as Thérèse's father and mother) to be linked across space and time in the same shot. It is an audacious move to link different times and spaces within the same shot. Duvivier then returns to the present. In 1877, the man and woman have married and have had five children, the youngest of whom is Thérèse (Simone Bourday). After the wife dies, Pauline, the second daughter, and Marie, the oldest, enter the Carmelite order. Thérèse prays to a small statue of Christ in the family home; Christ opens his eyes and moves his head towards her – he is now played by an actor, wearing a crown of thorns, with drops of blood on his face, and tells her: 'J'ai soif' ('I am thirsty').

The scene of the taking of the veil, when Thérèse enters the Carmelite order, is one of the most striking in Duvivier's career. It lasts for nearly fifteen minutes and charts the various stages of the initiation process, from Thérèse's arrival into the Order to her finally being led away. In the same way that he focuses on the rituals of Lourdes in *Credo*, Duvivier displays an equally anthropological fascination with the Carmelite rites. His camera lingers on religious art and artefacts, and the specific traditions of the Order. Even the later audience with Pope Leo XIII is meticulously filmed, lit and framed like medieval missal illuminations. Once again, Duvivier uses double exposures. A priest asks Thérèse to reflect on the life she is about to renounce and to think about what lies beyond the railings of the monastery. These *grilles* are superimposed onto Thérèse's face, along with intertitles: 'Obéissance', 'Humilité', 'Travail', 'Froid', 'Jeun', 'Solitude', 'Renoncement', 'Oubli', and

25 'By a strange predetermination, these exact same scenes were taking place, fifteen years apart, both at the Monastery of St Bernard and at the Hôtel-Dieu in Alençon.'

'Jusqu'à la Mort'.²⁶ Throughout this striking scene, Duvivier uses a range of techniques. The cutting of Thérèse's hair is filmed in an unbroken, two-minute-long close-up shot, preceded and followed by two extreme close-ups of her father's weeping face.

Once the hair has been shorn, Duvivier inserts a superimposed image of Christ, who reaches out to touch the back of Thérèse's head. While she kneels on the floor to the left of the screen, on the right-hand side, a second Thérèse has stood up and is being led off to another room. She leaves, but the two superimposed images of Thérèse and Christ remain in the frame.²⁷ After nine years in the Order, Thérèse again sees a vision of the Devil, who taunts her for the second time: 'Tu n'as pas la vocation ... tu n'aimes rien du Carmel! ... Tu aimes la joie! (*double exposure of dancing girls*) ... Tu aimes le soleil, tu aimes l'espace (*double exposure of forests, lakes, and trees*) ... Tu aimes la beauté, tu aimes le luxe (*double exposure of jewellery*) ... Sors d'ici! Tu seras Reine ... tu seras Mère! ... Ici, le froid, la faim, la solitude, la souffrance, et l'ennui ... Et la mort ... Et après la mort, RIEN (*Thérèse collapses*).'²⁸ These scenes contain moments as dramatic as anything Duvivier made in this period. As the *découpage* shows, content (faith, doubt) and form (double exposure, close-ups) are inextricably linked. Alain Masson has described Duvivier's films as a mixture of 'la passion du détail et le goût de la magnificence' (1996: 82).²⁹ It is an apt summation not just of the graphic impressiveness of *La Vie miraculeuse de Thérèse Martin* but also of Duvivier's silent work more broadly. Each film appears to alternate between intricate depictions of reality and a more expansive visual texture (whether landscape, climate, or city street).

26 'Obedience', 'Humility', 'Work', 'Cold', 'Fasting', 'Solitude', 'Renunciation', Oblivion', and 'then Death'.
27 A year earlier, in *La Passion de Jeanne d'Arc*, Carl Theodor Dreyer had subjected Renée Falconetti to similar treatment, shaving her head. It is surprising that few reviews of the time mention the links between the two films; Dreyer based his film on actual records of the trial of Joan of Arc, just as Duvivier worked from Thérèse's original memoirs.
28 'You do not have the calling ... you love nothing about the Carmelites! ... You love joy! ... You love the sunshine, you love the outdoors ... You love beauty, you love luxury ... Leave here! You will be a queen ... you will be a mother! ... In here, it is all about cold, hunger, solitude, suffering, and boredom ... And death ... And after death, NOTHING.'
29 'the passion of the detail and the taste of magnificence'.

Conclusion

History has not looked kindly on Duvivier's silent films, no matter that they constitute almost a quarter of his entire output. Maurice Bardèche and Robert Brasillach (1954: 337–8) wrote in *Histoire du cinéma* that, before the arrival of sound, Duvivier had directed 'un grand nombre de films d'une médiocrité repoussante, qui l'avaient classé une fois pour toutes parmi les commerçants de l'écran'.[30] In his 1968 retrospective of Duvivier's career, Pierre Leprohon sounded an equally cool note. Behind 'l'habilité du métier, le goût du paysage et des jolis effets' lay a penchant for 'l'artifice des situations [et] l'aspect conventionnel des caractères [et] des sujets qui manquent à la fois de vérité et de vigueur' (1968: 207).[31] Even Duvivier, in a 1931 interview with Nino Frank (1931: 11), admitted that he was dissatisfied with all of his silent films from 1926 up to his first sound film, *David Golder*, released in 1930: 'J'ai 'stagné', si j'ose dire' ('I stagnated, dare I say it').

Yet, if we look a little closer, we see that this genre eclecticism and sheer willingness to experiment are key driving forces. Duvivier's favoured working methods would be cemented during the 1920s – working fast, working to budget, proud of his adaptability, which secured him regular assignments and a chance to learn the craft of film-making 'on the job'. Pierre Lazareff (1928) wrote in *Paris-Midi* that Duvivier 'est l'un des *metteurs en scène* qualifiés pour donner au cinéma français la place que nous voudrions lui voir prendre'.[32] Hubert Niogret (2010) rates *Le Reflet de Claude Mercœur*, *Le Tourbillon de Paris*, and *Maman Colibri* particularly highly because they each resemble the very best American melodramas of the period in terms of *mise en scène* and narrative fluidity, and also because they offer dynamic domestic alternatives to films imported from elsewhere. Duvivier is playing rival national film cultures at their own game, borrowing their visual patterns (cross-cutting, costumes, performance style) and reworking them for eager domestic audiences. Thus, by *Au*

30 'a large number of films of a repellent mediocrity, which ranked him once and for all among cinema's *commerçants*'.
31 'the skill of his craft, the taste for the outdoors, and pretty effects'; 'artificiality of situations [and] conventional characters [and] subject matter lacking in both truthfulness and vigour'.
32 'is one of the directors best qualified to bestow upon French cinema the place that we would like to see it taking'.

bonheur des dames, Duvivier was in a prime position to head up a new, vigorous French cinema, one that borrowed liberally from its literary past but also offered convincing critiques of the modernity of French life – conspicuous consumption, and wealth, the rise of the urban metropolis, the relationship to its colonies, and so on. Duvivier's sensitivity to the relationship between environment and character was also a strong feature of his silent films and anticipated those more famous examples of the 1930s in which person–place interaction would be strengthened by means of expressive design and a visually dense *mise en scène*. And so, it is to the 1930s, and some of Duvivier's best-known work, to which we now turn.

References

Abel, R. (1984), *French Cinema: The First Wave, 1915–1929*, Princeton, Princeton University Press.
Anon. (1924a), 'La Machine à refaire la vie', *Comœdia*, 4123, 1 April, p. 2.
Anon. (1924b), 'Credo ou la tragédie de Lourdes', *L'Eveil provençal*, 28 August, np.
Anon. (1925), 'Credo ou la tragédie de Lourdes', *Cinémagazine*, 18, 1 May, p. 200.
Anon. (1929), 'La Divine croisière', *La Cinématographie française*, 28 September, np.
Bardèche M. and R. Brasillach (1954), *Histoire du cinéma*, Paris, André Martel.
Bonnefille, E. (2002), *Julien Duvivier: Le Mal aimant du cinéma français*, vol. 1, Paris, Harmattan.
Borger, L. (1998), 'Genius Is Just a Word', *Sight and Sound*, September, pp. 28–31.
Coutisson, J.-P. (1930), 'Au bonheur des dames', *Comœdia*, 817, 25 March, p. 6.
Croze, J.-L. (1926), 'L'Homme à l'Hispano', *Comœdia*, 5100, 11 December, p. 3.
de Puyfontaine, P. (1927), 'Le Mystère de la Tour Eiffel', *La Critique cinématographique*, 11 June, p. 7.
Desrichard, Y. (2001), *Julien Duvivier: Cinquante ans de noirs destins*, Paris, BiFi/Durante.
Duvivier, J. (1921a), 'Lettre d'Angleterre', *Hebdo film*, 295, 22 October, pp. 29–30.
Duvivier, J. (1921b), 'Le Cinéma à Londres', *Hebdo film*, 298, 12 November, pp. 19–21.
Duvivier, J. (1926), 'Mon retour de Jérusalem', *Comœdia*, 4895, 21 May, p. 3.
Flinn, M. (2014), *The Social Architecture of French Cinema, 1929–39*, Liverpool, Liverpool University Press.
Frank, N. (1931), 'Les confidences de M. Julien Duvivier', *Pour vous*, 117, 12 February, p. 11.

Gunning, T. (1990), 'The Cinema of Attractions: Early Film, Its Spectator, and the Avant-Garde', in *Early Cinema: Space, Frame, Narrative*, eds T. Elsaesser and A. Barker, London, BFI, pp. 56–62.
Lazareff, P. (1928), '*Le Tourbillon de Paris*', *Paris-Midi*, 1 August, np.
Leprohon, P. (1930), 'Entretien avec Julien Duvivier', *Cinémonde*, 69, 13 February, pp. 101–2.
Masson, A. (1996), 'La magnificence et le détail', *Positif*, 429, pp. 82–5.
Nardy, A. (1922), '*L'Ouragan sur la montagne*', *Bonsoir*, 20 September, np.
Nelson, B. (1995), 'Introduction', in *The Ladies' Paradise*, trans. B. Nelson, Oxford, Oxford University Press, pp. vii–xxiii.
Niogret, H. (2010), *Julien Duvivier: 50 ans de cinéma*, Paris, Bazaar and Co.
O'Brien, C. (2009), '*Sous les toits de Paris* and Transnational Film Style: An Analysis of Film Editing Statistics', *Studies in French Cinema*, 9:2, pp. 111–25.
Slavin, D. (2001), *Colonial Cinema and Imperial France 1919–1939: White Blind Spots, Male Fantasies, Settler Myths*, Baltimore and London: Johns Hopkins University Press.
Souillac, P. (1927), '*Le Mystère de la Tour Eiffel*', *Le Cinéopse*, 100, 1 December, pp. 1041–3.
Tenevain, A. (1928), '*Le Tourbillon de Paris*', *Le Cinéopse*, 1 May, np.
Tournier, G. (1922), '*Les Roquevillard*', *L'Echo de Paris*, 28 April, p. 5.

3

Sound, image, Gabin: Duvivier and the 1930s

> On connaît les défauts de ce brillant metteur en scène. Ces défauts, d'autres les appellent 'qualités'.[1]
>
> (Lucie Derain, reviewing *Le Paquebot Tenacity* in *Cinémonde*, 5 July 1934)

The story of the French film ecosystem of the 1930s has been well documented (Crisp 1993, 2002, 2015; Andrew 1995; Billard 1995; Phillips 2004; Vincendeau 2004; Jeancolas 2005; O'Brien 2005; McCann 2013; Driskell 2015). The coming of sound brought with it rapid industrial and cultural change and Duvivier adapted well. His projects were selected on the basis of personal taste and the final product often contained an expressive use of *mise en scène*. In the 1920s, Duvivier had dipped confidently into whatever material was offered him and he brought the same eclectic and assured approach to subject matter to his sound films. This confidence stemmed from the comparatively flexible working conditions that emerged in the early 1930s, where a 'can-do' climate was the norm. This was a time when smaller-scale film companies flourished and directors with strong artistic visions (such as Duvivier, Jean Renoir, and Marcel Carné) were encouraged to experiment with film's new sonic possibilities.

Several other factors accounted for Duvivier's continuing success. The development of panchromatic film allowed a greater control of shadow and light in the studio and aided the presence of typical motifs, such as glistening cobbles, rain-spattered pavements, and

---

[1] 'We all know the faults of this brilliant metteur en scène. Others call these faults "qualities".'

dark shadows. Duvivier's brand of poetic realism was underpinned by these sculpting properties of light, while his frequent designer Jacques Krauss fabricated décor that could be lit in expressionistic ways. The decade also saw an explosion of populist literature that chronicled the social transformations affecting French urban society. Novelists such as Ashelbé and Pierre Mac Orlan, alongside Georges Simenon and his socially inflected crime fiction, were preoccupied with criminal figures and the underworld milieu. As we shall see, Duvivier adapted novels by all three of these writers during this period. As he had done in the silent era, Duvivier worked on repeat assignments with the same technical and artistic teams. This time, his team included Harry Baur, Maurice Jaubert, Henri Jeanson, Jacques Krauss, Charles Spaak, and Armand Thirard. Such consistency of personnel helped to create a style that came to exemplify what Colin Crisp (1993) calls the 'classic French cinema'.

The coming of sound to French cinema in the early 1930s altered the film industry's artistic and economic imperatives (Crisp 1993: 104–14). New, acoustically improved sound stages altered performance styles and modified the contract between audience and actor. Trade journals questioned whether sound's arrival would compromise film's capacity for naturalism by requiring the use of the artificial studio. Having served his apprenticeship on Antoine's *plein air* films, Duvivier was interested from the early part of his career in the interaction between setting and character development. He did not abandon the graphic aspects of pre-sound cinema once sound became the industrial norm; instead, there is a remarkable continuity in his pre- and post-sound films. The use of double exposure is a case in point – Duvivier first applied this technique in *Haceldama ou le prix du sang* (1919), but it is freely used in *David Golder* (1930) and *La Charette fantôme* (1939), and many times in between. The incorporation of documentary-style inserts of real places to establish location is another example of this continuity from silent to sound practice, as is the use of lighting to create mood and the faith in literary adaptation (eleven of the eighteen films Duvivier made in France during the 1930s were drawn from novels or plays). The following analysis of four of Duvivier's early sound films illustrates these contextual factors. Aside from their sonic innovations, they remain fascinating examples of Duvivier's ongoing exploration of genre, adaptation practice, and atmospheric realism.

Experiments in sound

Duvivier's first sound film was *David Golder*, an adaptation of Irène Némirovsky's eponymous novel about a rich Jewish businessman (Harry Baur) who gradually comes to realise that his wife, Gloria, and his daughter, Joyce, love him only for his money. Golder was Harry Baur's first speaking role and his first of seven collaborations with Duvivier. The director admired Baur's acting style for 'sa versatilité, sa truculence, sa bonhomie, sa puissance' (Duvivier 1977: 41),[2] qualities that are abundantly on display here.

David Golder contains a complex sonic design that showcases the new potential of French sound cinema to record overlapping sounds and then exploit that combined sound as a dramatic device. The opening few moments reflect this. A montage sequence flashes up images of the Paris Bourse, railway lines, and a steamship, while various off-screen voices 'introduce' Golder ('Golder est une fripouille', 'Golder, c'est un grand bonhomme'[3]). We have not yet met Golder, but this *découpage* swiftly links Golder's larger-than-life persona to a world of transit and finance. Later, Golder's death on the ship that is returning him home after a foreign business deal is underpinned by a soundtrack that mingles Yiddish and Russian folk songs, the ship's horn, screeching seagulls, and Golder's conversations with a young man in French and Yiddish. In the film's final moments, the thrum of the ship's motor is overlaid onto Golder's weakening heartbeat, and a soft violin can be heard on the soundtrack. When Golder dies, the violin subsides and the ambient sounds of waves and the ship's engine build to a peak.

For many scholars, the most troubling aspect of *David Golder* is its anti-Semitism. Garçon (1984) notes that negative depictions of Jews were commonplace in 1930s French cinema. Lynn Higgins (2012) writes that Duvivier gives Jews an 'oppressive visual presence'; Soifer, an older German Jew who walks on tiptoe to save shoe leather, is given a hooked nose, a high voice, and an obsequious manner, while Fischl, Gloria's suitor, has an oily face and intimidating bulk (61). Burch and Sellier (1996) see a distinction between the 'good Jew' Golder, who is 'assimilated [and] who makes his capital work

---

2 'his versatility, his larger-than-life persona, his warmth, his strength'.
3 'Golder is a scoundrel'; 'Golder is a fine gentleman.'

for him', and the 'bad Jew' Soifer, an 'unproductive hoarder' (34). Simon P. Sibelman (2000) argues that the unambiguous reference to Golder's Jewishness alongside the connections constantly made in both novel and film between finance, capitalism, and conspiracy is a clear strategy by both Némirovsky and Duvivier to tap into France's strong anti-Jewish climate. For Sibelman, Duvivier's representational system is guilty of laying down a formal cinematic template for all future depictions of Jews in 1930s French cinema, providing the spectator 'with sufficient confirmation of its own pre-judgements concerning Jews, their heartless nature, and their utter "otherness"' (88). Crisp (2015) also sees Golder, and Duvivier's portrayal of modern capitalism, as problematic; he points to Golder's reaction to a former associate's suicide – 'Je m'en fous' ('I don't give a damn') – as evidence that '"not caring" is [Golder's] motto [...] he has become rich by being more ruthless than others' (38). Pierre Sorlin (1981) suggests that some, though not all, films from this period 'unwittingly contributed to reinforcing prejudices' (148). However, he also contends that Jews had to be presented to French audiences in ways that would make them immediately recognisable. Names, accents, physical characteristics, and connections with finance and business were vital to the identification of French Jews (140).

There is no indication in any of the interviews Duvivier ever gave either at the time of the film's release or subsequently that would suggest Duvivier was anti-Semitic. Duvivier actually presents Golder fairly sympathetically; it is his wife, daughter, and friends who are depicted negatively. Burch and Sellier (1996) see Golder's death as noble; he is the 'sacrificial father' who dies while guaranteeing his daughter (who, in any case, is not his) future financial prosperity. In terms of drawing out continuities with Duvivier's earlier and later work, the depiction of his wife and daughter comes dangerously close to pure misogyny (but that was already present in the novel): both Gloria and Joyce are vain, grasping, and materialistic. Some critics (Higgins 2012) detect in Golder the melodramatic and metaphysical panic of a man who is besieged by a *femme fatale*. Evidence of this is found in the harrowing scene when Golder revives from a heart attack. Gloria stands over his bed and screams that he is not Joyce's father and accuses him of not providing for their future. Golder's response to his 'castrating wife' is to grab her throat and slowly attempt to strangle her with her own pearls. Duvivier often 'doubles' this *femme fatale* figure, splitting it between mother and daughter. This dual/duel would return again, in equally disturbing form, in *Voici le temps des assassins* (1956).

Les Cinq gentlemen maudits (1931) marked a return to the colonial setting of *Maman Colibri* (1929). It was adapted from an André Reuzé novel,[4] and Duvivier directed two simultaneous multiple-language versions, one in French, the other in German (called *Die Fünf verfluchten Gentlemen**) that used the same décor, camera set-ups, and editing, but different actors.[5] While on holiday in Morocco, one of the five 'gentlemen' of the title attempts to remove the veil from the face of a native woman. All five are then cursed by a blind beggar and sentenced to die before the next full moon. One drowns, another dies in a plane crash, and another is stabbed. Jacques Le Guerantec (René Lefèvre) is determined to solve the mystery. It emerges that the curse is in fact an elaborate trick by Strawber (Robert Le Vigan) to acquire Le Guerantec's money; the blind beggar was a ruse, and two of the three men supposedly killed are still alive.

As the synopsis suggests, Duvivier destabilises the conventional suspicion of westerners towards the Moroccan 'other' by crafting a plot in which nothing is as it seems. This would become a hallmark of Duvivier throughout his career, in the form of shifting genres and narrative expectations, and the deception of audiences through narrative twists and a stylised *mise en scène*. The casting of high-calibre actors such as Lefèvre, Le Vigan, and Harry Baur became another noticeable facet of Duvivier's work. The film, however, feels disjointed. Despite its *noir*-infused narrative of double-crossing and duplicity, it is clear that Duvivier's interest lies more in filming the ambience and atmosphere of the foreign space. Like *David Golder*, the opening sequence is full of sound experiments. From the off, Jacques Ibert's score cedes to an exotic African chant as the opening

---

4 A 1920 version of the film had already been released.
5 The multiple-language version was a labour-intensive practice of remaking an entire film, often simultaneously, in which the same director would use the same sets and the same camera set-ups, but different casts, in order to make films in various languages that could then be exported to relevant territories without the need for subtitling or dubbing. The German-language-version stars Anton Walbrook in one of his earliest screen roles. He would go onto make *The Red Shoes* (1948), *La Ronde* (1950), and, with Duvivier again, *L'Affaire Maurizius* (1954).

credits roll. Once the credits end, we see the provenance of the sound – Moroccan tanners who use the rhythmic chanting for their work. The opening ten minutes or so are full of location shots of a tannery in Fez, an open-air market with its sights and sounds, children reciting the Qur'an, belly-dancers, snake charmers, muezzins and minarets, and the call to prayer.

Les Cinq gentlemen maudits was one of French cinema's earliest examples of colonial cinema. The cycle was started with Jacques Feyder's *L'Atlantide* (1921), but the genre exploded in popularity at the start of the 1930s with films such as *Le Grand jeu* (Jacques Feyder, 1934), *Itto* (Marie Epstein and Jean Benoît-Lévy, 1934), and *Les Hommes nouveaux* (Marcel L'Herbier, 1936). *Les Cinq gentlemen maudits* was made during the summer of 1931, at the height of interest in Paris' Exposition Coloniale (which had opened in May of that year). These cinematic depictions of the French empire gave spectators 'a sense of control over alterity, as it was brought to them in a contained form, in which potentially threatening difference was domesticated' (Ezra 2003: 57). The ethnographic feel of this opening segment is all of a piece with this discourse. Producers Marcel Vandal and Charles Delac developed a series of brochures that asked publicists to stress to French audiences how Duvivier had invented 'a new film genre' that united 'mysterious intrigue' with 'Moroccan ambience'.[6]

Throughout *Les Cinq gentlemen maudits*, Duvivier incorporates real sounds, authentic images, and found footage. Filming in Fez, Marrakech, and Moulay-Idriss lent an authenticity that recalled *Credo ou la tragédie de Lourdes* (1924), *Le Mariage de Mademoiselle Beulemans* (1927), and the numerous street scenes of Duvivier's Paris-based silent films. Elegant camerawork consisted of a mixture of crane shots, high- and low-angle shots, close-ups, and low tracking shots that evoke a sense of unease and disquiet. There is a sudden travelling towards a muezzin whose eyes are rolled upwards that evinces both fascination and repulsion towards the indigenous population. Later, in an exchange that reflected many of the prejudices French audiences would have had in 1931, one character admits that Morocco is a place of danger and superstition.

---

6 The film's promotional and publicity material is archived alongside reviews at the Bibliothèque Nationale in Paris.

After the critical success of *David Golder*, critics were less positive about Duvivier's follow-up (many condemned the plot) but still hailed the director's visual style, pacing, and direction of actors. *Les Cinq gentlemen maudits* also develops key Duvivier themes: false friends, doubles, and duplicitous behaviour are here transplanted from the Hexagon and mapped onto an exotic space. The aerial shots of roofs and the bright, white light that emphasise the oppressive heat of the North African sun lay down a blueprint for later Duvivier 'colonial films', most notably *Pépé le Moko* (1937).

What followed is a rarity in his body of work – a romantic comedy. *Allô Berlin? Ici Paris!* (1932) tells the tale of two telephone switchboard operators, one French, the other German, who 'meet cute'. The Parisian Lily (Josette Day, who would go on to become 'Beauty' in Jean Cocteau's *La Belle et la bête* [1946]) and the Berliner Erich (Wolfgang Klein) eventually fall in love, but this transcontinental 'comedy of remarriage' is jeopardised by the womaniser Karl (Hans Henninger) and the vampish Annette (Germaine Aussey), who each bully their way into Lily and Erich's blossoming relationship and pretend to be 'Lily' and 'Erich'.

On the surface, the genre coordinates of *Allô Berlin? Ici Paris!* are American, with Duvivier anticipating future screwball comedies from Howard Hawks and George Cukor. Its involuntary comic situations – characters talking at cross-purposes without realising it – anticipate Ernst Lubitsch's *The Shop around the Corner* (1940), while the scene in which Josette Day changes her clothes behind a curtain is replicated by Claudette Colbert in Frank Capra's *It Happened One Night* (1934). Closer to home, *Allô Berlin? Ici Paris!* nestles alongside René Clair's contemporary comedies such as *Le Million* (1931) and *Quatorze juillet* (1932). Not unlike Clair, Duvivier incorporates sight-and-sound gags and a strong dose of anti-authoritarianism, and combines romance and playful anarchy with darker, more transgressive elements. Coming between the bleakness of *David Golder* and the existential torpor of *La Tête d'un homme*, *Allô Berlin? Ici Paris!* demonstrates how skilfully Duvivier could change tack and grapple with lighter material. This tonal gulf between assignments would come to characterise Duvivier's entire professional approach, especially during the 1950s and 1960s.

Charles O'Brien (1998: 429) has noted how early 1930s French cinema is full of memorable moments due to the gratuitous materiality of certain sounds. *Allô Berlin? Ici Paris!* gives central place to sound and voice. The tour de force opening sequence reflects this cacophony: we see and hear a kaleidoscope of mouthpieces, earpieces, hands dialling, telephony parts, and '*allô, allô*' repeated on the soundtrack. We are left in no doubt of the vitality of this brave new world, in which telephonic communication will play a central role. Later, all of the female telephone operators, inspired by the unseen Erich, burst into song, surprising their switchboard clients and incurring the wrath of their supervisor. With the arrival of sound, Duvivier suggests, there is a strong need to maintain cinema's international perspective and significance (it is telling that the first image we see is a globe). Rather than film a multiple-language version, Duvivier made *Allô Berlin? Ici Paris!* a bilingual film. The French actors speak French, German ones speak German, and subtitles are added for the various domestic audiences.

More broadly, the film can be seen to extol Franco-German friendship and the importance of dialogue over conflict. Duvivier shuttles between Paris and Berlin, between Weimar taverns and Montmartre cabarets. This cutting between the two cities deepens the film's celebration of leisure, travel, and singing, and also, as one critic noted, generates 'la simultanéité malgré la distance' ('simultaneity in spite of distance').[7] Elsewhere, Duvivier alternates between silent-film grammar and the new stylistics of the sound cinema. He includes *pneumatiques* (a form of telegram),[8] letters, street signs, train station boards and timetables, clocks, several close-ups of faces and objects, double exposures, and kaleidoscopic images of telephones. Rapid cutting and a spinning camera reinforce the film's overtly burlesque moments. The Paris bus tour has a series of recurring visual punchlines, in which the tourists keep missing out on seeing the monuments because the driver, getting progressively more inebriated, is driving too quickly. Later, the 'President of the Transoceanic Republics' arrives in a rain-soaked Berlin, and the orchestra playing in his honour is drenched. Duvivier cross-cuts between teeming rain, the instruments, and the president's wet clothes.

Despite its gentle comic inflections, Duvivier's gloomier obsessions are on show. There is the loneliness of big-city living (the 'Automat' restaurant in Berlin in which lonely ladies telephone drunken men from across the other side of the room) and the subjugation of the

7 Jean Fayard, in *Candide*.
8 The address on the telegram is 'Rue Duvivier'.

worker. A song about to be performed by a *chanteuse* is announced by the MC as having 'paroles de Julien Duvivier' ('lyrics by Julien Duvivier'). While that self-reflexive moment comes as a surprise, the song itself is illustrative of Duvivier's wider concerns. Entitled 'Chanson lasse' ('Tired Song'), its lyrics are troubling: 'Las des hommes, las de l'espoir [...] Je ne veux plus rien que l'oubli.'[9] The scene is doubly revealing because during the performance, Duvivier tracks across the forlorn faces of the audience. Another recurring theme is the deception of Lily and Erich by duplicitous doubles. At one point, the two (wrong) couples visit two different bars: at 'Le Bal nègre', Annette tries to seduce Erich, while Lily brings Max, whom she thinks is Erich, to 'Au Lapin Agile'. Here, the double, the infidelity of appearances, and the ease with which people can deceive one another are skewed versions of the film's narrative hook: telephony can bring people together, but it can also trick and lie. In a typical move, Duvivier laces his romantic comedy with sadness.

Duvivier's final 'early sound' film was *La Tête d'un homme* (1932), adapted from Georges Simenon's novel. The author had been extremely frustrated with two recent adaptations of his work, *Le Chien jaune* (Jean Tarride, 1932) and *La Nuit du carrefour* (Jean Renoir, 1932) and thus decided to adapt and direct the next Maigret adaptation himself.[10] When producers Vandal and Delac became fearful of Simenon's unconventional suggestions for the film, the surer hand of Duvivier was brought in to replace him. Duvivier selected Harry Baur as Maigret (Simenon had wanted Pierre Renoir, brother of Jean, to reprise his role). In *La Nuit du carrefour*, Pierre Renoir imbued his Maigret with an air of all-knowing detachment; here, Baur's heft suggests a tussle with the criminal that is as much physical as psychological. *La Tête d'un homme* also starred Alexandre Rignault as the fall-guy Heurtin and Gaston Jacquet as Willy Ferrière, prolonging the link between Duvivier's silent and sound career. By far the most memorable performance was that of Russian émigré Valéry Inkijinoff – the star of Vsevolod Pudovkin's *Storm over Asia* (1928) – as the sinister villain Radek, who, like Raskolnikov in Dostoevsky's *Crime and Punishment*, kills not for profit or purpose but as a nihilistic gesture to a society he despises. Duvivier, along

9 'Tired of men, tired of hope [...] All I want to do is forget.'
10 'Only the author can judge how his novel must be incarnated', he confided in a *Paris-Midi* interview in April 1932.

with his production designer Georges Wakhévitch and cinematographer Armand Thirard, creates a succession of teeming, vibrant spaces in and around Montparnasse that prefigure the poetic realist aesthetic and early Hollywood *noir*.

The opening credits of *La Tête d'un homme* are revealing. Duvivier's adapation is 'inspiré du roman de Simenon' ('inspired by Simenon's novel'). This will be no direct transposition. Duvivier is not interested in maintaining suspense and guiding the spectator towards a conclusion in which everything is explained *à la* Simenon. In fact, in a ground-breaking tactic, Duvivier reveals the identity of the murderer very early on; the rest of the *policier* focuses on the cat-and-mouse dynamics between Radek and Maigret and examines the psychological intrigue between killer and detective.

Such a bold narrative choice foreshadowed later debates about the prevalence of *noir* in French film culture. In 1946, Nino Frank, writing for the leftist review *L'Ecran français*, saw *noir* as an articulation of a new version of the human condition that moved away from the traditional schema of the *policier*: 'La question essentielle ne consiste plus à découvrir qui a commis le crime, mais à voir comment va se comporter le protagoniste?' (Frank 1946: 14).[11] For Frank and others, post-1945 *noir* focused less on plot details and more on the inner workings of the criminal – their motivations, their psychology, and their repressed desires. What is particularly interesting, therefore, is to note that Duvivier was already doing this way back in 1932. As one review noted (Anon. 1933a: 117), Duvivier 'ouvre la porte à un genre difficile et jusqu'ici jamais réussi: le drame policier psychologique. [Duvivier] a composé un film remarquable, précis, nuancé et [...] parfaitement original et expressif'.[12]

The French director Patrice Leconte has called Simenon a 'false friend' because of the seemingly untranslatable nature of his visual images into cinematic form (Spicer 2010: 279). Yet Duvivier finds a set of visual equivalents in *La Tête d'un homme* that aligns the melancholic atmosphere that pervades Simenon's work with his own heightened visual sense. The landscape is dreary, rain-slicked and windswept, and full of fog, mist, and occluded corners. From a technical perspective,

11 'the essential question is no longer "who-done-it?" but how does this protagonist act?'
12 'opens the door to a difficult genre that has hitherto never been attempted: the psychological *policier*. [Duvivier] has created a remarkable film that is precise, nuanced and absolutely new and expressive.'

Duvivier tests out interesting classical procedures. The opening few moments of the film feature an unbroken travelling shot from Thirard that tracks Willy Ferrière through a crowded bar, and this is followed by a conversation between Ferrière and the barman filmed in a mirror. Duvivier switches from a wide master shot to a close-up of Radek and then cuts away to a note lying next to a foot. *La Tête d'un homme* ends with a daring use of camera placement. Radek lies trapped beneath the wheel of an omnibus, his hand and his head protruding at horrific angles. Sonically, too, the film is radical, whether in the use of off-screen noises, such as howling wolves and human breathing, which intermingle with the hubbub of Montparnasse bars; the hammering of a fist on a metal shutter as Radek lies dying; or the dead silence in the aftermath of the early murder. *La Tête d'un homme* thus fits alongside Jean Grémillon's *La Petite Lise* (1930) and Renoir's *La Chienne* (1931) as an adroit example of early sound cinema's application of dense, multi-layered soundscapes.

A few points need to be mentioned. Firstly, Duvivier continued his experimentations with new film technology with a transparent screen called the transflex.[13] When one of Maigret's associates questions a series of witnesses, he stands in front of a transflex upon which the background of the interrogation room and the witnesses are projected, and via a series of dissolves the witnesses appear to disappear while the detective stays in shot, giving the impression that he is moving from one location to another. Secondly, Duvivier cast the real-life *chanteuse réaliste* Damia as a mysterious woman who lives next door to Radek but who is not seen, by either Radek or the viewer, until the film's closing moments. Listed in the credits as 'la femme lasse' ('the weary woman'), Damia sings a haunting song that is heard multiple times, and its obsessive, hypnotic looping adds to the film's dream-like texture. The lyrics, written by Duvivier, are perfectly suited to the director's view of the world:

> Et la nuit m'envahit
> Tout est brumeux
> Tout est gris.[14]

---

[13] The transflex was created by Yves Le Prieur, the co-inventor of scuba and the air-to-air rocket.

[14] 'And the night invades me / All is mist / All is grey'.

At the end of *La Tête d'un homme*, as Radek assaults Ferrière's lover, Edna (Gina Manès), in his room, Damia's song once more floats into his apartment. Radek then barges into the singer's room, dragging Edna with him, and lies between Edna (the Body) and Damia (the Voice) in the ultimate creation of his feminine 'ideal'. For Edouard Arnoldy, Radek wants nothing more than to recreate an impossible fantasy, 'prendre à un corps sa voix, et une voix à un corps, pour modeler une créature parfaite, un *éternel féminin*' (2004: 137).[15] This is a radical addition to the Simenon text and reminds us that Duvivier's adaptation practices were rarely fixed. Trialling new formal and visual aspects was more important to Duvivier than replicating a style or practising literary fidelity. The third point to be mentioned is that the glittering reception of *La Tête d'un homme* raised Duvivier to the summit of French film-making; *L'Ami du film* (1933b) wrote that Duvivier was the 'meilleur *metteur en scène* français' ('best French director'). There were only a few dissenting voices, such as that of René Bizet (1933: 5) in *Pour vous*, who called for Duvivier's future films to be 'un art de suggestion plutôt que de visions brutales'.[16] As we shall see, Bizet's call for a less brutal cinema would fall on deaf ears.

Interlude: (re-)making *Poil de carotte* (1925, 1932)

In 1932, Duvivier turned to French popular literature once more and made *Poil de carotte*, based on Jules Renard's much-loved novel. Or, more accurately, Duvivier remade it, for he had already filmed a silent version in 1925. Both versions of *Poil de carotte* tell the story of freckled and red-headed François (the 'carrot top' of the title). He is the youngest son of the Lepics and has no friends, save for young Mathilde, whom he calls his 'fiancée', and Annette, the family housemaid. François' father is aloof and distant, his mother cruel and tyrannical. At school, he writes compositions entitled 'La famille est la réunion sous un même toit de plusieurs personnes qui ne peuvent pas se sentir.'[17] François tries to commit suicide but is saved from hanging at the last minute by the arrival of his father.

15 'to take a voice from one body and a body from one voice to create a perfect creature, an *eternal feminine*'.
16 'an art of suggestion rather than brutal visions'.
17 'The family is a group of people under the same roof who cannot feel for each other.'

For the 1925 adaptation, Duvivier cast Henry Krauss in the role of the father (after his mentor, André Antoine, turned it down). Krauss was a SCAGL stalwart with whom Duvivier had already worked on *Les Frères corses* (1917) and *Quatre-vingt treize* (1917), and his wife, Charlotte Barbier, was cast as Madame Lepic. François was played by André Heuzé. Renard's original text was composed of very short chapters, each flashing back to a particular event in François' life. Duvivier removed around two-thirds of the material and wrote a linear screenplay. He also departed from Renard by incorporating an additional subplot that focused on the romantic entanglements of the older brother (Felix) and a singer from a local cabaret.

Eric Bonnefille (2002: 51) calls *Poil de carotte* 'le sujet cinématographique' ('the cinematic subject') of Duvivier's entire life, and it is easy to see why. Christian Duvivier, the director's son, has often stated that the mutual antagonism between M. and Mme. Lepic in *Poil de carotte* mirrored his father's own Lille upbringing, where his mother and father hated each other. While that might seem too easy a reading, Renard's source material did allow Duvivier to show the debilitating results of familial unkindness and cruelty and the way in which they can humiliate an innocent child.[18] If François' father is coded as absent, more interested in local politics than his son's welfare, there is at least a glimmer of paternal love and compassion. On the other hand, Duvivier's misogyny fully emerges in his depiction of Mme. Lepic. With her negative attributes of greed, ugliness, and hypocritical piety, Mme. Lepic's portayal in both versions of the film is unrelentingly misogynistic and cruel. Richard Abel describes the 1925 Mme. Lepic as 'one of the most offensive images of women in the French cinema of the decade' (1984: 108). She beats François, pulls his hair, accuses him of theft, and even enters his dreams. Duvivier films her as a brooding presence, often in *contre plongée* or in extreme close-up, literally and figuratively dominating François and the rest of the family.

The film is a veritable treasure trove of hypermodern technique, and, along with *Au bonheur des dames* (1930), is Duvivier's most

---

18   Duvivier wanted to film the novel for a third time in the 1950s, with Gabin in the role of Lepic.

accomplished silent film. As well as the unusual canted camera angles and expressionistic lighting, he uses title cards sparingly so as to underscore the film's visual clarity and economy of style. When intertitles are used, it is for very specific purposes; the arrival of Mme. Lepic is followed by the card ('cancanière, hypocrite et méchante' ['nasty, hypocritical gossip']). When François contemplates suicide, he is discouraged by the thought of those who have shown him affection. Duvivier cuts quickly to Annette, a dog, and two cats. Double exposures reveal François' inner turmoil. As he writes his school composition, his mother's nagging face is superimposed onto the blank paper; Lepic's awareness of his son's exploitation by his wife is shown as a multiple exposure of François performing a series of menial jobs, and, with the rope around François' neck (a scene filmed in excruciating close-up, with no cutting), Duvivier superimposes images of the boy's own life onto his face. The most audacious move is during the extended family argument around the dinner table, when Duvivier films into a pivoting mirror, changing the audience's perspective by swivelling the mirror into and out of the frame. The result is a long, edit-free *plan-séquence* worthy of Renoir or Welles.

In 1932, Duvivier returned to Renard's story once more, this time setting the whole film during François' summer holidays against the backdrop of the luminous Corrèze countryside. The sound version starred Harry Baur and Robert Lynen as father and son, and Catherine Fonteney as Mme. Lepic. The film begins with François saying goodbye to everyone at school, intercut with the Lepics waiting indifferently for his return. More so than the 1925 version, the film depicts the Lepics as small-minded and *petit bourgeois*, unknowingly sowing the seeds of their child's misfortune.

The opening of the 1932 version of *Poil de carotte* is astonishingly complex for an early sound film. It last for nearly two minutes, containing eleven different camera movements (pans, tracks, dollies) and no cutting. Like the opening of *La Tête d'un homme*, this nimble establishing shot sets up character and setting, and also confirms Duvivier's early mastery of the exigencies of sound production. Elsewhere, Duvivier's direction is at times unostentatious (such as the delightful marriage 'rehearsal' when François and Mathilde march through fields, closely watched by farm animals[19]) or highly dynamic (while returning home on a horse and cart, he sees fathers playing with their sons and screams 'Personne ne m'aimera comme ça' ['No-one will ever love me like that']) as he whips the horse harder). In these scenes, Robert Lynen displays the raw naturalism shown in *Les 400 coups* (1959) by Jean-Pierre Léaud, to whom Lynen has often been compared.[20]

The climactic scene, where the father enters the barn and prevents his son from hanging himself, is one of the most powerful in Duvivier's work. 'Enlève cette corde' ('take off the rope'), orders Lepic as he struggles to remove the rope from around his son's fragile neck. As they both collapse to the ground, François tells his father: 'Je veux mourir' ('I want to die').[21] As in the 1925 version, father and son are movingly reconciled, with the father promising François that he will no longer be called 'poil de carotte'. Both films also conclude with Lepic's declaration that 'nous sommes deux' ('now there's two of us'). The wicked mother will no longer abuse François and the family unit is recast. This (re-)strengthening of masculine bonds, engineered by a strong patriarch, would become a key theme in Duvivier's later work.

Duvivier would work with Robert Lynen for a second time in *Le Petit roi* (1933)*, one of Duvivier's least known films. Lynen plays King Michel VIII, the young monarch of an unnamed central European country who ascends to the throne after the assassination of his father. When he falls ill, he retreats to the south of France to recuperate. While convalescing, he learns that a republic has been declared. Adapted from André Lichtenberger's 1910 novel, the film contains some obvious Duvivier motifs, most notably the possibility of a new life away from the rigid hierarchies of the monarchy. However, the overall critical consensus was negative and brought to a temporary end Duvivier's reputation, which had been so burnished after the consecutive critical successes of *Allô Berlin? Ici Paris!*, *La Tête d'un homme*, and *Poil de carotte*.

---

19 This sun-drenched scene is a world away from the oppressive gloom of *David Golder*.
20 Lynen joined the French Resistance and was tortured and shot by the Gestapo in 1944.
21 The British Board of Film Censors banned *Poil de carotte* in 1933 because it displayed scenes depicting a child driven to suicide.

Five little pieces: *Le Paquebot Tenacity* (1934), *Maria Chapdelaine* (1934), *Golgotha* (1935), *Le Golem* (1936), and *L'Homme du jour* (1937)

Before dealing with Duvivier's more celebrated films, it is worth exploring a number of his smaller genre pieces to see whether we can detect continuities of style. *Le Paquebot Tenacity* (1934) was based on Charles Vildrac's 1920 play. With a screenplay co-written by Vildrac with Duvivier, it is a delightful film, full of lightness and brightness. It is amusing, tender, and witty, yet stippled with sadness and the nagging sense that something better is always lying over the horizon, unattainable. The DNA of French poetic realism courses through *Le Paquebot Tenacity*, and, like *David Golder* and *La Tête d'un homme*, the film is a precursor to the 'classic French cinema' that would become so influential later in the decade. Bastien and Ségard (Albert Préjean and Hubert Prélier) find themselves in a Le Havre hotel as they wait to leave France for Canada. Bastien meets Émilienne (Nita Alvarez) and Ségard falls in love with Thérèse (Marie Glory). When they are forced to stay on shore for another week after the ship's engine malfunctions shortly after setting sail, the two men find temporary jobs. Bastien has an affair with Thérèse and eventually decides to stay in Le Havre. Ségard, having learnt of his friend's betrayal, boards the ship alone and leaves for Canada broken-hearted.

In this simple drama of two men who love the same woman, there is no real plot. Instead, Duvivier and Vildrac manufacture a series of complicating actions that gradually lead to extended moments of introspection and an irreparably damaged friendship. In this sense, the film is a proto-version of *La Belle équipe* (1936), in which male bonds are betrayed and broken by the arrival of a woman. While Thérèse is no vamp *à la* Viviane Romance, her ultimate rupturing of the homosocial bonds between Bastien and Ségard is another reminder of the destabilising presence of women in Duvivier's films.

The French response to the film was severe. François Vinneuil (1934) savaged Duvivier for making 'de déception en déception' ('disappointment after disappointment'); even future co-writer Henri Jeanson (1934) wrote that viewers should do one of three things: 'sifflent, baillent ou prennent la porte' ('whistle, yawn or walk out'). In stark contrast to this domestic reaction, the film was placed first in a top ten list of works released in Japan in 1935. Japanese director Heinosuke

Gosho regarded *Le Paquebot Tenacity* as one of cinema's purest examples of romanticism. He praised Duvivier for creating 'a lyrical poem' in which the Le Havre setting is not only 'perfect' for the theme of an unemployed couple who dream of a better life overseas but also 'glorifies' it. Gosho was particularly impressed by Duvivier's choices of settings – the Le Havre harbourside, the cobblestoned pavements, and the run-down hotel – and above all his use of the ship's whistle as an 'important element in intensifying the romantic atmosphere of the love story' (Anderson and Richie 1956: 80–1).

The backdrop of Le Havre indeed looms large. Characters wander along the harbour with cranes bisecting overcast skies and industrial detritus threatening to engulf them. The city's portrayal here clearly anticipates similar scenes in *Le Quai des brumes* (Marcel Carné, 1938). Yet, whereas Carné's Le Havre would be full of manipulative and untrustworthy individuals, Duvivier's version resembles a desired 'half-way house' for Bastien and Segard. Marooned there, midway between the gloomy *grisaille* of Paris and Canada's vast horizons, Bastien and Ségard find themselves gradually enmeshed into a joyous imagined community. They befriend the hotel staff and guests and the workers at the shipyard, and, the night before the *Tenacity* is due to sail, Bastien and Ségard sing with the other patrons in the bar, and passers-by and prostitutes join in. In a whirl of unbroken tracking shots, Duvivier lets in a chink of warmth that is all too rare in his early sound cinema. 'Tu chantes mieux que Préjean!' ('You sing better than Préjean!'), Louisette, the bar owner, tells Bastien/Préjean, in another of Duvivier's lighthearted intertextual moments. Yet, this being a Duvivier film, the overriding tone is melancholy.

The film enacts a variation of a strong narrative driving force in 1930s French cinema: escape (Crisp 2002: 95–116). In an apparent initial inversion of the conventions of poetic realist narratives, Bastien and Ségard's ship does actually set sail, and with both men on it. Such escape, however, in accordance with the in-built patterns of poetic realism, can only be temporary. The ship makes a swift u-turn and the duo is back on shore, kicking their heels. This promise of escape, so plangent in Duvivier's films of the 1930s, bubbles under the film's surface from the opening moments. In a Paris cinema, Bastien and Ségard watch a film set in some faraway exotic space, where women dance and banjos play. They decide to leave rainy Paris behind and head off to Canada towards a bright new future. Motifs of travel, freedom, and the (al)lure of the exotic run wide and deep. Yet escape is not thwarted, as would be the case in *Le Quai des brumes* and *Pépé le Moko*. Ségard does manage to leave for Canada at the end, even though he is the one who did not want to leave France in the first place. At one point, a local resident says to Thérèse: 'il y a ceux qui partent et ceux qui restent, on n'y peut rien, c'est la destinée'.[22] Concepts of inevitability and destiny would coalesce more fully in Duvivier's upcoming projects.

Maria Chapdelaine (1934) was an adaptation of Quebecois author Louis Hémon's 1913 novel and marked the first collaboration between Duvivier and Jean Gabin. A young woman (Madeleine Renaud) lives with her pioneer family on the Canadian frontier and struggles against a hostile climate and isolated landscape. She must choose between three suitors: a trapper (François Paradis: Jean Gabin), a farmer (Eutrope: Alexandre Rignault), and a French financier (Lorenzo: Jean-Pierre Aumont). She initially loves François; he leaves her to journey in search of furs with the intention of returning to marry her. He freezes to death and is devoured by wolves.

Winifred Woodhull (2003) notes that regional cultures and setting in French 1930s cinema are often framed as sites of tradition, communality, and authentic Frenchness so as to create sharp contrasts with the pitfalls of metropolitan (usually Parisian) life. The former spaces are presented ethnographically, concentrating on their pictorial or site-specific qualities with a nostalgic eye; the urban centres, conversely, are coded as exploitative and dangerous. Having already been to Morocco, and soon to depart for Algiers with *Pépé le Moko*, Duvivier once more turned his itinerant eye away from the Hexagon to French Canada. This story of a rural love triangle in a distant Francophone space clearly appealed to Duvivier the ethnographer. Shooting on location in and around Péribonka and Lake Mistassini in northern Quebec, Duvivier captures the grandeur and epic quality of that rugged wilderness in a similar way to in *Haceldama* and *Les Cinq gentlemen maudits*. Iroquois Indians were cast to provide local colour (there are scenes of dancing and drumming) and the daily life of the isolated community is beautifully rendered. An image

22 'there are those who leave and those who stay; you can't do anything about it: it's destiny'.

of a horse falling in the snow is an appropriate metaphor for the hardships faced.

Duvivier worked with four different cameramen on *Maria Chapdelaine* – Georges Périnal, Armand Thirard, Jules Krüger, and Marc Fossard – and each contributed to the film's impressive cinematography. They capture the seasonal rhythms of the landscape (harvest, farm labour, snowstorms) in a way that was rare in French cinema of this period. We see François framed multiple times in his surroundings, dwarfed by immense pine forests, the fast-flowing River Péribonka, and a huge waterfall. This 'mythic' entrance suggests a natural landscape both idyllic and overwhelming, and it is in turn mapped onto the emotions of the characters. Duvivier also incorporates silent techniques, such as a rapid montage of springtime images that suggest Maria's future happiness with François, and a series of ghostly images that kaleidoscope around Maria's mother as she lies dying.

Duvivier's adaptation of the novel is dynamic. Whereas Hémon's novel presents events consecutively and marks contrasts between the characters over several chapters, Duvivier cross-cuts, increasing the dramatic tension. One example of this is François trudging through the forest in a snow storm and Maria, back home, praying the rosary in the hope it will bring François back to her. Another occurs when Duvivier juxtaposes Eutrope's proposal of marriage to Maria with her father's regrets at his wife's deathbed for the miserable life he has given her. Here, Eutrope tries to give to Maria the life that her father was unable to provide for her mother.

After the commercial failures of *La Tête d'un homme*, *Le Petit roi*, and *Le Paquebot Tenacity*, *Maria Chapdelaine* was a box-office success, with record returns in cities all over France. The film won the Grand Prix du Cinéma Français in 1934 and earned Duvivier a special mention at the Venice Film Festival the following year. The *New York Times* called it a 'stirring, full-bodied and tremulously beautiful' film that 'possesses the vigor, the native wit and the homely warmth' of its down-to-earth characters and 'preserves the integrity of the Hémon work with a skill that gives the film the nobility of an epic poem' (Sennwald 1935).

Golgotha (1935) was the first sound film to portray Jesus Christ, and it centred on the last days of Jesus' life, from Palm Sunday to the Resurrection. Robert Le Vigan played Jesus, Gabin played Pontius

Pilate, and Harry Baur (Herod), Edwige Feuillère (Pilate's wife), and Lucas Gridoux (Judas) rounded out the cast.[23] Duvivier built his version of Jerusalem just outside Algiers, combining, at great cost, gigantic sets, existing structures, and various special effects. Jacques Ibert's almost constant score contributed significantly to the mood (Ibert is billed directly beneath Duvivier on the opening credit card). The visual quality is upheld by Jules Krüger's cinematography: he films the three crosses climbing up Golgotha in extreme long shot, and also films Judas' death (a return to *Haceldama*) from a distance. At the moment of Jesus' death, flashes of lightning and time-lapsed clouds rapidly bisect the sky. Duvivier and Krüger also alternate between close-ups for Pilate and Herod and *plans d'ensemble* that capture the teeming locale and the oppressive reactions of the crowds.

Like Mel Gibson's *The Passion of the Christ* (2004), Duvivier's film is less interested in Jesus' teaching and more centred on the political machinations within the Sanhedrin and between the Jewish leaders and Pilate. He does not focus on what Jesus says or does; rather, he depicts how others (Judas, Pilate, Herod, Caiaphas, the disciples at Emmaus) see him. That deflection is manifested in the title, which expands the narrative from a person to a place while also calling attention to the narrative's pre-ordained endpoint. It is a further reworking of the fatalism that had partially emerged in *Le Paquebot Tenacity* and would coalesce more fully in future Duvivier projects.

Golgotha is worth revisiting for its representation of Jesus. It opens with his entry into Jerusalem. With impressively fluid camerawork, Duvivier draws us into this circumscribed, fatalistic world with a long tracking shot that pans across the meticulously crafted maquettes of the city. We see the assembled crowds (five thousand extras were hired) and the Pharisees, the arrival in the distance, and a shot of the crowd from the point of view of Jesus. Yet Duvivier does not show us Jesus. Indeed, he is almost entirely absent from this introduction. Even when Jesus does appear, Duvivier shoots him from a low angle and at a distance, partially hidden by the disciples. He is presented as a mysterious character. Robert Le Vigan is given top billing, and yet Duvivier gives him few lines. He adopts a deliberately blank, expressionless look throughout the film, and throughout is

23 It is highly ironic that Herod is played by an actor murdered by the Gestapo and Jesus is played by an actor who ended up a Nazi sympathiser.

shot almost entirely from a distance, often in shadow, behind pillars, or obscured by other figures. While earlier and subsequent versions of the Passion (Cecil B. DeMille's silent *King of Kings* [1927]; George Stevens' *The Greatest Story Ever Told* [1965]) offered more melodramatically pious portrayals of Jesus, in *Golgotha*, he is rendered more as an icon or symbol than a fully fleshed individual, which emphasises his divinity and his 'difference'. The film is thus more comparable with Pier Paolo Pasolini's *The Gospel According to St. Matthew* (1964), which captures a more spiritual understanding of Jesus via a more stripped back visual and performative approach. Bonnefille (2002: 179) describes Le Vigan's performance as a mixture of 'douceur [et] douleur' ('softness and pain'); his sober, restrained poise is offset by the more exaggerated acting style of Harry Baur. It is not until twenty minutes of the film have elapsed that we see Jesus properly for the first time. Here, inside the temple, as Jesus drives out the moneylenders, Duvivier deploys a half-minute *plan-séquence* that tracks through the temple palisades behind Jesus as he moves from stall to stall. Another six minutes go by before we finally see his face in close-up.

This de-emphasising of Jesus continues all the way through the film. Later, when Jesus receives the forty lashes, Duvivier opts against showing us the whipping. Instead, he slowly zooms into the faces of witnesses staring through a barred window. Someone shouts 'Nous voulons voir' ('We want to see'), but Duvivier resolutely refuses. Those rapt onlookers return us to the heart of Duvivier's core concerns: the potential for human wickedness. A woman faints from the pleasure of seeing Jesus whipped. Roman soldiers sadistically taunt a blindfolded Jesus, poking him with a stick, and Herod ruthlessly mocks him. The crowd, as Jesus goes to Calvary, is like a lynch mob. When Pilate offers Jesus to the crowd, one can trace a throughline to *Panique* in 1946; these are two films in which good men are hounded to their deaths by crowds of hatred-filled bystanders.

More so than most Duvivier films, *Golgotha* has been the subject of multiple criticisms. Despite its striking compositions and transgressive approach to the presentation of Jesus, *Golgotha* has not aged well. Desrichard (2001: 38) called it a 'curieux et dangereux exercice' ('a curious and dangerous exercise'). Duvivier occasionally forces his visual equivalents. When Jesus tells Peter to 'feed my sheep', Duvivier cuts to a flock of sheep. Sorlin (1981: 147) wrote that

Golgotha was seriously weakened by the inconsistency of the casting ('Many reviewers laughed at Gabin's haircut and bare legs'). Jeanson, who would soon work with Duvivier on *Pépé le Moko*, wrote a lukewarm review for *Le Canard enchaîné*. *Golgotha* was boring, lacked conviction and emotional depth, and left audiences indifferent; in Duvivier's hands, Christ's road to Calvary 'n'est pas une tragédie [...] c'est un travelling' ('is not a tragedy [...] it's a tracking shot') (Jeanson 2000: 105).

After the exertions of *La Bandera* (1935, to be discussed later), Duvivier's next project took him to Prague, where he began work on *Le Golem* (1936), a quasi-remake of Paul Wegener's 1920 German Expressionist film *Der Golem, wie er in die Welt kam* (*The Golem: How He Came into the World*). Duvivier retells the story of the mythical clay creature that is brought to life in 1610 by a rabbi (Charles Dorat) to protect Prague's Jewish ghetto from persecution by Emperor Rudolph II (Harry Baur) and his chancellor (Roger Karl). The most noticeable visual aspect of *Le Golem* is André Andrejew's highly expressionistic décor. With its seventeenth-century castles, synagogues, inns, alchemy laboratories, and caged lions, the baroque aesthetic straddles horror and fantasy, and anticipates later works by Duvivier such as *La Charette fantôme* (1939), *Flesh and Fantasy* (1943), and *La Chambre ardente* (1962) in which these two registers overlap. Duvivier's touch is visible – long, slow tracking shots, wipe edits, documentary inserts of gibbets – but *Le Golem* was roundly criticised for its long dialogue sequences and, rarely for a Duvivier film, its unconvincing performances.

Whereas the Wegener version was a horror film, concerned with the morals of creating something that could not be controlled, Duvivier opts for a very different register. Most of his vision of *Le Golem* unfolds as a political drama that withholds the unleashing of the Golem until the final moments. The film begins in a synagogue, where the enslaved Jewish congregation prays for liberty, an end to the plague, and the awakening of the Golem. Duvivier's vision of Prague is a politically febrile one: in the background are scenes of grain theft, mobbed stagecoaches, armed guards, and hungry crowds rioting on the streets, while the emperor negotiates a series of mutually beneficial Czech–Spanish alliances. The violence meted out to the emperor's opponents is particularly graphic, with numerous scenes of torture, hangings, and Jews being fed to lions.

Some critics (Bilski 1988; Baer 2012) have read *Le Golem* as a reflection of contemporary historical developments in Europe, namely the growing oppression of Germany's Jewish population post-1933. They point to scene when Rachel (Jany Holt), the rabbi's wife, beseeches the congregation: 'Les meilleurs d'entre vous sont dans les mains des assassins', or when she writes on the Golem's forehead the words 'La révolte est la loi de l'esclave.'[24] When the Golem is finally awoken, he destroys walls and ceilings in the palace and then breaks open the gates of the ghetto, 'freeing' the Jews. Sibelman (2000) argues that *Le Golem*, like *David Golder* and *Golgotha*, evinces particular stereotypes of Jews that course through many French films of the 1920s and 30s. He points in particular at the role of Lang, who 'symbolises an extreme menace to the state' (91), and the scene of a cabal that depicts Jews as 'maniacal demons capable of calling upon the forces of Evil' (92). Yet Sibelman ignores the role played by Rachel, who bravely walks through the cages of lions to awaken the Golem, and fails to recognise the film's true villain, Emperor Rudolph, who has ensnared the Jewish community and left its members to starve. The numerous critics of *Le Golem* admonished Duvivier for the film's inability to reconcile the fantastical and realist elements of the story. In one telling review, François Vinneuil wrote that 'M. Duvivier est un remarquable ouvrier, un magnifique travailleur. Mais il n'a jamais eu et n'aura jamais le caractère d'un artiste.'[25] This hard-edged bifurcation of Duvivier's praxis would become a regular part of the post-war discourse on his work.

The final entry in this eclectic quintet is *L'Homme du jour* (1937). It starred Maurice Chevalier, in his first French-language talkie, as Alfred, a humble electrician who saves the life of Mona Thalia (Elvire Popesco), a celebrated actress, by giving her a blood transfusion. She rewards him by offering him the chance to develop his singing career, but he quickly becomes disillusioned with the public response to him. Unable to cope with the fame and publicity he receives ('the man of the hour' of the film's title), Alfred returns at the close of the film to his simple worker origins. This tale of a working-class man's rise and fall contains some playful experiments with sound, music, and performance.

---

24 'Your brothers are in the hands of murderers'; 'Revolt is the right of slaves.'
25 'Mr. Duvivier is a remarkable, magnificent worker. But he has never had, or ever will have, the hallmark of an artist.'

Le Paquebot Tenacity seemed like a deliberate sidestep after the darker early sound films, and *L'Homme du jour* is likewise a change of pace, sandwiched between the critically and commercially acclaimed *La Belle équipe* and *Pépé le Moko*. Graham Greene, one of Duvivier's most fervent admirers, noted that 'even in a comedy the shadow is there' (1972: 196). Here, the director splits his film down the middle, offering in the first half a Clair-style social comedy and in the second a more pessimistic examination of human nature that is more typical of Duvivier's worldview.

Indeed, the film amplifies one of Duvivier's key preoccupations: the role of the crowd. In *L'Homme du jour*, crowds gather wherever Alfred goes, capitalising on his popularity and eager to bask in his reflected celebrity glow. People stop him on the tram to thank him for saving Mona's life, a movie crew want him to make a film about 'le type qui a sauvé Mona Thalia' ('the bloke who saved Mona Thalia'), and, when a drunk Alfred tells his radio listeners where he lives and invites them to come over for cigars and flowers, Duvivier films real people and real traffic jams on the streets of Paris as the assembled crowds surround his front door. Yet the crowd progressively turns nastier. When Albert returns home to his normal life, he finds that his neighbours have turned against him and that someone has stolen his money, and he gets into a fight. Because of his fame and fortune, the crowd have now become jealous of him, and, in a foreshadowing of the 'foule imbécile' in *Panique*, the crowd begins to close ranks. Albert's neighbours send him a series of bogus letters to set up a meeting with Suzanne (Josette Day), a flower-girl who hopelessly loves him. These narrative turns recall *Le Tourbillon de Paris* (1928), anticipate *Tales of Manhattan* (1942), and remind us that social groupings for Duvivier are frequently riven with cynicism and cruelty.

The casting of Chevalier as an unassuming singer is clearly ironic given the actor's own career at that point. He was already a huge star in America (after films such as *The Love Parade* [1929] and *Love Me Tonight* [1932]) but had returned to France in 1936 after the relative box-office failure of *The Merry Widow* (1934). Chevalier sings four times during *L'Homme du jour*, performing some of the most popular songs of the period, such as 'Y'a d'la joie' and 'Ma pomme'. When budding *chanteur* Alfred arrives for an audition at the start of the film, he sings 'Y'a d'la joie' on an empty theatre stage. Duvivier alternates between head-on shots of Alfred singing and reverse shots of the theatre seats. This musical interlude plays out for a full three minutes, and Duvivier meticulously focuses on Chevalier's body language and his vocal skill. The scene ends on an ironic note – nobody has heard Alfred sing, as the director of the show and the theatre boss were out of the room. Alfred later sings 'Ma pomme' at a party organised by Mona. While he is performing, he magically transports himself back to the Paris bars that he is singing about; his 'body' and his 'voice' are in two places at once. Alfred eventually meets 'Maurice Chevalier', who is in Paris for a series of concerts. The actor playing 'Chevalier' wears a wig and glasses but then reveals himself to Alfred as Chevalier. Chevalier-as-Alfred and Chevalier-as-Chevalier then sing 'Prosper' together (in a triple Chevalier performance, because the two men are singing along to a record sung by Chevalier), and, in the final scene, Maurice Chevalier performs 'Mon vieux Paris' while Alfred and Suzanne watch from the theatre balcony. It is a dizzyingly self-reflexive finale, and highly sophisticated in its use of *trucages*. The doubling inevitably recalls *Le Reflet de Claude Mercœur* (1923) and anticipates *The Impostor* (1944), but Duvivier this time frames the duplication in a deft, conciliatory register. Albert and Suzanne have reunited, Chevalier is singing about the beauty of Paris, and Duvivier's pessimism is momentarily deferred.

Despite the presence of Chevalier and the lightness of its first half, *L'Homme du jour* was not a commercial success. The Ginger Rogers and Henry Fonda segment of *Tales of Manhattan* notwithstanding, Duvivier did not return to comedy – musical, romantic, or otherwise – until *La Fête à Henriette* and the Don Camillo diptych fifteen years later. Looked at now, *L'Homme du jour* feels out of place among Duvivier's more acclaimed accomplishments of this period. Yet beneath the surface lie some implicit political messages. Duvivier is suggesting that these opposed social groupings, as personified by Mona and Alfred, may interact with each other, but only temporarily. After his 'fifteen minutes of fame', Alfred confides to Suzanne that 'la place d'une dactylo c'est devant sa machine ... et la place d'un électricien c'est pas devant le projecteur'.[26] For Julian Jackson (1988: 139),

---

26 'a typist's place is behind her typewriter ... and an electrician's place is not in the spotlight'.

Alfred's return to his previous existence and to the virtue of 'knowing one's place' is a profoundly anti-Popular Front theme, and one at odds with La Belle équipe, which a year earlier had mirrored the mood of the 1936 bel été. Now, order needed to be restored, people must know their place, and all social mobility was illusory. Coming at a time when French cinema was often inflected with class discourse, Duvivier's comedy here suggests that the 'grand society' can indeed exist, but only along starkly fenced lines.

Fixing a style: Duvivier, Gabin, and poetic realism

Duvivier worked with the actor Jean Gabin five times in the 1930s. The director deployed Gabin's star quality, his allure, and his mythic quality to such an extent that he, more than any other director from this period, 'created' Gabin. As we have seen, Duvivier first cast him in *Maria Chapdelaine* (their friendship was forged on the transatlantic crossing from Europe to Canada). From this point, Gabin's popularity increased exponentially, and he became the recognisable face for Duvivier's poetic realist films *La Bandera*, *La Belle équipe*, and *Pépé le Moko*. Poetic realism has been used to classify a small group of dark, atmospheric French films of the mid-to-late 1930s that were a counterpoint to the theatrical and literary adaptations, 'diversion' films, and popular genres of the time. Generally speaking, poetic realism was a post-Second World War critical construct best defined as 'pessimistic urban dramas, usually set in Paris [...] in working class settings, with doomed romantic narratives often tinged with criminality' (Vincendeau 1996: 115–16). Several of these romantic narratives featured Gabin. As well as the Duvivier triptych, Gabin's genial escapee in Jean Renoir's *La Grande illusion* (1937) and doomed army deserter and factory worker in Marcel Carné's *Le Quai des brumes* and *Le Jour se lève* (1939) were examples of him playing out scenarios involving violence, the impossibility of redemptive love, thwarted escape, and death or suicide. The defining traits of poetic realism can be traced in the inner qualities of Gabin's characters from the 1930s, such as alienation, helplessness, assertive masculinity, and romanticism. It is in Duvivier's corpus that these qualities are best exemplified.

For Susan Hayward (2005: 173), the idealised representation of the 1930s working-class male (Gabin being the exemplar) 'has power over his immediate entourage – power to attract, dominate and seduce men and women of his own class'. Gauteur and Vincendeau (1993) too remind us that Gabin had more close-ups than any other actor in French cinema in the 1930s and was frequently framed centre screen, functioning as a diegetic and non-diegetic figure of identification. In *La Belle équipe* and *Pépé le Moko* especially, controlled use of *mise en scène* assists in the strengthening of Gabin's allure, for example in a band of light on his eyes or a tracking camera that follows his movements. Gabin excelled at playing tragic working-class heroes, and his worker identities in the 1930s sought to transcend the class divisions that the Popular Front government was also hoping to collapse. Yet these dreams of assimilation were frequently destroyed by social forces beyond his control – as the train driver driven to murder in *La Bête humaine* (1938) or an escaped prisoner-of-war in *La Grande illusion*, stripped of dignity by the horrors of combat. Such narrative patterns are also visible in Duvivier's films.

Gilieth (Jean Gabin) commits a murder in Paris. He flees to Morocco and joins the Spanish Foreign Legion. He is pursued by tenacious bounty hunter Lucas (Robert Le Vigan), who has also joined the Legion, and falls in love with a local woman, Aïscha (Annabella). Lucas and Gilieth reconcile at the end, as Arab fighters besiege their squadron. Gilieth dies but is honoured as a national hero.

Although Gabin did not have top billing (that honour went to Annabella, who wore dark make-up to portray Aïscha), his performance in *La Bandera* is regarded as laying the foundation for the 'Gabin myth', due to the combination of 'Duvivier's penchant for "men's stories"' and 'Gabin's physique and performance style' (Vincendeau 2000: 67). Moreover, Gilieth/Gabin the wayward son atones for his crime by dying for his country, thus conforming to a common colonial paradigm.

La Bandera was an adaptation of Pierre Mac Orlan's novel (Duvivier worked on the adaptation with Charles Spaak, with whom he would collaborate another seven times) and falls into the category of 'legionnaire film'. This was a genre that stressed an escapist, exotic mode rather than a nationalistic one; the main protagonist had usually run away to join the Legion after committing a crime back in France (Hayward 2005: 155). Though *La Bandera* begins in nocturnal Paris (the murder is committed in a studio-shot Paris street and Duvivier filmed the action as if it were a German Expressionist film) – most of it takes place in Spanish Morocco, shot on location amid the never-ending sand and sun.[27] Once in Africa, a whole range of mythological, imperialist, and visual representations are proposed. The film 'figures Africa as a lawless, anonymous zone, and as a female body whose contours are veiled' (Andrew 1995: 253). The film frames the Arab as the enemy: the legionnaires call them *salopards* (bastards), and, when they attack the fort, they remain invisible.

The second half of *La Bandera* shows the pressures the men come under while waiting for something to happen. Duvivier is not politically engaged here; he is not interested in exploring the reasons for the conflict. Rather, he concentrates on the daily lives of the legionnaires – their routines and suffering, and their recourse to a nostalgic mode. Marcel (Raymond Aimos) recounts stories about Paris to Spanish soldiers. He uses a matchbox for the Butte Montmartre, matchsticks for streets and people, and a ribbon for the Seine as props for his reconstruction. Marcel recalls the river: 'la Seine, elle vient, elle tourne et elle repart, mais elle ne part pas tout de suite. Elle a compris que quand on est à Paname, il faut y rester le plus longtemps possible.'[28] Marcel uses the arrival of the 'other' to extol the virtues of a long-departed but fully remembered space, a narrative turn that Duvivier would return to in *Pépé le Moko*. Eventually, camaraderie starts to fracture under pressure from the existential reality of war as-it-happens. The ennui of life in the barracks is intermingled with sudden death, poisoned water supplies, and surprise bombing raids. The urban claustrophobia of *La Tête d'un homme* has been replaced here by vast expanses of desert, but the dangers are still real and present.

La Bandera received overwhelmingly positive reviews, with many labelling it the best of Duvivier's career to that point. Henri Jeanson (2000), who had been so indifferent towards *Golgotha*, called it the perfect film. Jeanson also loved Gabin: 'Il ne joue pas, il ne truque pas […] Il a une nature et du naturel […] S'il a faim, on a faim aussi,

---

27 Duvivier dedicated the film to General Franco, who gave permission to shoot in the Spanish Sahara.
28 'the *Seine*, she comes, she twists and turns, she does not leave immediately. She understands that when you belong to *Paname* [Paris], you have to stay there as long as possible.'

s'il est saoul, on est ivre' (107).²⁹ If *Golgotha* was perceived a waste of Duvivier's talents, then his accomplishments not six months later on *La Bandera* meant that he was now a major player in the industry. Alistair Cooke (1971: 125) wrote that it resembled 'an exquisite newsreel taken away and baked brown to give you the feel of the air'. Duvivier's career, which had decelerated somewhat after the initial successes of *David Golder* and *La Tête d'un homme*, was now back on track.

In Duvivier's next film, five unemployed Paris workers share a lottery-ticket win, decide to pool their money, form a workers' cooperative, and transform an old dilapidated building on the banks of the river Marne into a *guinguette* (an open-air dance hall). Gradually, tragedy strikes, and the group of five – the 'beautiful team' – is reduced to just Jean (Gabin) and Charles (Charles Vanel), who are in love with the same woman, Gina (Viviane Romance). The film ends with Jean killing Charles and being arrested.

At first glance, *La Belle équipe*, like Renoir's *Le Crime de Monsieur Lange* (1935), seems to encapsulate the feelings of euphoria and political optimism engendered by the arrival to power of the Popular Front in 1936. Both Geneviève Guillaume-Grimaud (1986) and Dudley Andrew (1995) suggest that the plot provides ample opportunity to tick off Popular Front motifs, such as unemployment, the national lottery, leisure, travel, and fresh air. We are a long way from the Fordist–Taylorist production lines of Clair's *A nous la liberté* (1931); Duvivier instead presents a pre-industrial utopia where 'everyone is the president' and work is rendered as communal and artisanal. Despite the director's apolitical stance, *La Belle équipe* contains political ideas, the most notable of which are Mario's status as a political refugee from Spain (the Popular Front had not provided aid to Spain), the connection between building a *guinguette* and building a community, and the socialising effect of the song 'On s'promène au bord de l'eau' (co-written by Duvivier), which binds the guests at the *guinguette*'s opening in a collective moment of mass solidarity.

Christian-Marc Bosséno (1994: 30) notes that the Paris of *La Belle équipe* is 'an unliveable city'. Jean cannot bear his cramped apartment, Mario is a Catalan exile forever on the run from the police, and

---

29 'He doesn't perform, he doesn't make it false [...] He is completely natural [...] If he's hungry, so are we. If he's drunk, so are we.'

Charles is pursued by his ex-wife, Gina. Duvivier portrays Paris in a way that makes it understandable why the 'équipe' seeks to move away. Gina's apartment is codified as an animal's lair, with Duvivier's tight framing and skewed camera angles picking out the walls adorned with photographs of Gina in various semi-pornographic poses. At the men's block of flats, images of constriction and confinement are everywhere. The riverside *guinguette* thus embodies this desire to reconstitute a communal domestic masculine space elsewhere. Jean tells his apartment landlord that his rooms are dirty. The next logical step for him is to re-establish this social system elsewhere, in the countryside. Over the course of *La Belle équipe*, that *guinguette* assumes a gradually more symbolic role, 'born of [...] utopian impulse' (Flinn 2014: 168). Only beyond the borders of Paris can the men truly feel free, liberated from the city's toxic atmosphere. The film's opening credits, with a tracking shot along a country lane full of low-angle shots of trees and dappled sunlight filtering through leaves, cues up the restorative promise of the rural retreat. It is in the country, suggests Duvivier, where the men will re-establish and cultivate strong bonds of sentiment and a shared sense of purpose. Thus, *La Belle équipe* depicts the hopefulness of the *bel été* while recognising its frailty.

A final point about the ending of *La Belle équipe* needs to be made. Famously, the producers disagreed with Duvivier and Spaak about the original ending (Jean killing Charles) and requested the insertion of a *fin rose* in which Gina is jointly banished by the two men.[30] The original tragic ending is highly politically charged. It shows a much darker depiction of the travails faced by the newly enfranchised working class in which solidarity is cracked open and falls away. This being a Duvivier film, patterns of hope and disillusionment are rife, and Gina here embodies the usurping *garce* figure that threatens the integrity of the patriarchal order. She is emblematic of the forces that set out to destroy this imaginary male community. For Burch and Sellier (1996: 52), 'la misogynie viscérale de Duvivier s'accommode admirablement de son pessimisme'.[31] Some things never change.

---

30 At a test screening, audiences were shown both endings; the happy ending won out by 305 votes to 61.
31 'Duvivier's visceral misogyny blends admirably with his philosophical pessimism.'

In *Pépé le Moko*, Pépé (Gabin), a criminal on the run from the French police, lives freely in the Algiers Casbah, unopposed by local authorities. When Slimane (Lucas Gridoux), the local police inspector, sees that Pépé is in love with Gaby (Mireille Balin), the French mistress of a rich tourist, he seizes his opportunity to lure Pépé out of the Casbah. Gaby decides to return to Paris; on hearing this, Pépé leaves the Casbah, is arrested, and kills himself.

Pépé le Moko is Duvivier's best-known film and has been read in numerous ways: as a proto-version of film *noir* (O'Brien 1996), as an exemplar of French colonial cinema (Kennedy-Karpat 2013), as a study of fraught spatial relationships (Bayles 1999), as an inspiration for American remakes (Drazin 2011), and as the film that clinches the Gabin myth (Vincendeau 1998). It is based on a 1931 crime novel written by Détective Ashelbé, a pseudonym for Henri La Barthe. The dialogue was provided by Henri Jeanson, who also, oddly, reviewed the film for *Le Canard enchaîné*, describing it as having 'la vigueur, la netteté et le rythme d'un grand film américain' (2000: 148–9).[32] Indeed, subsequent analyses of the film (Beylie 1981, Vincendeau 1998) have read the film as a European version of Howard Hawks' *Scarface* (1932). The meticulous cinematography was by Marc Fossard and Jules Krüger, and the evocative set design by Jacques Krauss. Duvivier again cast well. Alongside Gabin, we find regulars such as Fernand Charpin, Marcel Dalio, Charles Granval, Lucas Gridoux, and Gaston Modot. For the key role of Gaby, a version of the 'jeune fille moderne' ('young modern woman') that we see in many of Duvivier's films, Mireille Balin was cast (she also starred that year with Gabin in Jean Grémillon's *Gueule d'amour*). In its bleakness, *Pépé le Moko* clearly fits into the French poetic realist model. Duvivier's film is about impossible desire and the implacable workings of fate, and reviews invariably contain terms such as 'mélodrame tragique' and 'romantisme désespéré' ('tragic melodrama' and 'hopeless romanticism'). These are themes that run deep in Duvivier's work.

Pépé le Moko is *the* key work of *cinéma colonial*, made at the pinnacle of France's infatuation with its North African empire. Duvivier had already demonstrated the strong allure of North Africa in *Les Cinq gentlemen maudits* and *La Bandera* (and earlier, in *Maman Colibri*). Like those two other 1930s films, *Pépé le Moko* is suffused

---

32 'the vigour, clarity and rhythm of a great American film'.

with colonialist ideology and culture, most notably in the representation of the colonial space and its 'other' inhabitants as both exotic and dangerous. The film frames the Casbah as a westernised fantasy of exotic bodies, dark shadows, and twisting, narrow passageways and motifs of divergence and disorientation are prevalent. When Frantz Fanon (1963: 38) described the colonial city as a world 'cut in two', he might have had the opening of *Pépé le Moko* in mind. This splitting can be seen twice. Firstly, in cutting from the Algiers police station in which French authorities discuss Pépé's ongoing freedom to images of the Casbah, Duvivier shuttles from the city's rationalist *quartier européen* to its haphazard colonial counterpart, and, secondly, Duvivier's representation of the Casbah cuts from real (documentary montage) to reconfigured (Joinville studios outside Paris with set design by Jacques Krauss) material. At the end of the two-minute sequence, the spectator is firmly anchored to the Casbah. Duvivier intertwines an impassive voiceover, footage of the Casbah filmed in low-angle close-up, vivid street names ('rue de la ville de Soum Soum', 'rue de l'hôtel du Miel'), and Mohamed Yguerbouchen's diegetic music.

As well as being an exemplar of colonial cinema, *Pépé le Moko* marks the culmination of Duvivier's virtuoso formal style in the early years of sound. For Vincendeau (1998: 11), the film offers 'an anthology of camera angles and movements, editing, lighting and music then in use in the best of the French cinema'. The climactic scene illustrates this flair. Pépé runs down the steps of the Casbah towards the port to see Gaby one final time, and Duvivier overlaps two shots to convey Pépé's frantic state of mind and heightened emotional state. The first shot is a *plan américain* of Pépé descending the steps, shot at Joinville. The second is a tight close-up of Pépé's face layered onto a glass transparency. When the two shots are combined with Vincent Scotto's music and a set of slow dissolves, Pépé's hallucinatory subjective experiences move him inexorably towards his death.

The presence of Henri Jeanson is critical in linking together the film's populist and colonial filaments. Pépé describes Ines, his partner, in negative terms (she is 'une espèce de Casbah portative' ['a Casbah you carry around with you']) but exclaims when he meets Gaby for the first time that 'j'ai un rendez-vous à Paris' ('I've got a date in Paris'). In a famous nostalgic exchange between Pépé and Gaby, the two reminisce about their childhoods in Paris, breathlessly citing evocative landmarks and place names: Rue Saint Martin, the Champs-Élysées, the Gare du Nord, Boulevard de Rochechouart, and so on. Later, Tania (played by ageing *chanteuse* Fréhel) comforts Pépé by singing 'Où est-il donc?', a plaintive ballad that contain the lyrics

> Où est-il mon moulin de la Place Blanche?
> Mon tabac et mon bistrot du coin? [...]
> Où sont-ils tous mes vieux bals musette?
> Leurs javas au son de l'accordéon[33]

This ritualistic cataloguing of common cultural motifs of working-class Paris reinforces the notion of the urban landscape as a dying space that can no longer be attained. Jeanson's dialogue throughout the film thus straddles the poignant and the romantic, serving in a wider ideological sense to cement the primacy of French national identity and symbolise the unattainability of a 'lost' Paris.

Pépé le Moko was remade in America as *Algiers* in 1938, with Charles Boyer taking on the role of Pépé. As was customary, the original was not released in America until 1941 and the end of the theatrical run of the remake. The American press were highly impressed with the original. *Time* wrote that Duvivier had 'caught such an accurate X-ray of a tortured mind [...] *Pépé le Moko* [is] an excellent example of a prime Hollywood weakness – obeisance to its technical proficiency [...] The French film studies its character with thought and patience' (Landazuri 2016).

Duvivier was able, with *La Bandera*, *La Belle équipe*, and *Pépé le Moko*, to combine commercial success with personal themes and approaches. *La Bandera* and *Pépé le Moko* were enormously popular at the French box-office, and *La Belle équipe* was also a success (see Crisp 2002: 318–31). Duvivier shows how popular and personal, genre and auteurism can co-exist, and work dynamically together.

Un Carnet de bal (1937)

Duvivier's box-office success would continue with *Un Carnet de bal* (1937). With its fragmented structure, undertones of melodrama and

---

33 Where is my moulin de la place Blanche
My tabac, My local bar [...]
Where are my *bals musettes*
With their dances to the accordion?

pessimism, wonderful array of performances, and fluid, visual style, it is a film worth revisiting. Working with writers Henri Jeanson, Jean Sarment, and Bernard Zimmer, Duvivier tells the story of Christine (Marie Bell), a recently widowed socialite who finds her first dance card (her 'carnet de bal'), from twenty years earlier. Seeking to satisfy her romantic curiosity – all those she danced with told her they would love her 'toute la vie' ('forever') – Christine sets off to track down the seven men. What has become of them? Duvivier (1937: 250) described the film as 'une histoire d'amour dont le principal personnage est le passé'.[34]

Un Carnet de bal is a *film à sketch* (a 'portmanteau' or 'episodic' film), a film genre that consists of several self-contained episodes tied together by a single theme, premise, interlocking event, or geographical space. Although *Un Carnet de bal* was not French cinema's first attempt at a *film à sketch* (Yves Mirande's *Billet de mille* [1934] got there first), it is by far its most accomplished. Its linked structure allowed Duvivier to broaden his favoured themes: disillusionment, the gap between reality and fantasy, the weight of the past, and male suffering at the hands of women. The expressive set design and the recurring use of Maurice Jaubert's 'Valse grise' ('Grey Waltz') are two examples of how Duvivier carefully positions visual and aural signifiers to reinforce atmosphere and thematics in a systematic fashion. *Un Carnet de bal* was the film that determined the sureness of the Duvivier 'touch'. It garnered the prestigious Best Foreign Film Award at the 1937 Venice Film Festival, was universally critically acclaimed on both sides of the Atlantic, and was the film that convinced Metro-Goldwyn-Mayer (MGM) boss Louis B. Mayer to offer Duvivier a contract to work in Hollywood.

As I have already discussed, an essential feature of Duvivier's career was his skill in casting actors of technical prowess and emotional truthfulness. *Un Carnet de bal* features an extraordinary reunion of the period's most prestigious actors – Harry Baur, Marie Bell, Pierre Blanchar, Fernandel, Louis Jouvet, Raimu, Françoise Rosay, and Pierre-Richard Willm. Dudley Andrew (1995: 125) has written that many of the most significant films of this era 'accumulate their energy on the different acting styles authorized by the variety [of] their scripts'. Andrew singles out *Un Carnet de bal* in particular, focusing

---

34 'a love story, with the past as the central character'.

on the contrasting performance styles of Harry Baur, Fernandel, and Louis Jouvet.

While *Un Carnet de bal* showcases the vitality and dynamism of French classical cinema's acting, Duvivier undercuts the film with pessimism and bleakness. One of the film's key interchanges comes early on, when Christine asks her friend Brémond 'Ne vous êtes-vous jamais demandé ce que des êtres que vous aviez perdus de vue avaient fait de leur vie?' His response is telling: 'Je me suis souvent demandé ce que la vie avait fait d'eux'.[35] A major Duvivier concern was always destiny, and how the choices one makes (in the case of *Un Carnet de bal*, twenty years ago) gradually alter, subvert, or correct initial ideas about love, life, and the future. The film is a voyage of discovery for Christine. She will see at first hand what life has done to her former dance partners.

Un Carnet de bal contains one unforgettable scene. Christine visits Thierry Raynal (Blanchar), a back-street abortionist whose office is situated directly behind the Marseilles docks. Raynal is blind in one eye, having lost it while in Africa, and he suffers from a form of *delirium tremens* contracted in the colonies. His affliction is starkly reflected in the episode's *mise en scène*: undulating floorboards, canted angles, Dutch tilts, a deafening clanking of machinery. Not only does Raynal not recognise Christine when she comes into the office but he also automatically lights the spirit lamp to sterilise his instruments; he does not think to ask whether Christine has come to see him for any other reason than for an abortion. All the way through this fifteen-minute scene, a sado-masochistic relationship is hinted at between Thierry and his mistress, Gaby (Sylvie), and the episode ends with Raynal shooting her just after Christine leaves (Duvivier implies that Christine's arrival is the catalyst for the murder). It is another version of Duvivier's 'paroxystic moments' that irrupts amid the other more sentimental sketches.

In many ways, Christine is the most fascinating character. Critics tend to regard her as blank, monolithic, and lacking in depth, like most of Duvivier's pre-war female characters. Yet Duvivier shows her in numerous different guises. She is cold and distant and seems incapable of displaying genuine feelings. She refuses to tell Georges'

---

35 'Have you ever asked yourself what the people you've lost have done with their lives?'; 'I've often asked myself what life has done to them.'

mother (Rosay) that she is indeed Christine, and not Christine's mother as Rosay thinks she is, and her first instinct when she meets Alain Régnault (Baur), a composer who is now a Dominican friar, is to try and seduce him. Christine is clearly framed as a narcissist. She seeks to seduce men in order to convince herself that she can be desired and loved, and panics at the idea of getting old. When she meets Éric (Willm) she asks him several times whether he thought she was beautiful that night at the ball. Eric never answers the question, and that, coupled with his decision not to spend the night with her in the Alpine hut, cuts to the heart of Christine's dilemma. Could it be that she is simply no longer desirable? Brémond had earlier told her that 'Vous êtes jeune puisque vous n'avez jamais aimé'.[36] Could it be instead that she is still young (but no longer desirable) because she has never *been* loved? Christine's childlike insecurities go hand in hand with a faulty memory. When she returns to the original dance hall with Fabien (Fernandel), she sees it now as a plain, unadorned space compared to her prior burnished memories of it. To seal the deception, Duvivier cuts between slow-motion shots of girls dancing at the ball in three-quarter time in long white robes, and the present day, with its dancefloor of humdrum provincials and upbeat music. In this brief scene, Duvivier's worldview is epitomised. 'Je suis partie pleine d'illusions et je reviens pleine de regrets,'[37] Christine tells Brémond on her return. This clash between illusion and regret cuts to the heart of Duvivier's films.

Towards the 'end of the day'

Duvivier's last two films of the decade are heavily imbued with feelings of remorse, sadness, and regret. He returned from Hollywood in 1938, scarred from the experience of *The Great Waltz* (1938) and eager to return to familiar territory. Both *La Fin du jour* (1939) and *La Charrette fantôme* (1939) draw to a close a period of immense creativity and experimentation from Duvivier, and allowed him an opportunity for future renewal. It is common for films of this later period of the 1930s to be read as reflections of prevailing social and political

36 'You are young because you have never loved.'
37 'I left full of illusions and I return full of regrets.'

concerns – the demise of the Popular Front, the growing external threat of fascism, and the seeming inevitability of the Second World War. Duvivier's final films are tinged with similar feelings of bleakness and a sense of an era passing, but arguably are continuations of a worldview that had gradually been coagulating for twenty years. Certainly, the visual patterns and motifs of *La Fin du jour* and *La Charrette fantôme* appear as natural extensions of Duvivier's thematic and formal preoccupations. By 1939, Duvivier was at the peak of his career. His Gabin triptych, the considerable success of *Un Carnet de bal*, plus a stint in America meant that anticipation was high for his next project. Duvivier returned from America in August 1938 and immediately began working on *La Fin du jour*. The action takes place in an old people's retirement home for actors and actresses that is threatened with closure. The strain of pessimism that had always been present in Duvivier's work in the 1930s reaches a climax.

La Fin du jour focuses on three ageing actors who are struggling with their memories and adjusting to the loss of their career and their acclaim: Cabrissade (Michel Simon), St.-Clair (Louis Jouvet), and Marny (Victor Francen). Bitterness afflicts each of them. Cabrissade has spent his professional career as an understudy rather than an actual actor; St.-Clair, a once-great actor, no longer gets curtain calls; and Marny never reached the summits of his previous acting career after the death of his wife, resorting to performing in second-rate plays rather than the works of Corneille and Racine. Duvivier's coup was to cast three of French cinema's most accomplished actors as these ageing *cabotins* (ham actors). The theatre backdrop also allows ideas about performance and storytelling to merge with Duvivier's wider concerns about lies, deception, and duplicity. As with *Un Carnet de bal*, memories overlap, are feigned, or are misremembered. Cabrissade admits to occasionally embellishing the truth 'non pas par méchanceté mais pour que les choses soient un peu plus jolies',[38] while St.-Clair sends old love letters to himself to prove that he is still the *tombeur de femmes* of his younger days. (Self-)deception for these actors is a means of displacing anxieties about ageing and death.

The trauma of ageing here runs alongside another Duvivier preoccupation – faulty or defective memory. Marny notes ruefully that 'Le drame, c'est d'avoir de la mémoire' ('Tragedy is remembering things');

38 'not out of maliciousness, but so that things can be a bit nicer'.

Madame Chabert, rejected by St.-Clair, says that 'Les hommes n'ont pas de mémoire' ('Men don't have memories'). Finally, Cabrissade is called up at the last minute to replace St.-Clair in a performance. Yet he is so overcome by stage fright that he forgets his lines. The curtain is brought down, and all Cabrissade can do is repeat the words 'Ce n'est pas ma faute ... Je suis vieux' ('It's not my fault ... I'm old'). It is a devastating scene, all the more poignant because Cabrissade dies shortly after this final embarrassment.

Duvivier and co-writer Spaak fleck *La Fin du jour* with some of their cruellest depictions of human nature. In *La Belle équipe* and *La Bandera*, Duvivier and Spaak also established communities, but these were composed of virile, masculine figures trapped in Paris and the colonies. Those groupings were gradually rent asunder by mutual suspicion, war, and the arrival of a grasping vamp; here, the community of Saint-Jean-la-Rivière is faced with encroaching death. This change is heralded by an early scene in which two old residents, condemned to live out their days together, begin fighting at dinner because one of them is served a bigger piece of sausage. *La Fin du jour* culminates with a series of paroxystic moments: there are violent confrontations between Marny and Cabrissade; there is another between Marny and St.-Clair; and there is Jeanette's suicide attempt, Cabrissade's death, and the mental breakdown of St.-Clair. It is in these moments of death and madness that the film's title – 'the end of the day' – can be read allegorically.

Bonnefille (2002: 283) reads the film as Duvivier's concession to a more poignant look at the human condition, in which his characters are treated tenderly. Indeed, there are glimmers of light. A couple decide to get married, having resisted for so long for fear of getting divorced. Marny is moved to tears when he is approached by a young fan who remembers the actor fondly, and, in one famous shot, Duvivier's camera glides down the corridors of the retirement home in the dead of night. As the camera passes each room, we hear the applause that nightly filters into the dreams of each long-retired actor. Yet Duvivier's bone-deep pessimism reveals itself once more when the camera stops outside Marny's room. The soundtrack changes from applause to mocking laughter and Duvivier cuts to a shot of Marny, visibly shaken as he awakens from this nightmare.

Duvivier concludes *La Fin du jour* on a sombre note: Cabrissade's funeral. Ageing actors stand together to say goodbye to one of their own. Marny improvises a eulogy and pays tribute to Cabrissade: 'Tu as aimé le théâtre [...] tu lui es resté fidèle, fidèle à ton amour de jeunesse, fidèle à ton rêve obscur et merveilleux.'[39] These words conclude *La Fin du jour*. Yet, unlike the characters in *Un Carnet de bal*, youthful dreams and possibilities forged in the past still remain intact; by 'staying faithful to one's youth', Duvivier crafts a more optimistic film, arguing that none of the old actors have betrayed their ideals, their love of the theatre, or their past.

La Charrette fantôme is a remake of the classic Swedish film *Körkarlen* (1921), directed by Victor Sjöström. Both films are adaptations of Selma Lagerlöf's 1912 novel. According to a Scandinavian legend, the *charrette fantôme* (ghostly carriage) conveys the dead to the afterlife. Whoever dies at midnight on the last day of the year is doomed to drive the carriage (whose creaking wheels can only be heard by those about to die) for a full year. In Duvivier's version, Sister Edith (Micheline Francey), suffering from tuberculosis, is determined to redeem David Holm, an alcoholic tramp (Pierre Fresnay), and return him to his wife and children. Fresnay's friend Georges (Louis Jouvet) died on the final day of the preceding year and is the current carriage driver. Edith fears that Holm might die, but he is redeemed and returns to his family.

La Charrette fantôme mixes fantasy and realism. Beneath the fantastical elements (the sound design, Jouvet's performance as the ghostly rider, dramatic diagonal shadows) lies a stark depiction of social misery. There are shafts of light in the gloom. Edith displays an unswerving faith in the capacity for human goodness and sees in Holm the opportunity for redemption, and the film's underlying social conscience is strong.

Despite its peculiar blend of style and tone, *La Charrette fantôme* in fact intersects with a number of other cinematic trends in French cinema. The backdrop of the Salvation Army and a community of drop-outs and alcoholics call to mind Renoir's *Les Bas-fonds* (1936); the harmony between lyricism, poetry, and social reality fits with the Carné–Prévert model of poetic realist aspirations; while the importing of a fantastical, dream-like tone into French realist cinema dates back to Louis Feuillade and the surrealism of Vigo and Clair and

---

39 'You loved the theatre [...] you were faithful to it, you were faithful to your love of youth, you were faithful to your obscure and marvelous dream.'

looks ahead to Cocteau's *La Belle et la bête* (1946) and Carné's *Les Visisteurs du soir* (1942). Duvivier himself was also returning to previous work in this genre, such as *Le Reflet de Claude Mercœur* and *Le Golem*. These films, as well as *La Chambre ardente* and *Marianne de ma jeunesse* (1955), reinforce the feelings of the uncanny and the *insolite* in Duvivier's world, and the perpetual coexistence between surface 'reality' and an underlying fantastical element that threatens to emerge.

Duvivier's boldly expressionistic *mise en scène* is perfectly suited to this pivoting between fantasy and realism. *La Charrette fantôme* is a compendium of the visual stylishness of French classical cinema. It opens with a pan across a scale model of snow-covered rooftops and then uses a wipe edit to transition from a model chimney to a full-size chimney that has been constructed on a multi-level full-size set. Edith's 'goodness' is telegraphed from the opening moments; Duvivier bathes Micheline Francey in high-key lighting and often captures her eyes in close-up. There are a number of memorable scenes, such as Jouvet, burning up with a fever, crawling across a roof to try and escape the carriage; an old woman trudging through a vast snowy landscape; and Holm's wife (Mila Parély) deliberating whether to poison her children before herself. In one particularly disturbing episode, a drunken Holm begins to beat his family. It resembles the Pierre Blanchar episode in *Un Carnet de bal* and is another example of Duvivier pushing his actors to paroxystic limits, drawing out of them performances that are touched by madness.

Released in February 1940, then removed from French screens until mid-1945, *La Charrette fantôme* has often been termed a *film maudit* because of its troubled reception, its perceived uneasiness of tone, and the fact that it was selected for the 1939 Cannes Film Festival (which was subsequently cancelled after the outbreak of war). It received lukewarm reviews on its release, due in part to its fantasy genre elements, which were regarded as un-French. American critics, who up to this point had been fervent admirers of Duvivier's directorial style, were likewise disappointed. For *Variety* (Ravo 1940), the finished product was 'strained and unconvincing', while the *New York Times* (Crowther 1940) called the film a 'meaningless picture, ponderous with morbid symbolism', regretting how 'three of the most talented men in French films [Duvivier, Fresnay, Jouvet] have gone hopelessly astray'. Maurice Bessy's breathless review for *Cinémonde* was one of the very few positive responses: Duvivier had offered up 'la plus incroyable réussite [...] à la fois mystérieux et merveilleux' (1939: 5).[40]

Finally, mention must be made of *Untel père et fils* (1945). Strictly speaking, *La Charrette fantôme* was Duvivier's last pre-war film, but, for the purposes of continuity, *Untel père et fils* will be discussed here. Duvivier's 'final' film of the 1930s had a curious production history. He was commissioned by Jean Giraudoux, then minister of propaganda, to make a film that exalted national values. Production started in Nice in December 1939 and continued throughout the *drôle de guerre* (phoney war). It was a prestigious production, featuring star actors such as Louis Jouvet, Robert Le Vigan, Michèle Morgan, and Raimu, with a sketch-like structure that linked it back to *Un Carnet de bal* and forwards to Duvivier's Hollywood work and *Sous le ciel de Paris* (1951). It was finished in May 1940, just as the Germans were starting their lightning advances across France, and, when Duvivier arrived in America in July 1940, he filmed some brief extra sequences, including a prologue with a voiceover by Charles Boyer that linked some scenes. As there were restrictions on what films could be exhibited during the Occupation, *Untel père et fils* was not shown in France until October 1945.

Set in Montmartre, the film starts in 1870 and briskly recounts the story of the bourgeois Froment family across four generations and three wars (Franco-Prussian, First World War, and Second World War), finishing in 1939 as war is declared. The broad historical sweep and time-lapsed depiction of a typical French family are maintained by having the same actors 'age' (somewhat unconvincingly) as the story unfolds (the film's original title – *La Relève* ['Continuation'] – is a better fit). The very first scene in *Untel père et fils* is documentary footage of German soldiers trooping past the Arc de Triomphe (Duvivier had this filmed in 1941 and incorporated it into the film).[41] Those images serve a deliberate purpose; they trigger the film's narration (by Charles Boyer). His opening voiceover promises a depiction of the 'real France' that most visitors never get to see: 'a country of simple, decent people, growing up, falling in love, raising children,

40 'the most incredible success [...] both mysterious and marvelous'.
41 This unsettling opening would be replicated in Jean-Pierre Melville's *L'Armée des ombres* (1969).

working hard [...] They did not want war, they wanted peace.'[42] The film's propagandistic inclinations are thus laid out: France is under threat once more from Germany, and France needs to prepare itself to protect the *patrie*. Throughout *Untel père et fils*, Boyer's voiceover regularly interjects with lists of French discoveries and achievements (Louis Pasteur, Victor Hugo's state funeral, the building of the Eiffel Tower). Such listings reinforce the film's ideological project: instil national pride at a time of deep unease.[43] Duvivier mobilises traditional French cultural representations, such as aviation, engineering, music, and art; there are also numerous scenes of dancing that can be read both as interludes of unrestrained self-expression and national cohesion in the face of political turmoil. When Uncle Jules (Raimu) visits the Moulin Rouge, Duvivier's sweeping camera captures the songs, the champagne, and the dancing. Like the *guinguette* in *La Belle équipe*, here is another communal site where French communities are entertained.

In another scene, set in 1918, Bernard (Lucien Nat), a schoolteacher, tells the story of how the actions of Marshal Joffre 'saved' Paris at the Battle of the Marne in 1914. Duvivier's staging here is important: Bernard is surrounded by children, centre screen, and he is the focus of their – and our – attention. As Bernard speaks, Duvivier slowly pans past the children's transfixed faces, eager to hear about Joffre and his exploits. This retelling of how Joffre would not let the German army cross the Marne is storytelling as both mythmaking and nation building. It is an explicit attempt to convince the 1918 children that France was, and is, worth fighting for. Those same children would now in 1940 be preparing to fight on the front lines. Here, Duvivier remobilises Joffre for the current historical moment; as Bernard reminds the children, for the second time, 'the fate of our country is being fought out on the Marne', and a tale of French resistance during the First World War can be salvaged and recycled.

---

42 The version of *Untel père et fils* I watched at the Cinémathèque Française was dubbed into English. This explains the use of English dialogue throughout the discussion of the film.

43 When the film was released in France in 1945, the voiceover segments with Boyer were cut. A new opening sequence was filmed in which Boyer described how the film had been banned by Joseph Goebbels.

The film ends in 1939, with a marriage and the announcement of the *mobilisation générale*. Newly married men head off to war for a third time, so that France may, in the words of the narrator, 'repel the forces of violence and wickedness'. The final scene is set in a cathedral, with choir music, and soft-focus lighting frames an elderly couple. Their prayer is the last line of the film: 'Please, our Lord, may our righteous cause triumph, so that France may live.' These would be the last words in a Duvivier French film until *Panique*, six years later.

The film was released firstly in America in 1943, with the symbolic title *The Heart of a Nation*, and did not reach France until 1945. The French reception was unanimously critical. *Carrefour* (Chalais 1945) called the film 'une galerie de glaces pour fantômes', while *Le Monde* (Néry 1945) denounced Duvivier's accumulation of 'les poncifs les plus usés et les situations les plus grotesques'.[44] As we shall see in Chapter 4, the cool reception of *Untel père et fils* was also intertwined with Duvivier's own trajectory during the Occupation. The fragmented set of events that led to its release (making it an exemplar of Jean-Pierre Jeancolas' [2005] concept of 'fifteen years' of the 1930s French cinema) has meant that the position of *Untel père et fils* in Duvivier's body of work remains indeterminate: is it a 1930s film that reinforces Duvivier's essential themes? Is it an 'American' film made for American audiences to counter anti-French sentiment and offer them examples of French resilience and resistance? Or is it a post-Liberation film out of sync with new political realities? The backlash against the film, and against its director, was starting to come into sharp focus.

Conclusion

Duvivier's achievements during the 1930s are highly impressive. There was little static 'filmed theatre' framing common in early sound cinema. Instead, Duvivier used dynamic travelling shots, close-ups, and cross-cutting. Works such as *Poil de carotte* and

---

44 'a hall of mirrors for ghosts'; 'the most worn-out clichés and the most grotesque situations'.

Allô Berlin? Ici Paris! modishly combined gags, avant-garde silent techniques, and use of natural landscape, and the *noir*-drenched *La Tête d'un homme* laid down a template for future *policiers* and 'atmosphere' films on both sides of the Atlantic. These early works (along with *Le Paquebot Tenacity* and *Maria Chapdelaine*) all demonstrated Duvivier's effortless flair with popular genre material. Later, Duvivier did much to establish the formal and aesthetic norms of French poetic realism. *La Bandera*, *La Belle équipe*, and *Pépé le Moko* each blended elements of populism and melodrama wrapped in an expressionistic *mise en scène*. The central concerns of these films – alienation, helplessness, assertive masculinity, romanticism – converged around the star aura of actor Jean Gabin, whose 'mythic' image Duvivier did much to craft. The period from 1935 to 1939 (from *La Bandera* to the ultra-pessimistic *La Fin du jour*) marked the greatest consistent phase of Duvivier's career. Duvivier's problematic approach to gender politics also emerges more fully in these films, in the highly negative depiction of Mme. Lepic in *Poil de carotte*, the *garce* figure of Viviane Romance in *La Belle équipe*, and the grasping mother and daughter in *David Golder*. Alongside these types sit Edith, the 'good woman' in *La Charrette fantôme*, and the alternately brittle and egotistical Marie Bell in *Un Carnet de bal*. Here, Duvivier displays complex portrayals of woman that go beyond the traditional misogynistic views ascribed to him. A final point to make is that Duvivier's films won multiple major prizes – *Poil de carotte* opened in Rome in 1935 for the fiftieth anniversary of cinema; *David Golder* won awards at Venice in 1932, as did *Un Carnet de bal* in 1938; *Maria Chapdelaine* garnered the Grand Prix du Cinéma Français in 1935; and *La Fin du jour* won Best Foreign Film at the 1939 National Board of Review Awards. Such success on the international awards circuit was evidence of Duvivier's films' cultural prestige. To borrow Italian novelist Italo Calvino's remark, after watching *Pépé le Moko*, French cinema smelled of real odours, as opposed to the Palmolive of American cinema (1976: 17). Indeed, in America, the Duvivier 'brand' would always be referred to as something 'not-quite-Hollywood'. There, critics admired his mature visual and narrative style, which was recognisably French. It was time for Duvivier to head to California.

References

Abel, R. (1984), *French Cinema: The First Wave, 1915–1929*, Princeton, Princeton University Press.
Anderson, J. and D. Richie (1956), 'The Films of Heinosuke Gosho', *Sight and Sound*, 26:2, pp. 77–81.
Andrew, D. (1995), *Mists of Regret: Culture and Sensibility in Classic French Film*, Princeton, Princeton University Press.
Anon. (1933a), '*La Tête d'un homme*', *Cinémonde*, 225, 9 February, p. 117.
Anon. (1933b), '*La Tête d'un homme*', *L'Ami du Film*, 24 February, np.
Arnoldy, E. (2004), *Pour une histoire culturelle du cinéma*, Liège, Éditions du Céfal.
Baer, E. (2012), *The Golem Redux: From Prague to Post-Holocaust Fiction*, Detroit, Wayne State Press.
Bayles, J. K. (1999), 'Gendered Configurations of Colonial and Metropolitan Space in *Pépé le Moko*', *Australian Journal of French Studies*, 36, pp. 39–57.
Bessy, M. (1939), '*La Charrette fantôme*', *Cinémonde*, 567, 30 August, p. 5.
Beylie, C. (1981), '*L'Auberge fameuse*', *L'Avant-scène du cinéma*, 269, pp. 4–5.
Billard, P. (1995), *L'Age classique du cinéma français: Du cinéma parlant à la Nouvelle Vague*, Paris, Flammarion.
Bilski, E. (1988), *Golem! Danger, Deliverance, and Art*, New York, Jewish Museum.
Bizet, R. (1933), '*La Tête d'un homme*', *Pour vous*, 223, 23 February, p. 5.
Bonnefille, E. (2002), *Julien Duvivier: Le Mal aimant du cinéma français*, vol. 1, Paris, Harmattan.
Bosséno, C.-M. (1994), 'Années 30–60: Le Cinéma français invente la banlieue', *Cahiers de la cinémathèque*, 59:60, pp. 26–32.
Burch N. and G. Sellier (1996), *La Drôle de guerre des sexes du cinéma français (1930–1956)*, Paris, Nathan.
Calvino, I. (1976), 'Autobiographie d'un spectateur', *Positif*, 181, May, pp. 13–23.
Chalais, F. (1945), '*Untel père et fils*', *Carrefour*, 19 October, np.
Cooke, A. (1971), *Alistair Cooke at the Movies*, London, Secker and Warburg.
Crisp, C. (1993), *The Classic French Cinema 1930–1960*, Bloomington, Indiana University Press.
Crisp, C. (2002), *Genre, Myth, and Convention in the French Cinema, 1929–1939*, Bloomington, Indiana University Press.
Crisp, C. (2015), *French Cinema: A Critical Filmography*, vol. 1, 1929–1939, Bloomington, Indiana University Press.
Crowther, B. (1940), '*La Charrette fantôme*', *New York Times*, 28 May, available at http://www.nytimes.com/movie/review?res=9D00E7DF1F30E43ABC4 051DFB366838B659EDE, accessed 15 September 2016.
Desrichard, Y. (2001), *Julien Duvivier: Cinquante ans de noirs destins*, Paris, BiFi/Durante.
Drazin, C. (2011), 'The Professional', in *The Faber Book of French Cinema*, London, Faber & Faber, pp. 101–27.
Driskell, J. (2015), *The French Screen Goddess: Film Stardom and the Modern Woman in 1930s France*, London, I. B. Tauris.

Duvivier, J. (1937), 'Un Carnet de bal', Cinémonde, 439, 18 March, pp. 250–1.
Duvivier, J. (1977), 'Mon ami Harry Baur', L'Avant-scène cinéma, 181, February, pp. 40–1.
Ezra, E. (2003), 'Empire on Film: From Exoticism to "Cinéma Colonial"', in Francophone Postcolonial Studies: A Critical Introduction, eds C. Forsdick and D. Murphy, London, Arnold, pp. 56–65.
Fanon, F. (1963), The Wretched of the Earth, trans. Constance Farrington, New York, Grove Press.
Flinn, M. (2014), The Social Architecture of French Cinema, 1929–1939, Liverpool, Liverpool University Press.
Frank, N. (1946), 'Un nouveau genre "policier": L'Aventure criminelle', L'Ecran français, 61, August, pp. 8–9; 14.
Garçon F. (1984), De Blum à Pétain, cinéma et société française (1936–1944), Paris, Cerf.
Gauteur, C. and G. Vincendeau (1993), Jean Gabin: Anatomie d'un mythe, Paris, Nathan.
Greene, G. (1972), The Pleasure-Dome: The Collected Film Criticism, 1935–40, ed. John Russell Taylor, London, Secker and Warburg.
Guillaume-Grimaud, G. (1986), Le Cinéma du Front Populaire, Paris, Lherminier.
Hayward, S. (2005), French National Cinema, 2nd edn, London and New York, Routledge.
Higgins, L. (2012), 'Némirovsky's David Golder: From Novel to Film and Back', Yale French Studies, 121, pp. 54–68.
Jackson, J. (1988), Popular Front in France: Defending Democracy 1934–1938, Cambridge, Cambridge University Press.
Jeancolas, J.-P. (2005), 15 ans d'années trente: Le Cinéma des Français 1929–1944, Paris, Nouveau Monde.
Jeanson, H. (1934), 'Le Paquebot Tenacity', Le Canard enchaîné, 4 July, np.
Jeanson, H. (2000), Jeanson par Jeanson, Paris, Éditions René Château.
Kennedy-Karpat, C. (2013), Rogues, Romance, and Exoticism in French Cinema of the 1930s, Madison, Fairleigh Dickinson University Press.
Landazuri, M. (2016), 'Pépé le Moko', Turner Classic Movies, available at http://www.tcm.com/tcmdb/title/86485/Pepe-Le-Moko/articles.html, accessed 14 September 2016.
McCann, B. (2013), Ripping Open the Set: French Film Design 1930–1939, Bern and Oxford, Peter Lang.
Néry, J. (1945), 'Untel père et fils', Le Monde, 20 October, np.
O'Brien, C. (1996), 'Film noir in France: Before the Liberation', Iris, 21, pp. 7–20.
O'Brien, C. (1998), 'Stylistic Description as Historical Method: French Films of the German Occupation', Style, 32:3, pp. 427–9.
O'Brien, C. (2005), Cinema's Conversion to Sound: Technology and Film Style in France and the U.S., Bloomington, Indiana University Press.
Phillips, A. (2004), City of Darkness, City of Light: Emigré Filmmakers in Paris 1929–1939, Amsterdam, Amsterdam University Press.
Ravo (1940), 'La Charrette fantôme', Variety, 20 March, np.

Sennwald, A. (1935), '*Maria Chapdelaine*', *New York Times*, 25 September, available at http://www.nytimes.com/movie/review?res=9C05E5D9113EE53AB C4D51DFBF66838E629EDE, accessed 17 September 2016.

Sibelman, S. P. (2000), 'Jewish Myths and Stereotypes in the Cinema of Julien Duvivier', in *France in Focus: Film and National Identity*, eds E. Ezra and S. Harris, Oxford, Berg, pp. 79–95.

Sorlin, P. (1981), 'Jewish Images in the French Cinema of the 1930s', *Historical Journal of Film, Radio and Television*, 1, pp. 139–50.

Spicer, A. (2010), *Historical Dictionary of Film Noir*, Lanham, Scarecrow.

Vincendeau, G. (1996), *The Companion to French Cinema*, London, BFI and Cassell.

Vincendeau, G. (1998), *Pépé le Moko*, London, BFI.

Vincendeau, G. (2000), *Stars and Stardom in French Cinema*, London and New York, Continuum.

Vincendeau, G. (2004), 'The Art of Spectacle: The Aesthetics of Classical French Cinema', in *The French Cinema Book*, eds M. Temple and M. Witt, London, BFI, pp. 137–52.

Vinneuil, F. (1934), '*Le Paquebot Tenacity*', *Action française*, 7 July, np.

Woodhull, W. (2003), 'France in the Wilderness', in *French Identity and Its Discontents: Nationalism, Colonialism, Race*, eds G. van den Abbeele and T. Stovall, Lanham, Lexington Books, pp. 55–68.

1 A man at work: Duvivier on the set of *Anna Karenina* (1948), courtesy of Photofest

2 Confronting the spectator: Camille Bert in the opening shot of *Haceldama ou le prix du sang* (1919), courtesy of La Cinémathèque Française

3 Piloting with concentration: Duvivier prepares to shoot *Au bonheur des dames* (1930), courtesy of Getty Images

4 The grasping woman: a father–daughter relationship turns sour in *David Golder* (1930), courtesy of Getty Images

5 Creating a myth: Jean Gabin in *Pépé le Moko* (1937), courtesy of Christophel Collection

6 Frenchie goes to Hollywood: Gabin (left) in *The Impostor* (1944), courtesy of Alamy

7 There's no fool like an old fool: Gabin's tenderness meets Danièle Delorme's duplicity in *Voici le temps des assassins* (1956), courtesy of Christophel Collection

8 Star quality, Hollywood style: Henry Fonda and Ginger Rogers in *Tales of Manhattan* (1942), courtesy of Alamy

9 The uncanny on show: Edgar Barrier and a set of masks in *Flesh and Fantasy* (1943), courtesy of Photofest

10 The quintessential Duvivier image: a bloodied Michel Simon at the mercy of the crowd in *Panique* (1946), courtesy of Alamy

11 Authorial tussles: Orson Welles comes between producer Alexander Korda, star Vivien Leigh, and director Duvivier on the set of *Anna Karenina* (1948), courtesy of Christophel Collection

12 A lighter touch: Fernandel and a broken egg in *L'Homme à l'imperméable* (1957), courtesy of Getty Images

13 The group fractured by guilt and suspicion: Bernard Blier, Noël Roquevert, Serge Reggiani, and Danielle Darrieux in *Marie-Octobre* (1959), courtesy of Alamy

14 Juju the Terrible and BB: Duvivier directs Bardot in *La Femme et le pantin* (1959), courtesy of Alamy

15 When an old master met a new waver: Duvivier prepares Jean-Pierre Léaud for filming in *Boulevard* (1960), courtesy of Alamy

16 The model professional: adept, efficient, versatile, courtesy of Wikimedia

4

'Piloting with concentration': Julien goes to Hollywood

> It is our guess that Monsieur Duvivier's first Hollywood effort will have a far-reaching influence on future west coast productions. He has shown that simplicity [...] can give screen drama a lovely quality rarely attained by lavishness of production.
>
> (*New York Herald Tribune* review of *The Great Waltz*, 25 November 1938)

Duvivier worked in America twice, firstly and briefly in 1938 and then again from 1940 to 1945. While there, he revitalised his own approach to film-making by imbricating 'Frenchness' into a very different industrial system. Duvivier's own reminiscences about his time in America oscillate between bitter disappointment and grudging respect. In 1946, after his return to France, he explained to *Cinémonde* that the role of the Hollywood director was to 'exécuter plus ou moins heureusement, des ordres de travail qu'il reçoit et [faire] mouvoir les acteurs' (1946: 18).[1] In other interviews, Duvivier talked positively about his respect for the efficiency of Hollywood, admiring how the best directors, like himself, kept to budget and deadlines, and how actors arrived on set on time and with lines learnt.

Subsequent critical readings of Duvivier's Hollywood production have been equally ambivalent. Yves Desrichard (2001: 60) comes down hard on Duvivier, considering this period the weakest of his career: 'ces cinq années de trahisons et de basses oeuvres'.[2] Similarly, Marc-Edouard Nabé (2010: 40) terms this period 'désastreux'

---

[1] 'carry out, more or less successfully, the orders one receives and move the actors around'.

[2] 'these five years of betrayals and menial jobs'.

('disastrous'), good only for 'une poignée de navets' ('a handful of duds'). Others are more dismissive of the Hollywood system itself and the way it gradually engulfed Duvivier's talent. Charles Drazin (2011: 127) argues that Duvivier found 'his artistic voice stifled', while Dilys Powell (1991: 76) notes that 'Duvivier [was] not at his best when transplanted.' More positively, Christian Viviani (1996: 89) states that, while most émigré filmmakers working in Hollywood saw their work 'mis entre parenthèses' ('put on hold'), Duvivier managed to incorporate his ongoing thematic impulses into his American films.

It is high time to re-evaluate Duvivier's American films. Contrary to previous readings of his time there, this was no blighted career move. Duvivier did not fall by the wayside as soon as he left Europe but continued to make innovative, challenging, and interesting films that were both critically and commercially successful. Pierre Billard (1995: 420) suggests that Duvivier was the most successful of the French émigrés in Hollywood because of his ability to apply methodical professionalism ahead of personal expression. Eric Bonnefille (2002: 272) notes too that Duvivier's great talent at this point in his career was his capacity to 'se couler dans le moule' ('fit into the mould'). Instead of being overwhelmed by the Hollywood system, Duvivier thrived, enjoying a form of privileged exile in which he was able to inculcate his own visual and narrative inclinations into the Hollywood system and avoid a complete standardisation of his own style. This career hiatus in America needs, therefore, to be read less as a kind of artistic obliteration, whereby a set of practices built up over two decades was suddenly jettisoned in favour of formulaic anonymity, than as a tale of rejuvenation, experimentation, and resistance to a wholesale integration of his style within a set of foreign practices. Viviani (1996: 91) has described the confrontation between Duvivier and Hollywood as 'un défi artistique qu'il remporta haut la main'.[3] As we shall see, Duvivier's experiences on the 'west coast' would provide a fruitful point of departure for his later work.

To America and back...

In September 1937, MGM boss Louis B. Mayer, impressed by the international success of *Un Carnet de bal* (1937), offered Duvivier a

3 'an artistic challenge that he won hands down'.

one-film contract to work in Hollywood. Duvivier accepted and left for New York in late October. In a letter to *La Cinématographie française* (Duvivier 1937: 5) on the eve of his departure, Duvivier explained his reasons for going:

> C'est moi qui vais faire cet essai. Il y a une nuance. Cet essai, j'ai le droit et le devoir de le tenter, de me plier à certaines méthodes de travail, de bénéficier de facilités de réalisation [...] Je suis fier d'avoir été, avec beaucoup de courtoisie, beaucoup de promesses, invité dans un pays où le cinéma a rang de deuxième industrie.[4]

He categorically rejected the notion, disseminated in the press, that his decision to work for MGM was all about money. Rather, the Hollywood system would allow him 'de se réaliser plus complètement, de travailler avec plus de tranquillité, d'aborder des sujets plus amples [et] d'entrer en lutte avec de nouveaux et passionnants obstacles'.[5] Duvivier ended the letter by predicting two possible outcomes – and the subsequent French reception – to his Hollywood career:

a) Si c'est un navet: La Machine-Californienne-A-Absorber-Les-Personnalités a fonctionné encore de plus [...] Sans doute, Julien Duvivier dérouté par des méthodes inaccoutumées, en possession d'un scénario douteux [...] a été digéré et rejeté par Hollywood [...]

b) Si c'est une réussite: Soyons heureux et fiers [...] Julien Duvivier a su planter sur les rives californiennes le drapeau de l'Art français! Vive l'Amérique! Vive Louis Lumière! Vive la France! (Duvivier 1937: 5)[6]

---

4 'It is I who am testing things out. There's a nuance. I have the right and the duty to try it out, to engage with certain work methods, to benefit from the resources for directing [...] I'm proud to have been invited, with great courtesy and generous promises, to work in a country where cinema is the second largest industry.'

5 'to fulfil myself more completely, to work more peacefully, to tackle broader subjects and go head to head with new and interesting obstacles'.

6 'a) If it's a dud: "The Californian Machine that Swallows People Up" will have worked once more [...] Without a doubt, Julien Duvivier, thrown off course by unfamiliar working practices, and working with a dubious script, [...] has been chewed up and spat out by Hollywood [...]; b) If it's a success: Let us be pleased and proud [...] Julien Duvivier has planted the flag of French art in Californian soil! Long live America! Long live Louis Lumière! Long live France!'

It was to be a prophetic statement, especially towards the end of his time in America, given the apathetic critical response that awaited *Lydia* (1941) and *The Impostor* (1944) back in France. The interview also reveals Duvivier's awareness of the dangers of working in this system. This would be a complete change of environment for him. He was leaving behind artistic flexibility for a market-driven and commercially motivated industry. He would presumably have been aware of the brief Hollywood experiences of French directors such as Jacques Feyder, Maurice Tourneur, and Claude Autant-Lara in the early 1930s and seen that the opportunity to work in the studio system often came at a heavy price. Feyder in particular arrived in America to great fanfare in 1929 after the successes of *Thérèse Raquin* (1928) and *Les Nouveaux messieurs* (1929), only to return to France three years later having made only two films for MGM.[7]

Duvivier left France in a blaze of publicity and was feted on his arrival in Hollywood. King Vidor hosted a reception in his honour in the presence of the likes of Frank Capra, John Ford, and Ernst Lubitsch, where he proclaimed that Duvivier was 'un "directeur" au sens propre du terme. On reconnaît sa griffe dans chacun de ses productions' (Chirat 1968: 16).[8] Yet Duvivier quickly became disheartened at the standardisation of MGM's product and looked on aghast at the unfettered power of producers such as Mayer whose sole objective was 'empêcher que leur public puisse désirer voir autre chose que ce qu'ils leur imposent' (Duvivier 1947: 18).[9] He was passed over on projects for which he felt he displayed a natural affinity (an adaptation of *Goodbye Mr. Chips*, and *The Shopworn Angel*, with James Stewart) and was dismayed that directors were locked into four-year

---

7 Pierre Billard calls Feyder's American career 'un échec artistique mais un intéressant stage de perfectionnement' ('an artistic failure but an interesting stage in his development') (Billard 1995: 49).

8 'a "director" in the proper sense of the term: you recognise his stamp in each of his films'. Bonnefille (2002a: 263) states that Vidor, who shared the transatlantic crossing with Duvivier, also dissuaded him from tackling a proposed remake of *Pépé le Moko*, starring Spencer Tracy. The remake did eventually happen, but *Algiers* (1938) was directed by John Cromwell and starred fellow French émigré Charles Boyer as Pépé. Cromwell allegedly kept a copy of Duvivier's original film running on set so that he could replicate as closely as possible the original's cinematography, editing rhythms, and camera set-ups.

9 'to prevent the public from seeing anything other than what was imposed upon them'.

contracts, which he saw as constrictive. For someone accustomed to the French artisanal, collaborative approach, Duvivier found it difficult to adapt to these new 'management by committee' surroundings, and as early as December 1937 a mischievous editorial in *Pour vous* hinted that Duvivier was already looking to head back to France as quickly as possible. Duvivier's first assignment was offered to him as a means to feel his way into the studio system. It was uncredited second-unit direction on *Marie Antoinette*, an ultra-sympathetic portrait of the Queen of France, based on Stefan Zweig's 1932 biography. Filming a series of *plans d'ensemble* and night-time crowd scenes when director W. S. Van Dyke fell ill, Duvivier saw at first hand the workings of 'la Machine Californienne' – the vast budgets (at three million dollars, *Marie Antoinette* was one of the most expensive films of the decade, with an almost unheard-of ten-week shooting schedule), the star actors (John Barrymore, Tyrone Power, Norma Shearer), the legion of screenwriters appointed to the project (Donald Ogden Stewart, Ernest Vajda, uncredited rewrites from F. Scott Fitzgerald), and the problematic nature of film credits and authorship.[10]

Finally, a project came to fruition. *The Great Waltz* (1938) was based on the Austrian composer Johann Strauss II. The opening title card hints that the film will be a loose adaptation – 'We have dramatised the spirit rather than the facts of his life' – which excuses the film from the prerequisites of the historical biopic and gives Duvivier free rein to mix history, fantasy, artifice, and kitsch. Duvivier exploited the MGM production unit to his utmost advantage, benefitting from a large budget, a ninety-piece orchestra, and some of MGM's most accomplished technicians (the costumes designed by Adrian, the sets by Cedric Gibbons, and cinematography by Joseph Ruttenberg, who won the first of his four Academy Awards). Dimitri Tiomkin composed arrangements of Strauss' waltzes, with lyrics by the librettist Oscar Hammerstein. The film starred Luise Rainer as Strauss' wife, Poldi, and the Polish soprano Miliza Korjus as his mistress, Carla Donner. Strauss was played by another French exile, Fernand Gravey.[11]

10 The following studio memo was circulated during post-production on the film: 'His [Duvivier's] name is not to be mentioned on screen, or in connection with paid advertising or publicity' (Eyman 2008: 256).
11 Gravey's name was anglicised to 'Gravet' in America to avoid confusion with 'gravy'.

The money-no-object freedoms and studio gloss afforded Duvivier on *The Great Waltz* encouraged him to be ever more audacious in his filming techniques. By 1938, MGM was already celebrated for its geometrically choreographed dance sequences in the likes of *The Great Ziegfeld* (1936) and *Broadway Melody* (1937), and Duvivier maintained that tradition with a series of waltzes and operatic interludes. The multiple musical numbers consistently mirror the swelling emotions of the characters, and Duvivier's highly mobile crane-mounted camera is instrumental in generating movement and thrust. 'The Blue Danube Waltz', Strauss' most famous composition, plays while women wash their laundry at the banks of the river. When Strauss and Carla dance together, Duvivier places his actors on a rotating turntable, which, complete with the spinning rear projection, captures the scene's energy and emotional heft.

Three sequences disclose the Duvivier 'touch'. Firstly, Strauss and Carla, riding in his carriage through the outskirts of the city at dawn, improvise the melody of 'Tales from the Vienna Woods', taking their cues from birdsong, the horses' hooves, the notes of a shepherd's flute, and the sound of a carriage horn. It is a knowing critique of the standard scene in musical biopics in which composers strain to find inspiration for their most famous piece of work. Here, artistic inspiration is demystified and emerges not from frenzied sleepless nights or a post-alcoholic moment of clarity but rather from the ambient sounds of a hyper-artificial Arcadian backdrop.[12] For Duvivier, it is the impromptu clash between the kitsch and the mundane that typifies composition and creation. Secondly, Carla looks back at Strauss from the rail of a ship as it pulls away from the harbour and into the night. She begins to sing 'One Day When We Were Young' as the ship slowly merges with the darkness and Strauss realises what he has lost. The image is a Duvivier archetype and recalls a similar scene in *Pépé le Moko*. Even in a lavish costume drama, the sheen of French poetic realism is visible. Finally, there is a remarkable *coup de cinéma* at the end of the film, when Poldi arrives at the opera house for the debut of Strauss' first opera. Rather than gliding the camera back in a reverse tracking shot, Duvivier opts for a rapid series of brief, Eisenstein-like cuts, each wider than the next, which frame the

12 The delays that resulted in the use of a crane for this sequence led to MGM placing a ban on future uses of cranes and jibs.

tiny figure of Poldi in time with the music against the splendour of the opera house.

Though it was not mentioned by critics at the time, Duvivier manages to infuse a transgressive political element into the film. Viewed retrospectively, *The Great Waltz* can be read as an example of American politics transposed into a *Mitteleuropa* context. The film plays out against the backdrop of the 1848 revolution, which overthrew the anti-reformist Metternich, and Strauss is coded as a fervent supporter of the Austrian democracy lobby (he writes a march for the demonstrators, he calls the future emperor a 'stuffed shirt', and he clashes with the emperor's guard). The demonstrators wield English-language signs that denounce tyranny and shout slogans that serve to make them appear decidedly American – they demand a constitution, a free press, and freedom of speech. This smuggling of a radical tinge is not entirely successful. It jars with the love triangle plot, and, when the revolutionaries achieve their goals midway through the film, the political subtext vanishes completely. Nonetheless, the film does suggest that political aspirations will always be fulfilled once the American ideals of freedom and citizenship are transplanted into Central Europe.[13]

With *The Great Waltz*, Duvivier injected a decidedly European flavour into the Hollywood mainstream by marrying two distinct art forms: film and music. He invigorated the musical biopic genre and set the standard for a foreign director by successfully finding compatibility in style, technique, and narrative. Yet there would be a sting in the tail. Duvivier was contractually obliged to return to France in August 1938 to begin work on *La Fin du jour*. During his passage back to Le Havre, MGM brought in Victor Fleming and Josef von Sternberg to complete what Duvivier presumed were minor dubbing inserts and retakes on the film. Yet MGM memos indicate that studio executives were highly dissatisfied with Duvivier's work. Too many scenes were filmed at night, the script was deemed too sophisticated and intricate for American audiences, and Korjus' role in particular required substantial re-editing.[14] There is some disagreement about

---

13 Some subsequent 'reflectionist' views have read *The Great Waltz* as a protest against Hitler and his March 1938 annexation of Austria to Germany, and seek to present an Austria proud of its traditions and cultures, which will remain indefatigable.

14 For more on the re-shooting and re-editing, see Sragow (2013: 270–81). Sragow quotes MGM executive Ed Sullivan: 'New policy at MGM [...] If a

how much of the film Von Sternberg shot, as Duvivier never mentioned in any subsequent interviews that his version of the film had been compromised or had had new scenes added. However, while he would later claim that he accomplished everything he wished on *The Great Waltz* – a multi-million-dollar budget, artistic control, box-office success, lack of interference from the producer – it is clear that working in Hollywood the first time around had been a sobering experience for him.

Released first in America in November 1938, then in Britain in December, and then in France in March 1939 (under the title *Toute la ville danse*), the film was roundly applauded. The American and British reception tended to focus more on Duvivier's technical prowess – a certain D. E. B. (1938: 279) at the *Monthly Film Bulletin*, like others, noted his 'outstandingly clever direction' – while the *New York Daily Mirror* (1938) praised a directing style 'continental in its broad sweep'. Domestic critics evoked the national pride generated by a French director who had elevated such a quintessentially Hollywood product to such a high level. Georges Champeaux (1939) set the tone: Feyder and G. W. Pabst had already 'failed' over the Atlantic, but Duvivier had triumphed with this 'éclatante réussite' ('dazzling success'). Maurice Bessy (1939: 4) agreed. Duvivier had 'brodé une dentelle unique [...] qui nous émerveille'.[15] The highest commendation of all came from legendary Hollywood producer David O. Selznick, who, during pre-production for *Gone with the Wind*, in March 1939 sent a memo to the film's production team that urged them all to see *The Great Waltz*. It was, he wrote, 'Hollywood's best technical achievement in many ways in several years. The photography [...] is the most outstanding job I have seen in a long, long time, as well as the way the camera is handled and the values that are got out of both sets and location shots' (Behlmer 2000: 196).[16]

There were a few dissenting voices. The *Post* called Duvivier's directorial style 'an empty exercise in technique' (Winsten 1938). Writing in *Sight and Sound*, Herman G. Weinberg (1939: 21–2) was more severe: 'The combination [of Duvivier and MGM] appears only to have

> director [i.e. Duvivier] doesn't measure up to the front office standard he is relieved immediately.'

15 'embroidered a unique piece of lace [...] which enthrals us'.
16 *The Great Waltz* was reputedly Stalin's favourite foreign film; he asked for a Russian version to be made.

been an embarrassment of riches – MGM's money and Duvivier's talent [...] There are some things even money can't do – and one of those is to provide a substitute equal to the lack of heart with which a man tackles a job he doesn't like.' For Yves Desrichard (2001: 50), Duvivier is an essentially invisible element in *The Great Waltz*: 'Mais où est, dans cette fantaisie, le réalisateur d'*Un Carnet de bal*?'[17] In hindsight, late 1930s MGM was probably the wrong studio for Duvivier, for, while his work on *The Great Waltz* certainly matched MGM's preferred in-house style – costume drama, lush décor, star actors, broad appeal to both popular and up-market viewers – the overall working conditions were very different from those he was used to in France. According to Thomas Schatz (1988: 254), MGM business practices at this time 'grew more rigidly efficient [and] the films themselves became more conventional, and innovation was implicitly discouraged'. Duvivier tried to comply with Hollywood's organisational system, with its raft of hierarchies, timetables, and deadlines, but it was not always a comfortable fit. This story of tensions arising when a designer accustomed to one film-making environment (autonomous and partnership-driven France) is transplanted into another (hierarchical, commercially-driven Hollywood) is a familiar one. My point here is that Duvivier's first experience can be seen as a test-case to examine whether European cinematic sensibilities needed to be recalibrated, harmonised, or simply jettisoned within the American system. By the time he returned to California in 1940, he was better prepared for the culture shock and was able, by virtue of his 'resourceful professionalism' (Bergstrom 1998: 91), to manage the change in conditions far more adroitly than his transatlantic compatriots.

... and back again

Duvivier returned to Hollywood in 1940 as part of a great wave of intercontinental emigration necessitated by the outbreak of the Second World War, fleeing first to Portugal with his Jewish wife and son and then on to New York in mid-July.[18] This time, he found himself in the company of two other distinguished French directors, Jean

---

17 'But where, in this fantasy, is the director of *Un Carnet de bal*?'
18 Also on the boat were Julien Green, Darius Milhaud, and Jules Romains.

Renoir and René Clair, and, within a few months of their arrival, each of the trio would release an American film: *Swamp Water* (Renoir, 1940), *The Flame of New Orleans* (Clair, 1941), and *Lydia* (Duvivier, 1941).[19] Duvivier was certainly the best prepared to adapt to these new surroundings. He had already learnt English, which proved invaluable when dealing with studio executives, actors, and crew.[20] He was already aware of the artistic and financial exigencies of the Hollywood studio system and the need to negotiate its rigid labour laws and hierarchical divisions. Such conditions were utterly foreign to Clair and Renoir, and made their transition to the Hollywood model more difficult.

Janet Bergstrom (1998) has noted that the directors who worked in America during the Occupation were always referred to, and always referred to themselves, as French. A discourse that emphasised Duvivier, Clair, and Renoir's Frenchness is to be expected, given that these were directors who were temporary émigrés, fleeing a conflict in Europe to continue working in what they hoped would be a receptive foreign environment. The critical reception of their films was generally prefaced with 'French' to differentiate their style from that of their American counterparts. The exiled directors also maintained a friendship network that extended across the entire period of their stay. Christian Duvivier recalls attending many Beverly Hills parties in the presence of Clair, Renoir, Marcel Dalio, Annabella, and Jean Lévy-Strauss, and recalls the animated political discussions that would ensue. Thus, Duvivier's experience also needs to be understood in this more personal sense, of 'surviving', of carrying on, of just working. In his review of *The Great Waltz* for *Le Figaro*, James de Coquet (1939) had noticed how Hollywood had offered Duvivier 'les moyens techniques les plus modernes' ('the most modern technical resources'), which had in turn rejuvenated his film-making style.

---

19 The Russian-born French director Léonide Moguy also emigrated, along with actors Charles Boyer, Victor Francen, Jean Gabin, and Michèle Morgan. Jacques Feyder went to Switzerland and Pierre Chenal went to Argentina during the Occupation.

20 In his conversations with François Truffaut (1983: 77), Alfred Hitchcock remarked: '[T]his may help you understand why Clair, Duvivier, and Renoir had difficulties in the United States. They aren't familiar enough with the American language and idiom.' In fact, however limited his English may have been, Duvivier did learn the language.

Two years later, it was time to see whether that successful one-film apprenticeship could mature into a more fully rounded body of work.

Lydia (1941)

It was while Duvivier and his family were in New York that he met film producer Paul Graetz. Graetz put Duvivier under contract and introduced him to producer-director Alexander Korda. Korda, a Hungarian-born émigré who had already worked in Hollywood in the 1930s (as well as in Germany and Britain) was on the lookout for a prominent star vehicle for his wife, Merle Oberon. Korda hired Duvivier to make *Lydia* (1941). It was a prestige production – a million-dollar budget, monumental sets by Korda's brother Vincent, elegant cinematography by Lee Garmes, and a screenplay by Ben Hecht, who had recently finished *Wuthering Heights* (1939), which had starred Oberon as Cathy. In *Lydia*, Oberon plays Lydia MacMillan, a wealthy old Bostonian spinster who runs a home for blind children. When she is visited by her former lover Michael Fitzpatrick (Joseph Cotten), the two recall their previous lives. They meet with two more former suitors – Bob (George Reeves) and Frank (Hans Jaray) – and they reminisce. Lydia tells the three that she has only ever loved one man, Richard (Alan Marshal), who left her before they could be married. As they revisit the past, each romance appears ideal and destined for happiness, but Lydia realises that the reality was far less romantic. Michael asks her who the real Lydia was, and she replies that there was never just one Lydia and that she was a different person to everyone who met her.

It is often written, incorrectly, that *Lydia* was a remake of *Un Carnet de bal*. While there are certain narrative similarities between the two (the six admirers in *Un Carnet de bal* now became four ex-suitors; the themes of lost love and the impossibility of repeating the past; the rather awkward framing devices), the character of Lydia is far more central to the film than was Christine in *Un Carnet de bal*. The latter remains on the fringes of Duvivier's *histoires d'hommes*, serving as a linking device to introduce the next famous French actor. *Lydia*, however, is one of Duvivier's rare *histoire de femmes*. Merle Oberon is consistently placed at the centre of spectatorial attention, exemplifying the dynamics of the Hollywood star system at the start of the

1940s. During this period, Hollywood produced an array of 'women's pictures', detailing the lives and emotions of women as never before. This prominence is clear from the film's title, the wording of the title card ('Merle Oberon in *Lydia*'), and the first shot of the actress, framed in long shot against a clouded sky at the top of a steep set of steps. As the orphanage is officially opened, a microphoned voice proclaims 'Lydia MacMillan, it shall be our privilege and honour always to serve the flag you have raised'. With this, Duvivier returns to the narrative patterns of female autonomy in *Le Tourbillon de Paris* (1928) and *Maman Colibri* (1929). In each case, he places a woman at the centre of the story, reaffirms the concept that a woman's true job is that of being a woman, and provides an escape into romantic love and sexual awareness (Basinger 1994: 13). *Lydia*'s dominant visual texture is one of reflective surfaces (mirrors, ballrooms, harps, marbled floors) and it is tempting to read the design in this film as an ironic counterpoint to the stable life that Lydia has chosen to lead. Like those earlier films, *Lydia* emphasises self-sacrifice and choice alongside a preferred lifestyle of glamour, wealth, and elegance. By rejecting a life of ostentation, Lydia conforms to one of the key archetypes of the 'woman's picture', namely the 'ordinary woman who becomes extraordinary' (Haskell 1973: 161).[21]

The act of remembering in *Lydia* is presented in contradictory, often mendacious ways. For instance, in a scene similar to the Marie Bell-Fernandel episode, the flashback to the first ball is introduced by Lydia's voiceover, which recalls the gilded ballroom, beautifully dressed with chandeliers and curtains, and the 'divine aggregation of musicians, hundreds of them, I think'. In that flashback, her entrance into the ballroom is filmed in slow motion, as if to accentuate the dream-like reshaping of the past event. Almost immediately, Michael corrects her memory, which leads to a second flashback to a far more modest ballroom with fewer musicians. Lydia then recalls that Bob 'spoke like Byron and Shelley' when wooing her, but the reality of the flashback shows us Bob repeatedly saying 'yep' as Lydia waxes lyrical about the sun and the stars. What we are told, what we remember, and what we are shown are not always the same thing;

---

21 Haskell (1973: 160–1) defines the extraordinary woman as one who 'begins as a victim of discriminatory circumstances and rises, through pain, obsession, or defiance, to become mistress of her fate'.

here, Duvivier offers a 'wry narrational commentary on Lydia's stubborn romanticism' (Bordwell 2011), undercutting her gilded nostalgia with a far more mundane reality.

Working in America meant Duvivier was obliged to negotiate the tricky terrain of the Motion Picture Production Code (a.k.a. the Hays Code). Officials at the Production Code Administration were concerned that Lydia's romantic involvement with Richard before he jilted her at the altar would go unpunished, and they demanded that she be held accountable for the sin of sex before marriage. Writers Ben Hecht and Samuel Hoffenstein argued that Lydia's decision to remain a spinster and devote herself to charitable causes for forty years provided sufficient 'compensating moral value' (i.e. a stern, moral lesson) (Miller 2016). The film was eventually passed uncut when Administration chief Joseph Breen suggested that, at her final reunion with Richard, Lydia should discover that he no longer remembers her. Almost inadvertently, this Hays Code-inspired decision provided the film with one of its strongest aspects – a deeply unsettling ending that is in keeping with Duvivier's own thematic emphasis on deception and disappointment.

Because *Lydia* bears a resemblance to *Un Carnet de bal*, similarities between the two have been drawn as a way of highlighting how Duvivier had been adversely affected by his relocation to America. Charles Drazin (2011: 125) notes that the French film 'inhabited a dream reality' but that *Lydia* belonged 'to the world of the Hollywood sound stage'. The final lines of *Lydia* sum up the impact of Duvivier's original: 'There was no real Lydia, Michael. There were dozens of them.' These hints at repetition and blurred perspectives suggest that Duvivier was aware of having to work in a different register, with a new set of narrative and tonal prerequisites.

Tales of Manhattan (1942) and *Flesh and Fantasy* (1943)

Duvivier's next two films, *Tales of Manhattan* (1942) and *Flesh and Fantasy* (1943), continued in the same vein as *Lydia*. They allowed Duvivier to showcase his 'touch', import high production values, and introduce his preferred narrative patterns. Duvivier had originally been brought to Hollywood on the back of the success of a *film à* sketch, *Un Carnet de bal*. Now he was encouraged to deploy that same formula again.

Released by 20th Century Fox, *Tales of Manhattan* (released in France as *Six destins*) was described by *Variety* (Anon. 1942) as 'probably the most ambitious picture ever to come out of Hollywood'. Here, Duvivier links together six separate stories by means of a jinxed tuxedo tailcoat that passes from person to person, bringing to each of its owners either good fortune or sorrow. At the start, the tailcoat belongs to a successful actor who is shot by his lover's husband; by the end, it adorns a black farmer's scarecrow. Along the way, the coat passes to a man whose fiancé finds an incriminating love letter in its pocket, a poor musician who rips the coat while conducting at Carnegie Hall, an alcoholic lawyer who wears the coat to attend a school reunion, and a conman who wears it while delivering a lecture on the virtues of abstinence.[22]

Like *The Great Waltz*, *Tales of Manhattan* is marked by an elegant, international style and contains some of the biggest box-office names of the period (Charles Boyer, who also produced, Rita Hayworth, Ginger Rogers, Henry Fonda, Charles Laughton, and Edward G. Robinson, among many others). It features ten credited writers (including Ben Hecht, Alan Campbell, and Donald Ogden Stewart, plus uncredited work from Buster Keaton). Eugen Schüfftan, the great German cinematographer (who had created a dream-like Le Havre for Marcel Carné on *Le Quai des brumes* [1938]), took an uncredited role for the location shooting on the streets of New York, while the glossy interior shooting was overseen by Joseph Walker, Frank Capra's long-standing cinematographer. By virtue of their shorter running times, portmanteau films require a different kind of storytelling. Duvivier's precise working methods and his reputation as an 'actor's director' were ideally suited for a narrative that requires a succession of balanced vignettes that both tell a story and fit into an overall thematic framework. Each writer brought with him a particular social issue or injustice to highlight (alcoholism, poverty), and

22 For many years, this final segment (starring W. C. Fields) was excised from the final cut; it was only restored after being discovered in a Fox vault in 1996. It is easy to see why producers cut the segment – its use of alcoholism as a comedy trope is out of place with the more engaged social concerns of the rest of the film.

Duvivier provided an internal artistic consistency. Each of the six segments fits a particular genre (*noir*, romantic comedy, morality tale, drama, farce, and all-black *drame social*) and segues fluidly from one to the next.

Tales of Manhattan is firmly embedded within the stylistic and narrative practices of the classical Hollywood cinema (CHC) style. Central tenets of the CHC style include the principles of continuity editing and invisibility (i.e. the camera should not call attention to itself), three-act structures (orientation, complication, and resolution), and a treatment of space that consists of centering, balancing, frontality, and depth (Bordwell, Staiger, and Thompson 1985: 1–59). Duvivier was generally faithful to the CHC style in each of his American films (indeed, one of the major reasons for his success in America was his adherence to pre-ordained narrative schemas), but occasionally his direction tilts towards the ostentatious. This had already been noticeable in *The Great Waltz*, but, in *Tales of Manhattan*, Duvivier manages to include noteworthy sequences. The first segment, featuring Hayworth as a *garce* figure not dissimilar from Viviane Romance in *La Belle équipe*, contains a series of agile *plans-séquences*. In the second, Duvivier films Ginger Rogers and Henry Fonda in an extended scene (alternating between mid-shots and close-ups) as she tries to make him roar like a lion, having mistakenly believed Fonda to be the recipient of a *billet-doux* that begins 'To my passionate lion'. In a scene that looks ahead to Fernandel's performative dexterity in *L'Homme à l'impérmeable* (1957), Duvivier shows his skill at choreographing lively comedy by showing Fonda roaring meekly, then loudly, and then filming Rogers and Fonda circle each other around the salon in a version of a mating ritual.

Though Desrichard (2001: 58) argues that *Tales of Manhattan* is the film in which Duvivier 'a abdiqué [...] toute ambition d'auteur' ('has relinquished [...] all ambition as an auteur'), some authorial touches remain. For a start, there is an underlying cruelty running through *Tales of Manhattan* that begins with a tailor preparing Boyer's suit and telling him that it will bring him good luck; by the end of the segment, he lies bleeding to death in the back of a limousine. As Charles Laughton starts conducting an orchestra, his tailcoat rips, and the audience begins to laugh at him. The reaction from the crowd – cynical, raucous, and brutal – replays an identical version from *Le Tourbillon de Paris*. Here, Duvivier highlights the way a crowd can quickly turn on an individual, reducing them to nothing (the irony here is that the 'crowd' is a well-dressed, Carnegie Hall-cultured elite).[23] The deceptiveness of appearances is also incorporated into the fourth story, in which Edward G. Robinson plays an alcoholic ex-lawyer who attends a school reunion at the Waldorf Astoria. At the end of the segment, he removes the tuxedo jacket to reveal an old striped shirt that he has been wearing while sleeping rough in Chinatown.

The most noteworthy segment is the final one, which has been analysed as an example of Hollywood's troublesome relationship with the African-American community. When a thief (J. Carrol Naish) dumps the burning coat from an airplane with $40,000 stuffed in its pockets, it lands in an impoverished rural black Southern shantytown. The coat is picked up by two farmers, Luke (Paul Robeson) and Esther (Ethel Waters), who believe it a miracle from heaven and decide to share out the money to all the residents. Scholars have called the segment hackneyed, due to its repeated stereotypical depictions of the African-American community. Robeson, a prominent civil rights activist at the time, was particularly appalled at the segment's casual racism and its depiction of the shantytown community as naïve and gullible.[24] He initially believed the segment might serve an instructive purpose in its depiction of the plight of the black rural poor, but later decried the portrayal of the 'Negro [as] childlike and innocent [in] the old plantation hallelujah shouter tradition' (Duberman 1989: 259–61). Most of the black and left-wing press castigated the film on its release, picketing ticket queues in Los Angeles. Robeson here is reframing similar arguments to those that continue to circulate around analysis of *Pépé le Moko*; namely, that the film contains an implicitly racist and colonialist ideology due to its untranslated Arab voices and representation of the Casbah as dangerous and erotic.

23 According to his son Christian, Duvivier lived in constant fear of the kind of ridicule that greets Laughton's character: 'My father was a perfectionist who had a horror of being embarrassed [...] The idea that this could happen was his recurring nightmare' (in Fraser-Cavassoni 2003: 74).
24 Disappointed with the stereotyping of blacks in *Tales of Manhattan* and the kinds of roles given to black actors in Hollywood, Robeson never made another film there again.

Yet the segment contains certain subversive elements. When he first finds the money, Luke tries to keep it for himself, dreaming of the 'two or three tractors' that might turn him into a profitable landowner. After a change of heart, he proposes a radical alternative to the rest of the community: to split the money up equally for the betterment of everyone. This Marxist solution certainly fits with Robeson's political views in the 1940s and early 1950s, when he was called before the House Un-American Activities Committee for his pro-communist sympathies, trips to Russia, and enthusiastic lobbying of communist art and culture. Luke encourages everyone to become sharecroppers:

> We're going to buy the land, do you hear? The land, and it'll be our'n [...] And we're going to work that ground, side by side, raisin' corn and cotton, and what we gets we shares. There won't be no rich and no more poor. Yes folks, a new day is dawnin'!

As in *La Belle équipe* of 1936, here we see the proposition of a Popular Front-like ideology of collective endeavour and joint ownership in the final moments of a major Hollywood studio production. Duvivier's detached foreigner's gaze exemplifies what Martin Scorsese (Scorsese and Wilson 1997: 98) has called the 'director as smuggler',[25] whereby filmmakers working with the CHC system could experiment with genre and narrative and could deploy a symbolic or suggestive *mise en scène* to talk obliquely to the socio-political issues of the day. This final part of *Tales of Manhattan* depicts to a remarkable degree the segregation and poverty within the black community, which was extremely rare in 1940s Hollywood cinema. Charles Musser (2008) argues that Duvivier's film and its smuggled political message are part of a wider body of work that emerged in America at this time. Pare Lorentz's film *The River* (1937), Erskine Caldwell and Margaret Bourke-White's book-length photo essay *You Have Seen Their Faces* (1937), and Richard Wright's *Twelve Million Black Voices* (1941) all amplified audience perception of the demoralising and often highly exploitative conditions

---

25 In *A Personal Journey with Martin Scorsese Through American Movies* (Scorsese and Wilson 1997: 98), Scorsese reveals how various Hollywood directors (especially André De Toth and Samuel Fuller) were able to transcend the B-movie forms for which they were known to include 'different sensibilities, off-beat themes, [...] even radical political views' in their otherwise conventional storylines.

faced by black sharecroppers. One reviewer called the segment's ideological boldness 'the most powerful indictment of the absentee landlord and sharecropper system in the South I have ever seen on the screen' (Burley 1942: 17). While Renoir worked extensively with the liberal and radical left during his time in Hollywood (Dudley Nichols, Clifford Odets), Duvivier preferred instead to further his professional credentials through serving the material as efficiently as possible. Yet, despite his political agnosticism, Duvivier is engaging in contemporary topics in this final episode.

Tales of Manhattan was a moderate box-office success,[26] and soon afterwards Universal approached Duvivier to direct another anthology film. *Flesh and Fantasy* (*Obsessions*, in French) had a supernatural inflection in which three unrelated stories were linked together by a conversation about the occult in a gentlemen's club.[27] Duvivier formed a co-production partnership with Charles Boyer (who would also star in the third segment) and reunited with his *Tales of Manhattan* stars Edward G. Robinson and Thomas Mitchell. Extra star quality was provided by Barbara Stanwyck (who made the film in between her two most memorable performances, as Jean Harrington in *The Lady Eve* [1941] and Phyllis Dietrichson in *Double Indemnity* [1944]).

In the first segment, Betty Field plays Henrietta, a bitter and unattractive woman secretly in love with law student Michael (Robert Cummings). She is given a white mask by a mysterious stranger (Edgar Barrier) who tells her that she must return at midnight. Michael falls in love with Henrietta but has not yet seen her real face. When she removes the mask, she has transformed into a beautiful woman. The second story is based on Oscar Wilde's short story *Lord Arthur Savile's Crime*. Podgers (Thomas Mitchell) is a palm reader who tells Tyler (Edward G. Robinson) that he will eventually kill someone.

26 It won a 1942 Box Office Blue Ribbon Award, earning around 2.6 million dollars.
27 There was to be a fourth segment in *Flesh and Fantasy*, in which Cliff, an escaped killer (Alan Curtis), takes refuge with a farmer and his blind daughter, Jane (Gloria Jean). The half-hour segment was shelved by Universal, and new footage was shot to bookend Duvivier's story, with framing scenes that reveal Cliff to be innocent of his crimes and allow him to return to the farm with Jane. It was eventually released as the 70-minute feature *Destiny* (1944), directed by Reginald Le Borg, but with no mention of Duvivier's name in the credits.

Tyler ends up strangling Podgers on a bridge, tries to escape, and is hit by a passing car. The accident is seen by the Great Gaspar (Charles Boyer), a trapeze artist, and leads into the final segment of the film. Gaspar has a recurring nightmare of falling from his high-wire, and each time encounters a woman (Barbara Stanwyck) he has never met. He eventually meets the woman and falls in love with her, but she is arrested for a prior crime.

Working within the Universal stable, with its long tradition of horror (*Frankenstein* [1931], *The Mummy* [1932]), one might have expected Duvivier to embrace a more menacing vision of the occult. *Flesh and Fantasy* was one of a number of films released around the same time (*Here Comes Mr. Jordan* [1941], *I Married a Witch* [1942, directed by Clair], and *The Uninvited* [1944]) that traded in the interplay between fate, mystery, and death. Yet, as with *Le Golem* (1936) and *La Charrette fantôme* (1939), Duvivier obliquely broaches the genres of horror and fantasy to project a more ethereal version of the supernatural. This may have been due to budgetary limitations – Universal was a more frugal studio than MGM – and so Duvivier chose to focus more on specific moments of the screenplay than the sustained visual excesses of *The Great Waltz* or *Tales of Manhattan*.

What on the surface seems a routine assignment for Duvivier reveals something far more unsettling. The setting of the stories is carefully chosen. The first takes place during Mardi Gras in New Orleans and allows Duvivier's tracking shots to accentuate the discomforting eeriness of the voodoo and the occult objects in the mask store and to underline the city's dream and fantasy elements. Henrietta is shown a series of masks (Lucretia Borgia, Joan of Arc, the Devil) before selecting a porcelain white fixed mask very similar to the one that Edith Scob would later wear in Georges Franju's *Les Yeux sans visage* (1960).[28] The highly stylised, oneiric depiction of London in the second film recalls G. W. Pabst's *The Threepenny Opera* (1931), and a further intertextual layer is added by setting much of the second half in a foggy Whitechapel (home of Jack the Ripper). Duvivier used two cinematographers, both of whom had just finished work on handsomely lit and framed films: Stanley Cortez (Orson Welles' *The Magnificent*

---

28 Duvivier would return to a similar costume shop and its assortment of grotesque masks, this time in a German village, in *La Chambre ardente* (1962). Behind Duvivier's sober, measured style, the *insolite* always lies in wait.

Ambersons [1942]) and Paul Ivano (Josef von Sternberg's *The Shanghai Gesture* [1941]). Both lend *Flesh and Fantasy* a gothic gloom, exploiting the relative plainness of the décor to project far more atmospheric embellishments than Duvivier had achieved in *Tales of Manhattan*. The uses of fog and the clarity of the monochromatic lighting in the second segment are particularly striking, as are its claustral visions of fatalism. Amid these baroque visual touches lies some early intersecting of the French and American *noir* style. A year later, Robinson would portray a similar role to Tyler in *The Woman in the Window*, in which he plays a professor drawn into a web of murder and blackmail, and in 1945 he would star in *Scarlet Street*, a remake of Renoir's *La Chienne* (1931). Both of these films would be made by another European émigré, Fritz Lang. Duvivier, like Lang, was road testing a European version of *noir* grafted onto its American equivalent.

Duvivier's fascination with the *insolite* is underlined via a series of compelling images. In the framing scene, one man reads the other a story, and the camera dollies into the image of a devil holding a stick of fire, like a Gustave Doré etching. Canted angles, distorted close-ups, and a dream-like montage in which Boyer tumbles repeatedly to his death both are visually ingenious and impart an evocative mood. As Tyler walks home from seeing Podgers for the first time, he sees a chalk drawing of a hanged man sketched onto the pavement. Podger's voice (via voiceover) constantly reminds Tyler that he is going to kill someone. Tyler's alter ego appears in a pair of glasses, in a shop window, inside a car, and in the reflection of a glass table, taunting him. All three segments are also further explorations of Duvivier's favoured themes of the deceptiveness of appearances, the 'double', and the vagaries of fate – are we born free or is life predetermined for us? Henrietta assumes a new personality when she wears the mask. As she walks through the various processions of Mardi Gras night, she is the centre of attention, but, whenever Michael asks her to remove the mask and reveal her true face, she refuses. When midnight strikes, she removes the mask, and she discovers that she is now beautiful. This inexplicable metamorphosis is never explained by Duvivier. The segment's fairy-tale setting and its sampling of 'Beauty and the Beast' and 'Cinderella' are deployed as a means to explore issues of self-determination. Duvivier ultimately suggests that the fortune tellers of New Orleans cannot tell one how to live one's life; only free will can.

The Impostor (1944)

The Impostor (1944) was Duvivier's final American film and the only one (partly) set in France. While the film's production designer, Eugene Lourié (1985: 101), described the film's plot as 'a highly melodramatic soap opera', *The Impostor* in fact shares several similarities with *La Bandera*. Clément (Jean Gabin) is a murderer saved from the guillotine by a Nazi air raid. He escapes to Africa during the post-Occupation exodus, usurps the identity of a dead solider, and 'becomes' Maurice Lafarge. Clément/Lafarge launches a brave attack on an Italian desert base and receives a medal. When he finally confesses, he is demoted and saves his battalion from defeat. He eventually becomes a hero who gives his life for France.[29] Filming took place in the San Fernando Valley (for the African jungle scenes) and the Universal Studios backlot (amid its outdoor complex of 'European streets'). Thematically, *The Impostor* reiterates two ongoing features of Duvivier's work: the recreation of a masculine micro-community and the themes of concealed appearances and confused identity.

According to Janet Bergstrom (1998: 92), *The Impostor* was specifically filmed to counter anti-French sentiment in America, to make the French defeat by Germany in May and June 1940 understandable to an American audience, and 'to make French people more sympathetic so that American public opinion would see France as an ally in need of and deserving liberation'. Universal's production notes reinforce the propagandist purpose of the film:

> Out of the stunned silence that followed the fall of France in June 1940, there came one voice that was loud and clear. 'Many Frenchmen refuse to accept surrender and servitude for reasons called honour, common sense and the superior interest of the nation [...] I, General de Gaulle, call upon all Frenchmen who wish to remain free to hear, and follow me'. One of those who heard was Julien Duvivier [...] He could not foresee how strong a force of freedom the Free French would become, nor could he predetermine how straight a line De Gaulle would follow through the confusion that was France. But Duvivier immediately perceived drama in the situation. He felt compelled to write a story, a story he now brings to the screen as a producer and director at Universal.[30]

---

29 The plot of *The Impostor* is almost identical to that of *Uncertain Glory* (1944), directed by Raoul Walsh and starring Errol Flynn.
30 From *The Impostor* production notes, Margaret Herrick Library, Los Angeles.

Bergstrom also reminds us how nearly all of the actors in *The Impostor* have or adopt French accents, so as to explicitly reinforce for American viewers the specific national-linguistic priorities of the film. Everything is specified to ensure maximum identification with France. The action opens with a map of France, traces a main road from Paris to Tours (where the film begins), and superimposes a date on the screen: '14 June 1940', the day German troops marched down the Champs-Élysées. French troops struggle to make sense of the scale and swiftness of the defeat ('What a beating', says one; 'No planes, no tanks', says another).

The casting of Gabin as Clément/Lafarge, in his second and final English-language role, forms a crucial part of the film's resonance.[31] As he did in *La Bandera* and *Pépé le Moko*, Duvivier accentuates Gabin's traits with controlled and low-key lighting to accentuate his physical features and confident gait. Importantly, Gabin's character is configured from the outset as politically sceptical – when Maréchal Pétain comes on the radio to deliver his armistice speech, all in the café listen intently, save for Gabin, who silently drinks wine and shows no interest in Pétain's talk of sacrifice. 'It's every man for himself now', he mutters. For Vincendeau (2006: 119), Duvivier's framing subtly positions Gabin as the one true Frenchman in the café; by turning his back on the crowd who are intently listening to the radio address, Gabin 'turns his back on Pétain and [...] collaboration' (119). Arriving at Dakar, Gabin hears another radio address, this time from de Gaulle, encouraging the French soldiers to continue fighting. Gabin's telling response – 'de Gaulle, who is de Gaulle?' – immediately establishes his lack of commitment to the central cause. He is coded as cynical and self-centred, only signing up for the Free French Army in French Equatorial Africa for money and for food ('Your patriotism finally moved you, did it?', asks his commanding officer, ironically). In a typically Duvivier touch, it is only *after* Clément becomes Lafarge, when Gabin's 'double' emerges, that he begins to embrace the values of camaraderie, sacrifice, and collective duty. The earlier, sceptical Gabin makes way for

---

31 Gabin had previously starred in *Moontide* (1942), directed by Archie Mayo. Bosley Crowther (1942a) began his review of that film for the *New York Times* as follows: 'You might almost think the lights and camera were working on a glamorous female star from the way they are concentrated on Mr. Gabin's roughly handsome phiz.'

a new incarnation: the man of action. Even when he is stripped of his rank and is transferred to Libya, he heroically sacrifices himself in the service of France by blowing up a strategic enemy point. Such actions are intrinsic to the 'Gabin myth' discussed earlier, whereby his characters function as heroic figures of redemption onto which the fantasy of an idealised Frenchman can be projected (Vincendeau 2000: 69). Moreover, whereas *La Bandera* promoted a romantic coupling between Gabin's Gilieth and Annabella's Aïscha, Gabin remains the 'outsider' in *The Impostor* (literally, as the only French actor in a film about French soldiers, and ideologically, as the 'other' Lafarge that the 'real' Lafarge's fiancée does not desire).

The Impostor is one of the very few films for which Duvivier retained a sole screenwriting credit. This allowed many personal traces that reference Duvivier's own back catalogue to be incorporated, such as the scene when the French soldiers reminisce about places they know in France, which recalls Gaby and Pepe's famous exchange in *Pépé le Moko*. Duvivier inserts multiple patriotic references, such as the scene when the 'Marseillaise' is heard on the radio ('it's the greatest call to arms ever written', says one character). Christmas Day in the desert brings packages from home of red wine and Gauloise cigarettes, and Lafarge at one point tells his battalion 'You fell in love in France. She is a beautiful woman, our France. And if you give her an even break, she will never let you down.' Such nationalistic interventions are all part of the film's propagandist strategy (for instance, audiences would have been familiar with the famous Marseillaise scene in *Casabanca* [1942] and its pro-Resistance undertones). Playing on anti-German sensibilities in American audiences presumably accounts for the scene when a solider sings 'Fee-Fi-Fo-Fum / I smell the blood of a dirty Hun'.

Finally, *The Impostor* neatly intersects with Gabin's career, throwing new light on the 'Gabin myth'. He served with honour in de Gaulle's Free French Forces in North Africa, won the Croix de Guerre, and was part of the military contingent that entered a newly liberated Paris in 1944. Likewise, Duvivier added to the references to *La Bandera* and *Pépé le Moko* by reminding audiences of three more of Gabin's most iconic roles. As well as recalling his soldier in Renoir's *La Grande illusion* (1937), Gabin's Clément evokes memories of Jean in Carné's *Le Quai des brumes* (1938), where he pitched up in Le Havre and assumed the identity of Robert Le Vigan's drowned painter.

Clément also talks to Lafarge's fiancée about his past life growing up in an orphanage; like François in Carné's *Le Jour se lève* (1939), Gabin's character seeks to explicate his current actions by returning to childhood experiences. Even in Hollywood, Duvivier was finessing the Gabin 'myth'.

From Bosley to Bazin: the critical reception

The heavily bifurcated critical reception of Duvivier's five Hollywood films in both America and France reveal in some measure how divided Duvivier himself felt as a foreign director for hire still wedded to a specific French style. In November 1938, Sawyer Falk, director of drama at Syracuse University, had given a lecture on *Un Carnet de bal* where he asserted that Duvivier's work 'comes close to being a great film'

1. Because it shows a superb handling of cinematic values as embodied in the sound-film;
2. Because its scenario shows a profundity and understanding of life;
3. Because there is a great sense of balance in the relationship of scenario parts;
4. Because of a superb feeling for design and artistic fidelity;
5. Because it uses acting to best cinema purpose.

(Polan 2007: 297–8)

For Falk, the film – released in America eight months earlier – exemplified French cinema's poised accommodation of various elements of the *mise en scène* and offered a blueprint for domestic studios looking to craft similarly high-brow, lush films. Falk's receptive discourse, at once admiring and envious, would be echoed in American press and trade journals during Duvivier's time in California.

Often, the keynote in the reactions to all five of his films was a 'European' sensibility – 'piloting with concentration', according to *Variety* (Anon. 1943) in its review of *Flesh and Fantasy* – and how that frequently translated into a leisurely directorial style that was skilled both in its visual sweep and in its ability to maintain a carefully modulated pace; Duvivier's favoured technique, according to *Variety*, was 'stressing characterization rather than movement'. Many reviews credited Duvivier for his careful selection and direction of actors. Bosley Crowther (1942b) of the *New York Times* praised his 'surprising evenness', 'delicacy', and 'gentle, detached comprehension of the irony and pity of life' in *Tales of Manhattan*. But it was not all one way. *Variety* (Anon. 1942) also criticised *Tales of Manhattan* for 'com[ing] up with very few original touches in this picture', and Crowther (1941) described *Lydia* as a 'hodge-podge of maudlin odds and ends' that was nowhere near as accomplished as *Un Carnet de bal*. *The Impostor* garnered unanimously bad reviews – *Variety* (Anon. 1944) deplored its lack of pace, and Crowther (1944) declared 'Duvivier has directed in a painfully commonplace way', calling the film 'monotone, occasionally broken by injections of laboured and ponderous fun'.

Because of the timelag between the American and French release of Duvivier's Hollywood films, the French press did not see them until a few years after they were made. Many critics rounded on the Hollywood system itself, blaming the mediocrity of Duvivier's work on the obliterating force of the system (a 'confection standardisée' ('standardised product', wrote one review; Arlin 1946) rather than the director's own shortcomings. Reviews often focused on the mismatch between Duvivier's obvious talent and the material he was obliged to serve: Yves Ducygne (1944) noted that, despite all the money that had been spent on *Tales of Manhattan*, the film was deficient – 'Plus pauvre, donc plus libre, Duvivier aurait fait mieux'.[32] Other reviews made the same point; *Cité-soir* (Arlin 1946) said *Lydia* was by no means a bad film, but 'nous ésperions tellement davantage de l'homme à qui nous devons *Poil de carotte*, *La Bandera* et *Carnet de bal*'.[33] Laurent Le Forestier (2004: 82) reads this discourse as an implicit affirmation of the French film industry and a barely concealed attempt to entice their fellow Frenchmen home: 'le message [...] est clair: le cinéma français, certes diminué par sa faiblesse financière, propose d'incomparables conditions d'épanouissement'.[34]

---

32 'With less money, and thus more liberated, Duvivier would have done much better.'

33 'we were hoping for so much more from the man who gave us *Poil de carotte*, *La Bandera* and *Un Carnet de bal*'.

34 'The message [...] was clear. French cinema, certainly diminished by its lack of resources, could offer incomparable opportunities for growth and renewal.'

Lydia was not released in Paris until July 1946, five years after it was made, and the critics lined up hard against it – *Paris-cinéma* called it a 'navet américain'(Laroche 1946), and elsewhere it was described as 'un spectacle assez morne' (Chalais 1946), 'une petite sotte sans intérêt' (Jeener 1946), or, worst of all, for *L'Ecran français* 'un film qui porte un nom qui [le] condamne: l'académisme' (Thevenot 1946).³⁵ *Tales of Manhattan* was released in October 1944³⁶ to a similarly apathetic response. André Bazin (1944) was disappointed – 'Duvivier nous apparaît ici standardisé, impersonnel [...] sans sincérité et sans qualités.'³⁷ *Flesh and Fantasy* fared little better – 'long, ennuyeux, inutile' ('long, boring, useless') was one response (Lenoir 1946). Jérôme Mansart (1946) in *Epoque* went even further, reproaching Duvivier for his 'décors mal bâtis [...] raccords mal soignés [...] séquences mal comptées [...] du travail mal ficelé'. He continued: 'Toute cuisinière a son plat préféré', but here, 'la sauce est fade' and 'le rôti brûlé'.³⁸ Time and again, the French critics recalled *Un Carnet de bal* – this was the film above all others that evoked the pre-Hollywood Duvivier and the one that he tried, unsuccessfully, to replicate three times in America.

The most divided critical response was reserved for *The Impostor*, with critics lining up to either denounce the film outright or search for mitigating circumstances regarding Duvivier's involvement. David Lardner's (1944: 60) op-ed in the *New Yorker* to coincide with the American release of the film began by describing Duvivier as 'one puzzling Frenchman'. He continued: here was a director invited to Hollywood, lavished with money and artistic freedom, who 'hasn't turned out a good picture since he's been there'. Bergstrom (1998: 95) observes that neither *The Impostor* nor Renoir's *This Land Is Mine* (1943), a similar propaganda piece designed to make the French surrender to Germany more palatable to American audiences, were meant to be shown in France. Yet both films premiered in Paris on 10 July 1946. French versions of *The Impostor* were preceded by the

---

35 'an American dud'; 'a rather gloomy spectacle'; 'an unimportant piece of silliness'; 'a film which bears a name that condemns it: academicism'.
36 In his radio interviews with René Jeanne and Charles Ford, Duvivier recalled that it was the first American film to be shown in the newly liberated France.
37 'Duvivier seems to us here standardised, impersonal [...] lacking sincerity or quality.'
38 'badly built set [...] badly put together linking shots [...] badly thought out sequences [...] badly structured work'; 'Every chef has his favourite dish [i.e. the sketch film]'; 'the sauce is bland and the roast is burnt'.

following explanatory title card, which was inserted at the behest of the film's French distributors, who were eager to deflect criticism away from what many perceived as a muddled, out-of-date film: '*The Impostor* [...] is a message. A message sent by the French in America to friends who must be reassured and to enemies who must be silenced.'

The film was dismissed in several quarters as facile propaganda, execrable melodrama, and 'une œuvre qui va desservir le cinéma français'.[39] It was a rare voice that tried to recuperate the film, and Duvivier's reputation. Only Claude Lazurick (1946) in *L'Aurore* drew favourable comparisons between *The Impostor* and Duvivier's pre-war work: 'Il a su créer, avec beaucoup d'habileté, cette atmosphère âpre et poignante qui est son royaume.'[40] While these negative appraisals can be attributed in part to the films' out-of-sync distribution patterns, there were more striking ideological reasons for their cool reception (to be discussed in Chapter 5).

Conclusion

Few critics have paused at any length over Duvivier's American films. Most discussions of his Hollywood hiatus frame it as a hit-and-miss period in which Duvivier quickly realised that a director was a mere *exécutant* (subordinate), stifled by the power of the producer. When director William Wyler, himself an émigré to Hollywood from Germany, was interviewed in 1939, he took the opportunity to rail against the increasing pre-eminence of the producer, lamenting their role in circumscribing talent and individuality. He concluded: 'Take a man like Julien Duvivier, the French director [...] He made magnificent pictures in Paris, where he had charge of everything. But in Hollywood he couldn't make a picture. Why? He wasn't given a chance to express himself. Someone else was always overruling him' (Crowther 1939: 5). Wyler was referring to Duvivier's rather troublesome experiences making *The Great Waltz* in 1938. As we have already seen, while that shoot was not particularly taxing

---

39 'a work that is going to do a disservice to French cinema'.
40 'He has been able to create, with a great deal of skill, this cruel and poignant atmosphere that is his trademark.'

for Duvivier, the post-production travails certainly were. Producer interference and his sense of disempowerment as a director were things that Duvivier would look back on with some bitterness. His second sojourn in California was a more successful one because he had learnt to compromise with and adapt to the visual and stylistic imperatives of the CHC style. There remained some residual disappointment that the financial largesse of a studio system did not always allow for great flexibility or creativity on the part of the director. If Duvivier remained dubious about Hollywood, then that is partly to do with his implicit criticism of a system that systematically reduced the role of the director to a cog in the machine. In 1946, he told Pierre Leprohon (1957: 56): 'Réaliser un film, en Amérique, c'est très exactement le "mettre en scène". Le metteur en scène de théâtre qui reçoit une pièce, dont le texte sera dit par des acteurs engagés préalablement, n'a d'autre tâche que de créer l'atmosphère de l'œuvre dramatique à lui confiée.'[41]

Duvivier the auteur might well have viewed Hollywood and the pressures of the CHC style as a potential brake on his creative independence and thematic consistency. By Duvivier's own definition, the auteur was the person in charge of the entire film, from storyboard to Universal City backlot to Los Angeles premiere, and so any deviation from that trajectory would understandably lead to isolation and under-appreciation. In many ways, Duvivier's approach to working was not conducive to the American system; he himself admitted that standardisation in Hollywood was the norm and that only Orson Welles had ever truly managed to free himself from the creative shackles of the industry to create deeply personal works.

Yet, if we look closer, we can agree with Viviani's (2008: 124) appraisal of 'Duvivier *américain*' – 'un bilan plutôt honorable' ('a pretty respectable track record'). While none of Duvivier's American films were as fully realised, either conceptually or technically, as his best work in France, that is not to downplay their visual diversity, thematic coherence, and internal critiques of genre. Duvivier was able to manipulate what Graham Petrie (1985: 4) calls 'the horizon of expectations', the terms by which European émigré directors, actors, and technicians

---

41 'To direct a film in America is simply a matter of "staging" it, much like the theatre director who is handed a play and a cast, and whose sole task now is to simply construct the atmosphere of that play.'

leave their own countries to work in America. For Petrie, the results are usually paradoxical, as the Europeans are first welcomed for 'promising to bring something artistically adventurous and thematically daring to American cinema, and then all too often berat[ed] and condemn[ed] for doing just that' (4). This part of Duvivier's hiatus in Hollywood has important industrial implications. It shows that accomplished French directors could adapt their own particular style to individual circumstances by deploying notions of adaptability, professionalism, and authenticity where appropriate. We have seen that, throughout his career, Duvivier's work continually pushed at the boundaries of rigidly defined national cinema styles and incorporated various genres, styles, registers, and tones. Instead, his willingness to interface with multiple genres (fantasy, musical, war film) quickly and inexpensively made him ideally suited to the industrial imperatives of Hollywood.

Duvivier's trip to Hollywood is comparable to the one taken by Max Ophüls, in that his experiences there allowed him to make more complex and challenging films when he eventually returned to France. Like Duvivier, Ophüls worked in Hollywood, making five films in three and a half years (most notably, *Letter from an Unknown Woman* [1948] and *Caught* [1949]) before returning to France to a period of revitalisation and energy with *Madame de...* (1953) and *Lola Montès* (1955). What Ophüls learnt in Hollywood he was able to incorporate back into his French films – the restless camera, the dollies, and the crane shots. Similarly, Hollywood offered Duvivier a cosmopolitanism he embraced eagerly.[42] The international casts, European sensibility, and specific moment of national history in *The Great Waltz* constitute an example of Duvivier working within the confines of what André Bazin (1957: 11) called 'le génie du système' ('the genius of the system'). Though that system sometimes confined him, Duvivier was able to exploit it to toggle between lavish musical and sombre chamber piece. Such meandering across genres would serve Duvivier well in the years ahead, as he set sail for post-Liberation France.

---

42 At the end of *Boulevard* (1960), Jojo (Jean-Pierre Léaud) walks past a cinema playing *L'Amérique insolite* (1960), a documentary by François Reichenbach. Its English-language title was 'America as Seen by a Frenchman'.

References

Anon. (1938), 'The Great Waltz', *New York Daily Mirror*, 25 November, np.
Anon. (1942), 'Tales of Manhattan', *Variety*, 5 August, np.
Anon. (1943), 'Flesh and Fantasy', *Variety*, 22 September, np.
Anon. (1944), 'The Impostor', *Variety*, 9 February, np.
Arlin, J. (1946), 'Lydia', *Cité-soir*, 31 July, np.
Basinger, J. (1994), *A Woman's View: How Hollywood Spoke to Women, 1930–1960*, London, Chatto & Windus.
Bazin, A. (1944), 'Six destins [i.e. Tales of Manhattan]', *Le Parisien libéré*, 15 October, np.
Bazin, A. (1957), 'De la politique des auteurs', *Cahiers du cinéma*, 70, April, pp. 2–11.
Behlmer, R. (2000), *Memo from David O. Selznick*, New York, Modern Library.
Bergstrom, J. (1998), 'Emigrés or exiles? The French directors' return from Hollywood', in *Hollywood and Europe*, eds G. Nowell-Smith and S. Ricci, London, BFI, pp. 86–103.
Bessy, M. (1939), 'Toute la ville danse [i.e. The Great Waltz]', *Cinémonde*, 543, 15 March, p. 4.
Billard, P. (1995), *L'Age classique du cinéma français: Du cinéma parlant à la Nouvelle Vague*, Paris, Flammarion.
Bonnefille, E. (2002), *Julien Duvivier: Le Mal aimant du cinéma français*, vol. 1, Paris, Harmattan.
Bordwell, D. (2011), 'Play It Again, Joan', *Observations on Film Art*, available at http://www.davidbordwell.net/blog/2011/10/25/play-it-again-joan, accessed 12 March 2015.
Bordwell, D., J. Staiger, and K. Thompson (1985), *The Classic Hollywood Cinema: Film Style and Mode of Production to 1960*, New York, Columbia University Press.
Burley, D. (1942), '"Tales of Manhattan" Minus Uncle Toms', *New York Amsterdam News*, 3 October, p. 17.
Chalais, F. (1946), 'Lydia', *Carrefour*, 22 August, np.
Champeaux, G. (1939), 'Toute la ville danse [i.e. The Great Waltz]', *Gringoire*, 16 March, np.
Chirat, R. (1968), *Julien Duvivier*, Lyon, Premier Plan.
de Coquet, J. (1939), 'Toute la ville danse [i.e. The Great Waltz]', *Le Figaro*, 15 March, np.
Crowther, B. (1939), 'The Director Dissents', *New York Times*, 16 April, p. 5.
Crowther, B. (1941), 'Lydia', *New York Times*, 19 September, available at http://www.nytimes.com/movie/review?res=9502E1D8123DEF32A2575AC1A96F9C946093D6CF, accessed 16 September 2016.
Crowther, B. (1942a), 'Moontide', *New York Times*, 30 April, available at http://www.nytimes.com/movie/review?res=9C0CE4DA143EEE3BBC4850DFB2668389659EDE, accessed 16 September 2016.
Crowther, B. (1942b), 'Tales of Manhattan', *New York Times*, 25 September, available at http://www.nytimes.com/movie/review?res=9E0CE3DB163CEE3BBC4D51DFBF668389659EDE, accessed 16 September 2016.

Crowther, B. (1944), 'The Impostor', *New York Times*, 27 March, available at http://www.nytimes.com/movie/review?res=9904E7D6153DE13BBC4F51DFB566838F659EDE, accessed 16 September 2016.
D. E. B. (1938), 'The Great Waltz', *Monthly Film Bulletin*, 5:60, 21 December, p. 279.
Desrichard, Y. (2001), *Julien Duvivier: Cinquante ans de noirs destins*, Paris, BiFi/Durante.
Drazin, C. (2011), *The Faber Book of French Cinema*, London, Faber & Faber.
Duberman, M. (1989), *Paul Robeson*, New York, New Press.
Ducygne, Y. (1944), 'Six destins [i.e. *Tales of Manhattan*]', *Résistance*, 14 October, np.
Duvivier, J. (1937), 'Pourquoi je vais à Hollywood', *La Cinématographie française*, 15 October, p. 5.
Duvivier, J. (1946), 'De la création à la mise en scène', *Cinémonde*, special edn, December, p. 18.
Duvivier, J. (1947), 'Les Libres propos de Monsieur Platon', *Cinémonde*, 656, 25 February, p. 18.
Eyman, S. (2008), *Lion of Hollywood: The Life and Legend of Louis B. Mayer*, New York, Simon and Schuster.
Fraser-Cavassoni, N. (2003), *Sam Spiegel*, New York, Simon and Schuster.
Haskell, M. (1973), *From Reverence to Rape: The Treatment of Women in the Movies*, New York, Penguin.
Jeener, J. B. (1946), '*Lydia*', *Le Figaro*, 3 August, np.
Lardner, D. (1944), 'Baffling Case', *New Yorker*, 1 April, p. 60.
Laroche, P. (1946), '*Lydia*', *Paris-cinéma*, 44, 6 August, np.
Lazurick, C. (1946), '*L'Imposteur* [i.e. *The Impostor*]', *L'Aurore*, 14 July, np.
Le Forestier, L. (2004), 'L'accueil en France des films américains de réalisateurs français à l'époque des accords Blum-Byrnes', *Revue d'histoire moderne et contemporaine*, 4:51, pp. 78–97.
Lenoir, J. (1946), 'Obsessions [i.e. *Flesh and Fantasy*]', *Gavroche*, 29 August, np.
Leprohon, P. (1957), *Présences contemporaines*, Paris, Nouvelles Editions Debresse.
Lourié, E. (1985), *My Work in Films*, San Diego, New York and London, Harcourt Brace Jovanovich.
Mansart, J. (1946), 'Obsessions [i.e. *Flesh and Fantasy*]', *Epoque*, 4 September, np.
Miller, F. (2016), '*Lydia*', *Turner Classic Movies*, available at http://www.tcm.com/tcmdb/title/82210/Lydia/articles.html#oo, accessed 6 September 2016.
Musser, C. (2008), 'Paul Robeson and the End of His "Movie" Career', *Cinémas: Revue d'études cinématographiques*, 19:1, pp. 147–79.
Nabé, M.-E. (2010), 'Le cauchemar Duvivier', programme for Cinémathèque Française, March–May, Paris, La Cinémathèque Française, pp. 38–42, available at http://www.cinematheque.fr/cycle/julien-duvivier-45.html, accessed 13 September 2016.
Petrie, G. (1985), *Hollywood Destinies: European Directors in America 1922–1931*, London, Routledge.

Polan, D. (2007), *Scenes of Instruction: The Beginnings of the U.S. Study of Film*, London and Berkeley, University of California Press.
Powell, D. (1991), *The Dilys Powell Film Reader*, ed. Christopher Cook, Manchester, Carcanet.
Schatz, T. (1988), *The Genius of the System: Hollywood Film-Making in the Studio Era*, London, Faber & Faber.
Scorsese, M. and M. Wilson (1997), *A Personal Journey with Martin Scorsese through American Movies*, London, Faber & Faber.
Sragow, M. (2013), *Victor Fleming: An American Movie Master*, Lexington, University Press of Kentucky.
Thevenot, J. (1946), '*Lydia*', *L'Ecran français*, 57, 31 July, np.
Truffaut, F. (1983), *Hitchcock/Truffaut*, New York, Simon and Schuster.
Vincendeau, G. (2000), *Stars and Stardom in French Cinema*, London, Continuum.
Vincendeau, G. (2006), '"Not for Export": Jean Gabin in Hollywood', in *Journeys of Desire: European Actors in Hollywood*, eds A. Phillips and G. Vincendeau, London, BFI, pp. 115–23.
Viviani, C. (1996), 'Duvivier américain: Le Savoir-faire et l'inspiration', *Positif*, 429, pp. 89–91.
Viviani, C. (2008), 'Julien Duvivier entre Paris et Hollywood: Le Cheminement des images', *Revue françaises d'études américaines*, 115, pp. 121–36.
Weinberg, H. G. (1939), 'Old Wine in a New Bottle', *Sight and Sound*, 8:29, pp. 21–2.
Winsten, A. (1938), '*The Great Waltz*', *The Post*, 25 November, np.

5

1946–56: darkness and light

> Moi, quand j'ai fait un film, c'est terminé, je l'oublie, c'est le prochain qui m'intéresse.[1]
>
> (Duvivier in Niogret 2010: 65)

In most circles, Duvivier's return to France after his time in America was highly anticipated. *Le Film français* summed up the prevailing mood in two editorials, firstly in May 1945 – 'Souhaitons donc le retour prochain et définitif de l'un des hommes dont le cinéma français a besoin' (Anon 1945: 3)[2] – and then a month later – 'Julien Duvivier a été à Hollywood mais vraiment il ne s'est pas américanisé et c'est avec impatience que le cinéma français attend la rentrée d'un de ses meilleurs artisans' (Idzkowski 1945: 1).[3] In no uncertain terms, Duvivier was being asked to kickstart the French film industry, restoring it to its pre-war position of prestige.

Yet he was not universally welcomed back. Pockets of the industry responded cynically to his imminent arrival. This friction was manifested two-fold. Firstly, there was the lukewarm critical response to his American films, which, as I have already noted, were not released in France until the period 1944–6. The French press often studiously ignored their existence altogether. It was the man who had made

---

1 'When I've made a film, it's over, and I forget about it. It's the next one that interests me.'
2 'Thus, let us wish for the imminent and definitive return of one of the men French cinema needs the most.'
3 'Julien Duvivier may have been working in Hollywood but he has not been "Americanised". French cinema is waiting impatiently for the return of one of its finest artisans.'

Un Carnet de bal (1937), and not *Lydia* (1941), who was returning to France. Such anti-American bias was part of a wider set of cultural polemics about the role of French film culture in the aftermath of the war that was exacerbated by the 1946 and 1948 Blum–Byrnes trade agreements.[4] Much of the criticism of Duvivier's American films came from left-wing critics (such as Georges Sadoul and those at *L'Ecran français*) who sought to expunge Duvivier's American exile and aggressively recuperate him as a French director now back to making French films in France.

Secondly, insinuations were made that Duvivier was an opportunist who had turned his back on France in 1940 to take advantage of the lucrative professional breaks and financial opportunities available in Hollywood. It was no coincidence that the adverse response to Duvivier's American films occurred as these attitudes began to harden. The longer the likes of Duvivier, Clair, and Renoir stayed in America, the more disparaging the tone of the French press. Henri Diamant-Berger wrote a scathing article in *Paris-Cinéma* in 1945 in which he accused the three of 'un reniement de la France' ('a renunciation of France') (see Billard 1998: 278–9). As Laurent Le Forestier (2004: 78–97) reminds us, the response to the return of the three directors was a kind of double reproach – on the one hand, the trio were admonished for having left France in the first place and not resisting 'sur place' like Carné, Bresson *et al.*, and on the other there was anger that they had still not returned home, despite the Liberation and the end of the war in Europe. The negativity surrounding the reception of the trio's American films can thus be attributed to this symbolic absence.

Panique (1946): the homecoming

Panique est le film le plus significatif de ma carrière, car il veut dire quelque chose.[5] (Duvivier 1946a: 10)

---

4 In the first six months of 1946, thirty-eight American films were released in France; in the same period in 1947, that number had reached 338.
5 '*Panique* is the most significant film of my career because it has something to say.'

It was against this background noise that Duvivier's first project on his return to France was made. *Panique* (1946) was an adaptation by Charles Spaak and Duvivier of Georges Simenon's 1933 novel *Les Fiançailles de M. Hire*.[6] In Villejuif, a commune outside Paris, the reclusive Monsieur Hire (Michel Simon) photographs a murder committed by Alfred (Paul Bernard). Alfred and his girlfriend Alice (Viviane Romance) both conspire to use Hire's voyeuristic affections towards her as means of deflecting police attention away from Alfred and towards Hire. After incriminating evidence is planted in his apartment, Hire becomes the chief suspect and is eventually hounded to his death, falling from a rooftop gutter after trying to escape from a crowd baying for his blood.

Panique is *the* key transitional film in Duvivier's career, marking not just his reintegration back into the French industry after a period of almost six years in isolation in Hollywood but also the incorporation into his work of a tone and a visual style that would grow ever bleaker and more misanthropic. Pierre Billard (1995: 460) describes it as 'un féroce pamphlet sur la lâcheté des êtres';[7] as well as cowardice, it is also a film about revenge, duplicity, and the persecution of an outsider. *Panique* inaugurated a cycle of far darker Duvivier films, such as *Sous le ciel de Paris* (1951), *L'Affaire Maurizius* (1954), and *Voici le temps des assassins* (1956), that suggested that the malign forces of fate and destiny that had been seeded through Duvivier's work in the late 1930s and throughout his time in America remained firmly embedded in his preferred narrative structures and visual patterns. As a traumatic response to France's post-Liberation mood of suspicion and retribution, *Panique* can be compared to Fritz Lang's *Fury* (1936) and Henri-Georges Clouzot's *Le Corbeau* (1943), where seemingly rational individuals could be whipped up into a mob frenzy. Looked at today, *Panique* is a deeply coruscating work, exploring the scapegoating of a man ironically innocent of the crime of which he is accused. Simon's moving central performance once again highlighted Duvivier's unerring reputation as a director who could coax unexpected layers of guilt, unease, and sympathy from his actors.

6 The novel was later adapted for a second time, in 1989, by Patrice Leconte, and entitled *Monsieur Hire*.
7 'a savage tract on human cowardice'.

The historical context of *Panique*'s production is important. Margaret Butler (2004: 119) states that post-Liberation films such as *Les Portes de la nuit* (Marcel Carné, 1946), *Un Revenant* (Christian-Jaque, 1946), *La Fille du diable* (Henri Decoin, 1946), and *Panique* are all permeated with guilt, disillusionment, betrayal, and revenge and that each interpret social realignment in austere terms. These blackly realist films are not so much critical of social institutions as metaphysically bleak, offering audiences a dispiriting view of humanity and an often absurdist view of existence. In particular, *Panique* welds the visuals of pre-war French poetic realism with a new bitterness and a drab, no-exit reality to illuminate the nation's post-Liberation climate of *épuration* (purges) and male identity crises. During production, Duvivier (1946a: 10) explained his reasons for making the film:

> Pourquoi *Panique*? Parce que c'était pour moi une réaction inévitable. J'arrivais d'Hollywood où j'avais vu pendant cinq ans des films optimistes avec le happy end inévitable [...] Aussi avais-je envie de traiter un sujet plus en rapport avec la situation actuelle [...] Que dit *Panique*? Il dit que les gens ne sont pas gentils, que la foule est imbécile, que les indépendants ont toujours tort [...] et qu'ils finissent inévitablement par marcher dans le rang. Évidemment, nous sommes loin des gens qui s'aiment, ceux-là sévissent sur les écrans d'Hollywood, mais j'ai bien l'impression que nous traversons une époque où les gens ne s'aiment pas.[8]

The film can thus be read as a rebuffing of a particular kind of cinema, the one of neat narrative conclusions and bright optimism that Duvivier had encountered in America. Now he was ready to begin work on a film that had far more in common with everyday reality. Although the Occupation years are not alluded to, *Panique* is clearly rooted in a contemporary present tense, much as *Au bonheur des dames* (1930) and *La Belle équipe* (1936) had been, responding to

---

8 'Why *Panique*? Because it was an inevitable reaction for me. I'd come back from Hollywood where for five years I'd watched optimistic films with obligatory happy endings [...] I also wanted to deal with a subject that was more in tune with the present situation [...] What is *Panique* about? It's about unkind people, it's about the idiotic crowd, it's about independent people who are always wrong [...] and who inevitably end up falling in line with the rest. Obviously, we are far from people who love each other, who are all the rage on the screens of Hollywood, but I have the strong impression that we are living in a time where people do not love each other.'

changes in the political and social fabric. As has been pointed out elsewhere (Phillips 2004), what was also particularly troubling about Duvivier's rationale here was his uncomfortable deployment of 'nous' ('we'). Here, the first-person-plural pronoun implicates the audience, pointedly accusing them of consenting to the current realities of score settling and scapegoating.

In Simenon's novel, Hire is explicitly Jewish, but in Duvivier and Spaak's version the word is never mentioned. Some critics have nonetheless pounced on the film's *mise en scène* to extrapolate recent historical resonances. Edward Ousselin notes that Hire is the only bearded character in the film, that there is an extra-diegetic sound of a train at the moment Hire falls from the roof, and that the bus's revolving signboard at the start of the film includes the destinations Villejuif ('Jewish town') and Gare de l'Est ('Station of the East'). Such choices 'allégorise[nt] le destin de 76,000 juifs déportés de France sous le régime de Vichy' (Ousselin 2007: 71).[9] Conversely, Florianne Wild (1996: 179) argues that *Panique* is less about 'Jewishness' than the coming to terms with France's recent history and the disgrace of the French during the Occupation. By jettisoning the explicit anti-Semitism of the Simenon source text, Duvivier and Spaak universalise their story, setting it in an any-space-whatever 'où les gens ne s'aiment pas' ('where people do not love each other') and making Hire's physical appearance and social awkwardness the markers of his marginalised status. They shift focus onto the arbitrary bleakness of human nature and provoke a deep collective sense of unease.

That bleakness is diagrammed onto the *mise en scène*. Unusually for a Duvivier film, the majority of *Panique* was shot on a studio set (at Nice's Victorine Studios). While this discards Duvivier's typical documentary-style engagement with the urban space, the decision to shoot on a sound stage imbues the film with an unsettling claustral quality. Production designer Serge Piménoff and cinematographer Nicholas Hayer craft a series of grim, desolate scenes that appear almost *noir*-ishly abstract. At one point, Alice and Alfred discuss their future together near a church where canticles are being sung. Later, Alice discovers Hire's secret identity, and we are introduced

---

9 'are an allegory for the fate of the 76,000 Jews deported from France under the Vichy regime'.

to another of Duvivier's doubles, the astrologer, Dr. Varga. In one of Duvivier's most memorable scenes, Hire is hemmed in by other cars at a fun-fair bumper-car ring. As onlookers stare at him (one remarks 'Je parle de la grande chasse, la chasse à courre!'[10]), Duvivier foreshadows the film's closing moments. He films the bumper-car drivers with front-on point-of-view shots as they drive past or collide into Hire from all directions, laughing at him and staring at a point just past the lens. Elsewhere, extensive use of close-ups reveals Alfred and Alice's treacherous faces, whereas Hire is often shot front on, in a way that both neutralises and fragments him. Critics also referred to the film's 'plans poisseux et poreux' ('sticky and porous shots'), as if the progressive fear and hatred of the crowd had begun to seep into the film itself. This role of the crowd in Hire's demise continued a thread already established in Duvivier's work, such as *Golgotha* (1935) and *Tales of Manhattan* (1942). Many reviews of *Panique* both at the time and subsequently contained the words 'veule' and 'veulerie' ('spineless'; 'spinelessness') to describe the actions and motivations of the crowd.

One final point to make here is about the film's gender politics. Burch and Sellier's work (1996) on 'evil women' in post-war French cinema argues that the social conflicts of the 1930s had, by 1946, been replaced by a 'battle of the sexes', in which political fears had been displaced onto gender relations. In *Panique*, Alice seduces and betrays the inveterate romantic Hire and colludes in his downfall. So, while *Panique* is another example of Duvivier's problematic representation of women, it is also the case that Alice's representation in barely concealed misogynistic terms is part of a wider post-war canvas that focused on the victimisation of men by manipulative women. This emphasis can be seen as a paranoid interpretation by men of their own predicament at the Liberation, which led to a scapegoating of women for war-time collaboration. As I have already noted, women are frequently presented as duplicitous and scheming in Duvivier's films, and the casting of Viviane Romance a decade after her destructive role as Gina in *La Belle équipe* is telling. Here, Duvivier reinforces pre- to post-war continuities via the representation of this *sale garce* (evil bitch). And it would not end end here. Alice's diabolical persona would continue to mutate, firstly into Mlle. Chamblas in *Au royaume*

10 'I'm talking about a big game hunt, with hounds!.'

des cieux (1949) and then, most memorably, into Christine in *Voici le temps des assassins* (1956).

While the film's commercial returns were reasonable – selling nearly 2.5 million tickets[11] – the critical response to *Panique* was highly divergent. As might be expected from a journal of the far left, *L'Humanité* was severely critical of Duvivier: 'Si c'est pour mettre sa technique au service de pareilles œuvres qu'il est revenu d'Hollywood, il pouvait rester là-bas' (Gaillard 1947).[12] Other critics were particularly uncomfortable with the film's ending. *L'Ecran français* (Vidal 1947: 5) did not care for the 'sadisme collectif' ('collective sadism'), and Lo Duca (1946: 6) in *Cinémonde* described the final moments as 'une violence affreuse, comme nous n'en avions pas vue depuis longtemps sur nos écrans'.[13] 'M. Hire meurt surtout victime de la bêtise et de la cruauté de la foule', stated the film's synopsis in *Opéra*; not so, argued its resident critic Jean Fayard (1947) in the same review: 'M. Hire meurt surtout victime de la cruauté de Spaak et de Duvivier.'[14] In the aftermath of the Liberation, it seems, critics wanted to be salved. But Duvivier was in no mood to pander to genteel taste. For Colin Crisp (2015: 140), 'only a Belgian scriptwriter [i.e. Spaak] and a French director who had been absent from France during those recent events could have dared to make a film so powerfully (if implicitly) critical of the French people's role in them'.

The tepid response to *Panique*, and to Duvivier's return more generally, mirrored Marcel Carné's diminishing fortunes. In the late 1940s and early 1950s, Carné's reputation likewise began to dramatically ebb, and, despite the burnished success of *Les Enfants du paradis* (1945), he never again reached the sustained critical heights of his 1930s poetic realist output such as *Hôtel du nord* (1938) and *Le Jour se*

---

11 It was a still a long way back from the box-office successes of the 1946–7 season, such as Clair's *Le Silence est d'or* (4.2 million tickets), Claude Autant-Lara's *Le Diable au corps* (4.8 million), and Alexandre Esway's runaway hit *Le Bataillon du ciel* (8.7 million).
12 'If the reason why he came back from Hollywood was to make films such as these, then he can stay there.'
13 'an awful violence, the likes of which we had not seen on our screens for a long time'.
14 'M. Hire dies chiefly the victim of the stupidity and the cruelty of the crowd'; 'M. Hire dies chiefly the victim of the cruelty of Spaak and Duvivier.'

lève (1939). Carné's *Les Portes de la nuit* had been particularly admonished for its nostalgic embracing of a pre-war aesthetic that had, by post-Liberation, become 'all too familiar and predictable' (Hayward 2005: 170).[15] Most damning of all was that Carné had not left France at all during the Occupation.

Panique did not fit into the bracket of poetic works that had emerged during the war (films such as Carné's *Les Visiteurs du soir* [1942] and Jean Cocteau's *La Belle et la bête* [1946]). It had far more in common with the 'black realism' of *Le Quai des brumes* (1938, which had also starred Simon and featured another remarkable scene at a bumper-car ring) and the Duvivier–Gabin films of the 1930s. Yet, unlike Carné, Duvivier cleverly grafted the pessimism of those earlier poetic realist works onto a new set of political and social contexts. The result remains one of the high points of European post-war *noir*. The last line of Henri Jeanson's (2000: 330) review of the film for *Le Canard enchaîné* announced 'Cinéma français pas mort. Julien Duvivier continue.'[16] But it would not be as easy as that.

Interlude: Duvivier the film critic

Shortly after the filming of *Panique*, Duvivier was approached by his friend Maurice Bessy, journalist at the film magazine *Cinémonde*, to write a series of reflections on the current state of the French film industry. Using the pseudonym 'Monsieur Platon' – in reference to the Greek philosopher – Duvivier's weekly columns were wide-ranging and thought-provoking interventions, and stand as a fascinating summary of the director's thoughts about his own craft. Writing as Platon between November 1946 and February 1947, Duvivier extolled the virtues of recent foreign releases (he greatly admired Disney's *Fantasia* [1940], Noel Coward's *Blithe Spirit* [1945], and the emotional heft of David Lean's *Brief Encounter* [1945]); criticised the Blum–Byrnes agreement; defended René Clair; urged audiences to see *La Belle et la bête*, believing Cocteau's film would restore French cinema's pre-war international prestige; and vociferously

---

15 Duvivier (1947a) did not like *Les Portes de la nuit* and criticised Carné's decision to rebuild the sets in the studio and not shoot on location.
16 'French cinema is not dead. Julien Duvivier goes on.'

backed Italian neo-realism, especially the films of Roberto Rossellini. Those who suggest Duvivier never had a sense of humour would be surprised by his mischievous review of *Panique*, which had just premiered at the Palais de Chaillot: 'il y a dans *Panique* une poésie du mouvement, une symphonie de la foule [...] Quant à son mordant et à sa virulence, il s'apparente au *Corbeau*, avec cependant plus d'ampleur' (Duvivier 1946c: 6).[17] A fortnight later, in his end-of-year round up, M. Platon awarded the following prizes: 'Le film le plus bouleversant de l'année: *Panique*. La scène la plus poignante de l'année: la mort de Michel Simon en *Panique*. La meilleure actrice française de l'année: Viviane Romance en *Panique*' (Duvivier 1947b).[18]

These contemplations are valuable for a number of reasons. They clearly epitomise a series of cultural debates that were taking place in post-war France about the need to restore French cinema to a position of cultural pre-eminence, more urgent now given the domination of American films in French cinemas and the rise of other European cinemas to positions of value. By loudly championing a film such as *Macadam* (Marcel Blistène, 1946), Duvivier foregrounded the embryonic post-war French *noir* and reminded readers that French cinema has always excelled at 'ces drames d'atmosphère, évoluant d'une poésie désespérée à un réalisme violent' (Duvivier 1946b: 5).[19] The term *drame d'atmosphère* inevitably recalls earlier films such as *Pépé le Moko* (1937), and so Duvivier-as-Platon is also committed to a process of cultural rehabilitation, turning back to recent film history – and the exalted status of poetic realism exemplified by the likes of himself – to suggest that post-war atmospheric, or *noir*, French cinema might again attain those lofty heights. Duvivier also emphasises through his criticism how intensive theoretical confrontations with the medium could be explored through the practicalities of film-making. There is a move from theory to practice advocated throughout the Platon pieces that incrementally plots out

---

17 'There is in *Panique* a poetry of movement, a symphony of the crowd [...] As for its intensity and venom, it resembles *Le Corbeau*, yet with more depth.'
18 'The most earth-shattering film of the year: *Panique*. The most poignant scene of the year: Michel Simon's death in *Panique*. The best French actress of the year: Viviane Romance in *Panique*.'
19 'these "atmospheric dramas", which develop from desperate poetry to violent realism'.

a preferred Duvivier 'style' that would eventually be channelled into his later films. Perhaps most importantly, Duvivier also sketches out his own definitions here of the auteur, anticipating the *Cahiers du cinéma* debates to come. 'Platon' sees auteurism as both collaboration and the singular vision of the director, and thus diagrams a possible third way in the auteur debate. On the one hand, he looks back to his time in Hollywood, and in France of the 1930s, in which large-scale industrial and small-scale artisanal teams worked together to fashion a final shared output. On the other, he also regards 'la création pure' ('total creation') as the ultimate goal of a single artistic vision (Duvivier 1946d: 18). As we shall see, Duvivier was adept at straddling both tendencies.

Anna Karenina (1948)

If Duvivier thought that his return to France would bring to an end his period of enforced migration, then his next project triggered a fresh wave of peripatetic film-making. From this point until *La Grande vie* (1960), he would work in studios in England, Italy, Germany, and Spain and only return to France periodically. Duvivier headed off to London's Shepperton Studios to honour an earlier contract he had signed with Alexander Korda in Hollywood to adapt Leo Tolstoy's monumental novel *Anna Karenina*.[20] The film, shot in English and released in 1948, was expensive, designed to capitalise on the casting of Leigh, still famous from her Oscar-winning role in *Gone with the Wind* (1939), and to relaunch the Korda brand in an international market. Korda assembled a diverse European production crew. Working alongside Duvivier were a German cinematographer (Henri Alekan), a Russian set designer (André Andrejew), an English costume designer (Cecil Beaton), and a French co-writer (the playwright Jean Anouilh).

Duvivier soon encountered many of the same problems he thought he had left behind in Hollywood, namely around authorial control and the triangular relationship between the director,

---

20 There have been over a dozen adaptations of Tolstoy's novel, from 1911 to Joe Wright's 2012 version, starring Keira Knightley and Jude Law. Greta Garbo played Anna twice, in 1927 and again in 1935.

producer, and star. Duvivier and Anouilh's original plans to update the story of a married socialite and her destructive affair with Count Vronsky to contemporary France were strenuously rejected by Korda, who wanted the original nineteenth-century Russian context to be scrupulously maintained. As a result, Anouilh was fired from the project and replaced by Guy Morgan. Korda had also wanted to cast Leigh's husband, Laurence Olivier, as Anna's lover Count Vronsky, but had to settle for Irish newcomer Kieron Moore instead.[21] Leigh clashed repeatedly with Duvivier over their differing readings of Ralph Richardson's Karenin, Anna's detached, aristocratic husband. She felt that his overtly sympathetic portrayal mitigated Anna's eventual decision to commit suicide and argued instead that he needed to be uncaring and cold, whereas Duvivier wanted to invest him with a touching humanity. Duvivier would ultimately win out, as the film contains two examples of Karenin's compassion that do not exist in the novel (namely, the scene when he offers Anna his hand after he has pushed her to the floor after discovering her love letters, and when he tells her that he does not understand her after she has accused him of never having loved her).

For a film so fraught with tension, it is remarkable that Duvivier managed to fashion a singular vision of Tolstoy's story and intersperse his controlled visual style and sumptuous *mise en scène*. For instance, Duvivier's version is far less 'Russianised' than earlier adaptations. Despite Korda's insistence upon the Russian setting, Duvivier (1947c: 14) told Marcel Idzkowski that he had deliberately reined in the luxuriousness described by Tolstoy to fashion a version of the text that was 'resserré, étriqué, banal, inconfortable' ('squeezed, tightened, unremarkable, uncomfortable'). The only excessive visual marker that signals 'Russia' is the heavy snowfall that accompanies Anna's first trip to Moscow and her return to St. Petersburg, while Henri Alekan's deep-focus monochrome cinematography and André Andrejew's baroque production design concentrate instead on generic *grands salons*, palaces, train stations, and opera houses to evoke a specific time and place.

Duvivier's adaptation practices come to the fore in *Anna Karenina*. Irina Makoveeva (2001: 122) terms Duvivier's version of Tolstoy an

21 Olivier was filming *Hamlet* at the time. The lack of chemistry between Leigh and Moore was a recurring complaint among reviewers.

'illustration-adaptation', in which the film carefully follows the literary source, finding cinematic equivalents for certain elements. The debt owed to Tolstoy's original is explicitly rendered in the film's first and last shots, in which pages from the novel are projected onto the screen (at the start, 'All happy families resemble one another, every unhappy family is unhappy after its own fashion'; at the end, 'And the light by which she had been reading the book of life [...] went out forever'). This book-ending practice is a common adaptation device, suggesting that the film will convey as much as possible from the source text. Duvivier's adaptation is the most faithful to the incidental details of the novel, such as Alexei's habit of cracking his knuckles and Anna's black ballgown.

Duvivier did make quite radical changes. Most of the subplots, aside from the Anna–Vronsky–Karenin triangle, were either curtailed or suppressed. The marriage plot between Konstantin Levin and Kitty Scherbatsky, for instance, is reduced to barely three minutes. Structurally, the film follows the novel in the parallel development of two separate narratives: Anna and Vronsky on one hand, and Kitty and Levin on the other. Duvivier shows Anna preparing to leave for Italy with Vronsky at the same time that Kitty and Levin are getting married, neatly foreshadowing the destinies of the two couples. At the same moment, Levin becomes a husband and future father and Anna is becoming Vronsky's mistress and parting from her son. Duvivier deviates again when Karenin and Serezha attend the wedding while Anna remains sick at home. This alteration is in tune with Duvivier's overall narrative thrust: here, Anna is definitively breaking from the family, remaining isolated and on its fringes. By altering each of the characters in the love triangle (Anna is less passionate, Vrosnky is less assertive, Karenin is less cold), Duvivier shifts focus from the determinism of adultery to the dynamics of class- and gender-defined groups.

Duvivier obsessively recreates the social landscape, showing aristocratic life in St. Petersburg and Moscow, Karenin's work meetings, and Levin's country lifestyle. He is clearly at home exploring the rigid conventions that exert themselves on aristocratic social norms. Karenin instructs Anna how to deport herself in public, General Serpuhousky informs Vronsky that marriage is vital in maintaining a successful career, and Princess Betty refers to Liza Merkalova, who is married but skilled enough to be able to have a lover. Anna's high-society women's group is also forensically detailed, not least the cynical countess, who admits that she would enjoy Roman gladiators spilling blood. Makoveeva (2001) notes how many of the secondary characters from Tolstoy's novel, often omitted from earlier or subsequent adaptations, are reintegrated into the film and function as part of a wider social community.

The end result of Duvivier and Leigh's co-creation of Anna is both static and dynamic. Sue Harper notes that the style of *Anna Karenina* is extremely mannered, and Duvivier's dense visual texture suggests Anna's joyless past. Anna is portrayed throughout as a beautiful victim, whose passion resembles 'a tableau from Madame Tussaud's' (Harper 1992: 221); the *New York Times* (Crowther 1948) was less kind, writing that 'Miss Leigh slowly disintegrate[s] into a whining, maudlin, vain, self-pitying dame'. Duvivier repeatedly emphasises Anna's tragic situation. The first time we see her, she already cuts a melancholic figure, looking sadly out of a frost-tainted train window, while her mental breakdown and approaching death (heralded via the figure of a hammering train worker) are reminiscent of the final moments of *Pépé le Moko*. As Anna faces the advancing train and her disordered mind recreates the snowstorm of long ago instead of registering the rain in her present, Duvivier's final directorial flourish in his rather visually restrained film is to use a bird's-eye shot of Anna's body lying on the train tracks.

With returns of only £150,000 from a budget of £700,000, *Anna Karenina* was not a financial success, despite Leigh's name above the title. In one critic's words, Duvivier's film 'was beautifully mounted and magnificently produced, even within the limitations that black and white film imposed, but unfortunately it seemed never to come alive' (Edwards 1977: 160). The general feeling was that *Anna Karenina* was a disappointment in terms of its status as a Duvivier adaptation. *Franc-tireur* (Néry 1949) called the new version 'figé, curieusement fragmenté, et, par instants, déformé' ('rigid, strangely fragmented, and occasionally deformed'). Other critics regarded Korda's current successes, such as *The Winslow Boy* (1948) and *The Fallen Idol* (1948), as more successful versions of adapted material. For such a prodigious *adaptateur*, such remarks foreshadowed a shift in French cultural attitudes at the end of the 1940s towards literary adaptation and costume dramas.

Au royaume des cieux (1949) and *Black Jack* (1950)

After a planned film fell through (backed by Alexander Korda, it was to be shot in Tahiti in colour), Duvivier returned to France. He teamed up with Henri Jeanson for the first time since *Un Carnet de bal* to work on a story of a *maison de correction* (reform school) for young girls. Maria (Suzanne Cloutier), an orphan in state care, is sent to the sinister Haute-Mère facility, run by its sadistic and cruel director Mademoiselle Chamblas (Suzy Prim). Maria's boyfriend Pierre (Serge Reggiani) vows to come and free her, Chamblas' increasingly dictatorial style leads to a riot, and, when Chamblas tries to flee, she is savagely attacked by the school's guard dog. Mademoiselle Guérande (Monique Mélinand) takes over the running of Haute-Mère, and Maria and Pierre are reunited.

The plot of *Au royaume des cieux* (1949) is similar to that of G. W. Pabst's *Diary of a Lost Girl* (1929) and, closer to home, shares visual and tonal qualities with the war-time *réalisme fantastique* of Marcel Carné and Jacques Prévert. It displays a feverish style in which the brutality of Chamblas intermingles uneasily with undercurrents of sadism, suicide, and a pathological eroticism (many of the girls have committed crimes of murder and prostitution). The film also featured the debuts of several young French actresses, such as Colette Deréal, Juliette Gréco, and Christiane Lénier. Cloutier herself would later star opposite Orson Welles as Desdemona in *Othello* (1952).

Several post-war French films about orphans reflect the idea that, for children whose parents were lost in prisoner-of-war camps, from deportation or from bombing raids, their childhood had been stolen (Butler 2004: 169). Even though the opening intertitles dedicate the film 'à l'enfance malheureuse' ('to unhappy childhoods'), Duvivier is not interested in the social realist implications of these neglected, orphaned youngsters. In a typical move, he charts what happens when Maria's 'goodness' (the allegorical overtones of her name are clear) comes into contact with the institutional vice and cruelty overseen by Chamblas. This dialectical focus also informs the film's formal style, such as the alternating between the hyper-realist setting of Haute-Mère and the dream-like catacombs, which double as solitary confinement; the crescendoing sound of ringing church bells throughout the opening and closing credits; and Victor Arménise's fluid interchange between close-up and tracking and panning shots.

Duvivier creates a striking atmosphere from the outset. As Maria is driven to Haute-Mère, a police car traverses a series of desolate landscapes. It is raining hard, and this consistent rain will eventually build to an inundation on Christmas morning that washes away a church. Pierre takes advantage of the rising water to free Maria. The metaphorical links between storms and floods inside and out Haute-Mère are clear to see. Chamblas tries to break a hunger strike by bringing the girls a large pot of soup, and Duvivier cuts from close-ups of their faces to the steaming pot. Later, girls run screaming down the corridors, breaking open bottles of wine they find in the storeroom, and march ominously towards Chamblas, who is barricaded in her room. Duvivier's brief interventions are models of narrative concision, like the *plan subjectif* as Chamblas tidies the desk of her predecessor seconds after the latter has been pronounced dead. Chamblas has waited twenty years to assume the role of director at Haute-Mère, and Duvivier reinforces her newly acquired power with a close-up of an ink stamp.

The film features a rarity – a happy ending. Maria and Pierre are reunited at the close, and, for the girls who remain behind, the appointment of Mademoiselle Guérande and the instructive power of Maria's redemptive love offer hopeful shafts of light. After his despairing portrayal of human behaviour in *Panique*, Duvivier offers moments of relief in *Au royaume des cieux*; both Guérande and the chaplain (Jean Davy) show compassion to those in the institution. Yet continuities with *Panique* remain. The wickedness and evil of that film are manifested again in Chamblas. Duvivier makes her a man-hating, sexually repressed shrew who treats the girls in her care sadistically. It is another troubling representation of femininity in Duvivier's work and one that is eventually avenged not by human agency but by a dog. As in the later *Voici le temps des assassins*, Duvivier lets an animal do what human characters seem powerless to do: mete out justice. That the dog's name is Goliath again adds to the film's allegorical, almost mythical register.

If *Au royaume des cieux* was seen as a partial return to form for Duvivier by critics who were still coming to terms with *Panique*, then *Black Jack* (1950) left them completely nonplussed. Considered one of Duvivier's minor works, *Black Jack* was a Franco-Spanish-American production, shot in Mallorca, and – rarely for a Duvivier film – was an original screenplay, co-written by Duvivier with Charles

Spaak (with additional dialogue from Robert Gaillard and Michael Pertwee). The story amplifies several of Duvivier's long-standing thematic concerns, such as complex intertwining destinies, characters who are not who they initially appear to be, and expatriate cynicism.

Described as 'a delicious drama of imposture, an involuntary comedy of con men and women, and an intermittently suspenseful thriller where good confronts evil' (Nissen 2013: 145), *Black Jack* tells the story of Mike Alexander (George Sanders), an ex-pat American now living in Mallorca who trades in drugs, guns, and illegal immigrants using his yacht *Black Jack*. When Mike tries to go straight, he is drawn into an even murkier world of contraband and racketeering. Cast alongside Sanders were Patricia Roc (as Ingrid, Mike's love interest), Agnes Moorehead (as a double-crossing racketeer), Herbert Marshall (as a narcotics agent), and Marcel Dalio (as a cowardly captain familiar to French audiences from Jean Renoir's *La Grande illusion* [1937] and *La Règle du jeu* [1939]). The film owes a clear debt to the likes of *To Have and Have Not* (Howard Hawks, 1944) and *The Third Man* (Carol Reed, 1949) with its focus on smuggling refugees by boat and distributing black-market drugs in post-war Europe. Dalio's presence is also a reminder that *Black Jack* shares some thematic DNA with *Casablanca* (Michael Curtiz, 1942). Indeed, many of the plot points of Curtiz's film are replicated: an American man stranded in north Africa saddled with a healthy dose of cynicism and world-weariness, a sultry climate, crime and illicit activities in the background, and the possibility of redemptive love with the arrival of an outsider (Ingrid Bergman then, 'Ingrid' here). Curtiz had woven fragments of *Pépé le Moko* into *Casablanca*. Was Duvivier here repaying the favour?

Like *Anna Karenina* before it, *Black Jack* had an erratic production history. The original shooting schedule was due to last eight weeks but went on for almost seven months. Sanders later sniped that part of the delay was due to Duvivier's fastidiousness – he 'would not shoot unless the sky was exactly to [his] liking, which to my way of thinking happened rather rarely' (Sanders 1960: 86). The effect of this extended shoot is most visible in Sanders' physical appearance. In the early scenes, he appears svelte, by, the end of the film, he has put on a considerable amount of weight.[22] He is not helped by a rather

---

22 Sanders later admitted that the delays on the film had made him drink and eat more.

cumbersome script that is littered with anachronisms – Sanders is asked to deliver lines such as 'Is this on the level?' and 'Honey, I'll be back', despite his cut-glass upper-class English accent.[23]

Black Jack's on-location compositions, with snippets of spoken Spanish and flamenco music, lend a neo-realist immediacy and direct engagement with an exotic atmosphere. This incorporation of authentic sights and sounds is a typical Duvivier touch – he would finesse these glimpses of the 'Spanish exotic' in *La Femme et le pantin* (1959) – and reminds us that he was never more comfortable than when filming on location and bringing a foreigner's eye to a foreign locale. As he did in *Pépé le Moko*, Duvivier shuttles between Mallorca's *quartier européen* and its local centre with an ethnographic fascination. *Pépé le Moko* looms large in other respects. For instance, when Mike and Ingrid dance for the first time, Mike describes himself as 'a crook with an ambition – to stop being one, and pull out fast, for keeps'. Just as Pépé had been fascinated by the arrival of Gaby, seeing her as his chance for redemption and to leave the Algiers Casbah for good, so Mike regards Ingrid in the same way. When they kiss for the first time, he tells her that 'the world is ours in two days' time'. It is not hard to see why Duvivier would be attracted to this type of story: a world-weary cynic with a skewed moral compass ('I don't steal, I don't hurt people, I just sell things people need') playing out a classic trope of American crime cinema – the crook prepared to do 'one last job' before pulling out and going legit. *Black Jack*, for all its narrative slackness and disjointed visual style, is another of Duvivier's *histoire d'hommes* inflected with his customary pessimism.

After Mike kills Nikarescu by pushing him under the water with his foot (a death scene that would be copied in *La Chambre ardente* [1962]), he destroys the drugs, tipping them over the side of the boat. In Ingrid's eyes, Mike is a reformed man, no longer involved in the grubby business of narcotics. Chasing Mike on his boat, the shore patrol authorities shoot him just after he has told Ingrid he loves her. As he and Ingrid enter international waters and leave the jurisdiction of the Spanish police, he dies. The last line is 'I'm free, free', and in a voiceover, as the end credits roll, Mike's ghostly voice returns: 'Call

---

23 It did not help that rushes had to be sent to the mainland for processing, making it impossible to view progress on a daily basis. Much of the external post-synching seems muffled and even the sound in the studio-shot scenes does not always appear to match the actors' voices.

no man happy until he is dead.' The Duvivier worldview (supplemented by Spaak) was still intact; the Hollywood 'happy ending' overruled. Mike continued a line of protagonists (Pépé, Cabrissade, Anna Karenina, Lafarge) for whom death meant freedom.

Narrative experiments: *Sous le ciel de Paris* (1951) and *La Fête à Henriette* (1952)

Over the course of a day in Paris, a poor elderly woman (Louise Sylvie) seeks food for her cats; a student (Christiane Lénier) tries to resist the advances of her employer; a truanting young girl (Marie-France) is reunited with her mother; a girl (Brigitte Auber) from the provinces is stabbed to death in the street by a sculptor (Raymond Hermantier); the sculptor is killed by a policeman, who also accidentally shoots a worker celebrating his wedding anniversary (Jean Brochard); the injured man undergoes emergency open-heart surgery; and the surgeon (Daniel Ivernel) who performs the operation has just failed his intern exam.

As this synopsis makes clear, *Sous le ciel de Paris* (1951) is an elaborately structured film that follows seven people whose lives intersect across the city. It mixes a bright, optimistic tone with a darker, more pessimistic outlook on Parisian life. This tonal unease is established at the outset, when a fisherman disturbs a corpse floating down the Seine. Thus, what on the surface appears to be a picaresque comedy quickly shifts into a far darker meditation on life in the city. Pierre Leprohon (1968: 245) sees the central tenets of *Sous le ciel de Paris* as 'la domination de l'auteur sur son récit' and 'sa position de meneur de jeu'.[24] This 'domination' stems in part from the narrative framework but also from Duvivier's visual skill. And if, as Leprohon suggests, *Sous le ciel de Paris* is a film about the control a director exercises, then it is because themes of destiny and predetermination are subtly woven throughout.

Despite its focus on multiple protagonists and its criss-crossing urban trajectory, *Sous le ciel de Paris* is not an anthology film in the same vein as *Tales of Manhattan* or *Un Carnet de bal*. While those

---

24 'the power of the author/auteur over their story'; 'their status as game master'.

films placed various characters within ten-minute sketches, *Sous le ciel de Paris* is what the French call a *film choral*, in which various unconnected tales eventually intersect within a unifying frame. Duvivier had been thinking about making the film since the release of *Panique*, and initially wanted four different writers to each contribute a section to a film that would revolve around four seasons in Paris. Co-writing with the actor René Lefèvre (who had starred in René Clair's films as well as in *Les Cinq gentlemen maudits* [1931]), Duvivier narrowed the film's narrative timeframe down to a single twenty-four-hour period and shot in the late summer of 1950 at Billancourt studios and on location in Paris. As he had done with *Au royaume des cieux*, Duvivier avoided star casting. Brigitte Auber would go on to work on Hitchcock's *To Catch a Thief* (1955), and Paul Frankeur would become a regular for Luis Buñuel, but the rest of the cast were a mixture of theatrically trained actors, non-professionals, and unknowns. The title song, added in post-production, became a huge popular hit in France (in the film it is sung by Jean Bretonnière, but it would eventually form part of Édith Piaf's songbook). The song can be heard several times in the film, beckoning us back into the fictional world and binding together the destinies of the various characters. It is another example of the importance of popular song in Duvivier's cinema, standing here as a marker for populist Paris (Maurice Chevalier and Charles Trenet are mentioned in passing later in the film), solidarity, and the authentic sights and sounds of the capital.[25]

To bolster this sense of destinies intertwining, Duvivier included a voiceover that bookends the film and comments on the action. This omniscient chorus-like narration, written by Henri Jeanson and delivered by François Périer, carries with it a Prévertian mixture of irony, black humour, and tenderness. The opening section contains a series of wry, witty pronouncements, accompanied by the sound of a spinning roulette wheel: 'Les Parisiens ne se doutent pas que pendant ce temps-là, le destin pense à eux tout en rodant sa roue'[26] and 'Suivons le donc, c'est sa tournée. Il règle tout, le destin, sauf

---

25 A second song, 'Cœur de Paris', by André Claveau, is played over the film's opening and closing credits.
26 'The Parisians have no idea that in the meantime, fate has something for them, and is honing his wheel.'

ça: l'aurore aux doigts gris-perle lui échappe.'[27] The technique is theatrical, but it is not contrived. Unlike the post-production addition of the voiceover in *Untel père et fils*, this voiceover introduces individual characters, magnifying them and drawing attention to their character and personality while at the same time commenting ironically on the unfolding events.

The way *Sous le ciel de Paris* oscillates between light and darkness marks it out as a quintessential Duvivier film. What starts as a gentle love letter to Paris transforms into something far darker and more misanthropic: women who beg for money are treated with indifference, a girl is abandoned by the boy she befriends, a fashion student is sexually harassed by her employer, and a solitary sculptor – whose artworks are deformed, bloated depictions of the female form – stalks the streets. *Sous le ciel de Paris* also incorporates strands of other Duvivier films – Denise's lottery-ticket win recalls *La Belle équipe*, the open-heart surgery evokes the blood transfusion in *L'Homme du jour* (1936), Mathias' psychopathy returns us to Radek in *La Tête d'un homme* (1932), and the penniless Sylvie could be related to anyone from *La Fin du jour* (1939).

One storyline in particular that resonates with the rest of Duvivier's work is the arrival of Denise from the country. She disembarks at the Gare de Lyon and is immediately taken aback by everything she sees. Duvivier updates a similar scene from *Au bonheur des dames*, recalling Dita Parlo's Denise, who also stepped out from a Paris train station, wide-eyed before the hustle and bustle of the modern city. Yet, whereas Denise Baudu would eventually marry Octave Mouret and rise to the pinnacle of the Paris *demi-monde*, migration proves fatal for Denise Lambert, who will eventually be killed on a gloomy back street behind the Sacré Cœur by a psychopath. Margaret Butler suggests that it was Duvivier's status as an exile during the Occupation years that provided him with a keen sense of the polarities between the urban and the rural. Thus, the inclusion of the 'girl from the country' who is first seduced but then assassinated by the temptations of the city is an admittance by Duvivier of the fundamental incompatibility in French national identity between the rural and the urban (Butler 2003: 233). Yet, despite this dark

---

27 'Let's follow him; it's his round. Fate, he fixes everything up, except this. The pearl-grey dawn is beyond his grasp.'

strain, Duvivier remains a moralist and looks to provide resolution at the end – the evil and the ambitious are punished, the good and the brave are rewarded, and a neighbour brings milk and meat for the old lady's cats.

One of the most prominent aspects of the film is its use of location shooting. From the opening helicopter shots, Duvivier incorporates extensive footage. Moving from Rue Mouffetard to a fashion shoot at the Palais de Chaillot, the unspooling topography of Paris – left and right bank; east and west; populist and luxurious – offers a series of spatial anchors that bring order to the film's fragmented narrative. While much of the city is showcased (Le Marais, the Champs-Élysées, Les Invalides, Bercy, Ménilmontant, Montmartre), Duvivier is less interested in the tourist side of Paris than in the routines and rituals of its inhabitants. With its focus on the *petits gens*, *Sous le ciel de Paris* harks back to the populist films of the 1930s by Clair and Carné, who similarly explored the quotidian lifestyles of groups of Parisian 'types'. Indeed, Périer's first voiceover is accompanied by a languorous travelling shot across the roofs of the city that cannot help but remind us of the opening of Clair's *Sous les toits de Paris* (1930). Duvivier casts his wide gaze across the city and scatters the story with incursions into real-life places. He takes in *haute couture* fashion shoots (with gowns provided by Dior), sit-in demonstrations at factories, and medical procedures at the Hôtel-Dieu hospital. This time-capsule vision of 1950s Parisian fashion, music, and architecture once again reinforces Duvivier's ongoing fascination with the authentic. Nicolas Hayer, who had already lensed *Panique* and Clouzot's *Le Corbeau* and would go on to work with Melville and Rohmer, alternates between handheld cameras and studio work to establish the film's luscious black-and-white cinematography.[28] Scenes at the Palais de Chaillot, the Tuileries, and the Seine quaysides are shot with a luminous high-key lighting, shifting to a murkier grey for the factory scenes and an expressionistic chiaroscuro for the scene when Mathias murders Denise.

The film's afterlife was considerably prolonged when it was well received in other European territories (winning a top prize in Sweden) and secured an American release in 1952, with the title

---

28 Hayer was also the cinematographer on *Le Petit monde de Don Camillo* (1952).

Under the Paris Sky. Looked at today, it is the innovative direction and narration that lends *Sous le ciel de Paris* its singular appeal. Its use of voiceover, on-location engagement with Paris, reliance on handheld cameras, and restless jumping from one storyline to another all suggest a film-making style that might, were the conditions right, be regarded as closely aligned to the spirit of the New Wave.

Indeed, that precursory engagement with the technique and narrative structure of the New Wave blossomed with *La Fête à Henriette* (1952), shot in between the two Don Camillo films. An intensely self-reflexive film, it is one of Duvivier's most enjoyable works and affirms his position as one of French cinema's most radical experimenters of the 1950s. Like *Sous le ciel de Paris*, *La Fête à Henriette* takes place over the course of a day. It centres on Henriette (Dany Robin) and how she spends Bastille Day in Paris with her fiancé, Robert (Michel Roux). At a ball, Robert abandons Henriette for young starlet Rita Solar (Hildegarde Neff); Henriette then crosses paths with Maurice (Michel Auclair), a small-time crook who persuades her to assist him in a robbery.

The delightful twist here is that the film just described is in fact a film-within-a-film. *La Fête à Henriette* is a part-Brechtian, part-Pirandelloesque fiction that deliriously charts the pleasures and pitfalls of screenwriting as the duo of *scénaristes* (Louis Seigner and Henri Crémieux) comes up with their next film, 'une simple histoire d'amour' ('a simple love story'). To complicate this smooth creative process, the two writers are diametrically opposed. Henri Jeanson and Duvivier's script assigns the two men differing artistic temperaments – Seigner the romantic optimist; Crémieux the cynical, sadistic *noir* specialist. The film luxuriates in this in-built tension. On numerous occasions, the writers intervene to show up the fictional nature of the story, and, depending on their individual moods, pivot between light comedy, satire, high burlesque, and *noir* drama, and agonise over whether their fictional heroine Henriette should be given a happy ending, as Seigner insists, or suffer an unhappy one, as Crémieux demands. A large portion of *La Fête à Henriette* is devoted to the articulation and justification of these points of view. Crémieux tells his partner: 'Tu mens quand tu essaies de prouver au public que la vie est rose bonbon et que tout est bien qui finit bien, je ne me prêterai pas à cette escroquerie intellectuelle'; Seigner replies: 'Et moi je ne laisserai pas imposer un pessimisme systématique par un démagogue de la caméra.'[29] Of course, it is tempting, as many have done, to read this working relationship between the two writers as an exaggerated version of the Duvivier–Jeanson dynamic. One of the writers tends towards dark, bitter material; the other prefers it 'fleur bleue' ('mushy').[30] Duvivier, who in 1936 had been compelled to impose a happy ending at the close of *La Belle équipe*, clearly revelled in this witty deconstruction of the conventions and audience expectations of narrative cinema.

The structural ingenuity of *La Fête à Henriette* frees up Duvivier to incorporate a range of stylistic and technical extravagances. The film's opening titles begin with 'Les films **** présentent un film de ?????' instead of the usual cast and credits as the writers remark that their last script had been banned by the censors. Scanning the newspaper for inspiration, Crémieux reads out *faits divers* that might serve as a starting point for their new film. One story is about a man arrested for stealing a bicycle to replace his stolen bicycle; another refers to a priest and a communist mayor who came to blows. The references to *Bicycle Thieves* (Vittorio de Sica, 1948) and Duvivier's own *Le Petit monde de Don Camillo* (1952) are clear, as is a later reference to Carné and Prévert's *Les Portes de la nuit*, when they introduce a blind man into the story who 'incarne le destin' ('epitomises fate'). The final scene, as fireworks light up the sky and the two lovers unite, recalls Clair's *Quatorze juillet* (1932) and the sort of romantic comedy for which he was famous. As the film's tone pivots from light to dark, the ever-developing screenplay is dramatised on screen. When the writers eventually reach a compromise, they are interrupted by the 'real' Michel Auclair, who informs them that their 'original' screenplay has already been filmed, with the title 'La Fête à Henriette'. To complete this dizzyingly ludic circle, Auclair then proceeds to read the end credits out loud, including his own name, to us.

---

29 'You are lying when you try to prove to the public that life is sugar sweet and that "all's well that ends well". Well I won't go along with such intellectual dishonesty'; 'And I won't have such systematic pessimism foisted upon me by a demagogue of the cinema.'

30 Duvivier (1959: 16) admitted that the main source of inspiration for the writing duo was Charles MacArthur and Ben Hecht, Hollywood screenwriters from the 1930s. Bonnefille (2002b) notes that Duvivier and Jeanson were at one point lined up to play the roles of the two writers.

Duvivier divides the two story worlds with a series of visual demarcations. The 'real' events take place in a hotel salon while the 'fictional' story is set in a Paris primarily filmed on location. Duvivier deploys a quasi-Brechtian reflexivity, using a set of techniques more suited to a Godard film, to call attention to its own artificiality, in turn distancing the spectator. So, Crémieux imagines that the heroine might be Swedish and blonde, living on the left bank with a Japanese poet; he then changes his mind and this time proposes that the heroine is a petite brunette who grifts at the Bastille. As Crémieux speaks, Duvivier cuts to shots of an actress matching those descriptions crossing the Boulevard Saint-Germain and pretending to be hit by a car on the Place de la Bastille. When the plot(s) become(s) too far-fetched, the scenes are filmed with the camera tilted at a 45-degree angle. Three potential heroes are then introduced – a swimmer, a postman, and a ballet dancer – who turn and acknowledge the camera as they are listed in turn. These interruptions to the traditional smooth exposition of the fictional universe not only reinforce the impression that 'it's just a film' but also expose the artificiality of filmic boundaries. Such devices jam the transmission of an orthodox story and work to contradict and undermine the norms characteristic of most film genres and performance modes.

La Fête à Henriette anticipates later films about the role of the director and/or writer in the creative process. Sometimes, the plot simply stops (grinding to a halt because the two writers do not agree), rolls back on itself, and starts again, this time with a different approach or plot line.[31] As it had been in *Pépé le Moko* and *Un Carnet de bal*, Jeanson's acerbic wit is also in evidence, with streaks of anti-clericalism ('la scène de l'archevêque et la petite fille a dû faire tiquer les censeurs'[32]) and anti-militarism ('l'intervention du général – objecteur de conscience'[33]).

---

31 Woody Allen's *Melinda and Melinda* (2004) shares the central conceit of *La Fête à Henriette*. Allen's film begins with two playwrights – one a tragedian, the other a comic writer – arguing about whether the same story (a distraught woman interrupts a dinner party) can be told as a comedy or a drama. Recall too that the opening monologue of Allen's *Manhattan* (1979), delivered by Allen himself, is restarted and rewritten multiple times.
32 'the scene with the archbishop and the schoolgirl must have shocked the censors'.
33 'and the general becoming a conscientious objector'.

Perhaps rather fittingly, given the film's doubled approach to storytelling and the artistic process, the critical response was heavily divided. Critics called it dull, vulgar, faux-populist, and sloppy. Others were more forgiving, especially Marcel Huret (1952), in *Radio Cinéma*: 'rarement [...] le cinéma a parodié le cinéma avec autant de lucidité féroce [...] Julien Duvivier fait preuve d'une adresse cinématographique souvent remarquable.'[34] The film was moderately well received in America, where it would be remade – with a shift in genre towards romantic comedy – in 1964 as *Paris When It Sizzles*, with William Holden as the writer and Audrey Hepburn as his secretary.

What is most ironic is that in 1952, a full two years before Truffaut's damning article condemning a 'certain tendency of French cinema', Duvivier arrived at a similar prognosis. *La Fête à Henriette* clearly articulates a problem that was beginning to beset the film industry at the start of the 1950s, namely the tension between producing conservative crowd-pleasing films and more self-reflexive challenging narratives. Duvivier holds up the conflicts inherent within artistic creation for ridicule: by trying to appease the censor, the producer, and the audience simultaneously, films invariably regress to tried-and-tested formulas and unimaginative rehashings of traditional storylines. This is precisely the line of argument held by Truffaut and *Cahiers* at the time, and the fact that the film concludes with an entirely predictable happy ending seems like a droll acknowledgement from Duvivier that French cinema had by now become irredeemably rigid and prescribed.[35] That is why the formal ingenuity on display in both *Sous le ciel de Paris* and *La Fête à Henriette* makes it difficult to understand how Duvivier ever acquired the reputation of a hack director. His free-form variations on the *film à sketches* in pre-war France and war-time Hollywood were now finessed for a third time in the 1950s via an adventurous interweaving of episodic stories, a *mise en abyme* playfulness, and a visual style that oscillated between *noir* and *rose*.

---

34 'Rarely [...] has the cinema parodied the cinema with such fierce lucidity [...] Julien Duvivier reveals his frequently remarkable filmmaking skills.'
35 Robert Guédiguian's 2000 film *À l'attaque!* is a near-remake of Duvivier's film, charting the trauma of the creative process between two clashing personalities who decide to write a contemporary political film.

Box-office successes: *Le Petit monde de Don Camillo* (1952) and *Le Retour de Don Camillo* (1953)

Le Petit monde de Don Camillo (1952) was the first in a series of five films made in the 1950s and 1960s based on Giovanni Guareschi's well-loved 'Don Camillo' stories. Guareschi's original tales were highly satirical representations of the political divisions and comic tussles between the Italian Roman Catholic Church and the Italian Communist Party. The film was a Franco-Italian co-production – one of over four hundred in the period 1949–59 – in which the original author, the setting, and one of the two stars were Italian, and the director, the screenwriter, and the other star were French. With its comic situations that articulated the ongoing contradictions of a nation undergoing rapid social and cultural transformation in the post-war period, *Le Petit monde* is a prototype of the *commedia all'italiana* (Italian-style comedy) tradition in which films 'perform an analytical form of "social autopsy" on the anthropological changes being wrought by the "economic miracle"' (Lanzoni 2008: 50).

In the aftermath of the Second World War, Don Camillo (Fernandel) is the Catholic priest of Bassa, a fictional small town in north Italy's Po valley, where a communist mayor, Peppone (Gino Cervi[36]), has just been elected. The two men are continually at odds with each other, and their relationship is complicated by the fact that, during the war, they were Resistance fighters. The film details the vigorous but often amiable bickering between them as they fight for their constituents' support. Peppone frequently rails against the town's Catholic 'reactionaries', ordering them to be shot, while Don Camillo denounces what he sees as 'godless Communists'. Broader conflicts are settled between Don Camillo and Peppone in a similarly conflicting but ultimately unified fashion, such as the organisation of a farmers' strike against the region's wealthy landowners, a procession to prevent the river Po flooding, and the thwarting of a Romeo-and-Juliet-style youth suicide.

Don Camillo and Peppone clearly represent the two faces of Italy in the late 1940s, split into two main blocks: Catholics against communists. Released at a time when Italy was undergoing a

---

36 Several commentators have noted how Cervi's moustache in the film is the same shape and colour as that of Guareschi and Joesph Stalin.

remarkable economic recovery, *Le Petit monde* thus reflects these post-war tensions of social reconstruction and the beginnings of Cold War schisms. The two main political forces in Italy at this time were the Christian Democratic Party, influenced by the Vatican, and the Communist Party; the future of post-war Italy, as these two rivalries play out, is at the core of the Don Camillo series. Duvivier's film, like the four sequels, features a series of discussions about the future of the nation. In Guareschi's original stories, the Communists are the only political party with a mass grassroots organisation in the town. For Duvivier and his co-writer René Barjavel, the recurring tension in the film is between these competing ideologies. Bassa (the *petit monde*, or 'small world') of the title is a microcosm of post-war Italy, a country strongly divided between communists and those who wanted a right-wing republic.

Duvivier had originally proposed Don Camillo to Jacques Tati, but it seems inconceivable now that anyone other than Fernandel could have played the role. French box-office figures would seem to warrant the description of Fernandel as 'the biggest French star of the 1950s': every year between 1950 and 1960, the actor appeared in at least one film listed in the top twenty, with attendance figures of at least five million (Simsi 2000). The actor brings a combination of compassion, vocal exuberance, and facial expressivity to the role, most notably in the celebrated scenes where Don Camillo talks to Christ on the crucifix in his church. When Christ replies – via Jean Debucourt's voiceover – with wise advice and occasional words of disapproval and reprimand, Fernandel's reactions are masterful examples of physical acting.[37]

Don Camillo plays an explicitly political as well as a religious role. At one point, Duvivier films Fernandel front on as he walks alone down a street brandishing a large crucifix towards the massed silent ranks of communists. Elsewhere, the series of ideological scuffles between the priest and the mayor is often conveyed in broadly physical terms, such as the scene in which Don Camillo kicks Peppone on the bottom while the latter is praying, or the fight in the church belltower when Peppone tries to silence the priest's bellringing as a symbol of protest over his recent election. The *New York Times* (Crowther

---

37 In the dubbed version released in America, Orson Welles provided the voice of Jesus.

1953) described the film's 'guileless simplicity and calculated comedy' as the reason it works so well, and much of this dynamic stems from the interplay between Fernandel and Cervi. That boxing scene in the bell-tower is about as violent as the film gets in its vision of two rival ideologies butting together. Peppone and Don Camillo flex muscles and unleash a few jabs, but nothing more. The symbolic nature of this 'gentle' violence is underlined a later scene, at a fun-fair, when Peppone shies a coconut at a *papier-mâché* figure of Don Camillo.

Duvivier depicts a world in which everyone wants to build something in the service of the community, whether it is a community hall (built with money stolen from the fascists in the Second World War), a kindergarten, or a marriage that will salve the infighting between Catholics and communists and prevent two young people from killing themselves.[38] The future of the town – and its place in this new post-war order – is cemented by this marriage, and the baptism of Peppone's newborn son (whose middle name will be Camillo). It is perhaps the abiding friendship between Don Camillo and Peppone that lies at the heart of the film's ideological leanings. Duvivier admitted that what he best appreciated in these characters was 'leur qualité d'hommes' ('their quality as men') (Lorcey 1990: 298). This maintains a link with one of Duvivier's key themes – male camaraderie and interaction – this time framed in a comic register.

Duvivier was only hired after a number of Italian directors, including Vittorio de Sica, turned down the film. It is for this reason that Bonnefille (2002: 93) describes it (and its sequel) as an anonymous piece of hackwork: 'il n'y a [...] pas grand-chose à sauver de cette plate comédie sans imagination'.[39] While it does not contain the structural inventiveness of *Sous le ciel de Paris* or *La Fête à Henriette*, the film reveals a barely hidden political message. Peppone and Don Camillo put their differences to one side and unite when the integrity and safety of the village is threatened, secretly milking the village cows during the strike. *Le Petit monde* thus becomes both a utopian and a humanist fable, wherein individual ideology is trumped by shared interest and the common good. Despite the bickering between Don Camillo and Peppone, it is their collective action during difficult times

---

38 The scene of attempted suicide between Gina and Mariolino was removed from the Italian version of the film.

39 'there is [...] not a great deal that can save this flat, unimaginative comedy'.

that lifts the film into the realm of allegory. When the town is faced with rising waters, hunger, industrial action, or youth suicide, the two rivalling worldviews harmonise and set aside hard-wired political affiliations. The village locals – mainly all communists – who feared that Duvivier would mock them need not have worried. *La Belle équipe* was an earlier prototype that focused on solidarity and shared intentions; Duvivier evidently saw in Guareschi's stories the importance of fighting side by side for the same purpose. *Le Petit monde* ends with Don Camillo leaving the town after causing a mass public brawl. He receives a warm send-off from Peppone and the communists. A question was left hanging: would Don Camillo return?

Duvivier was not convinced, even after filming had ended, that the film would be a success. When it was released in June 1952, 6.6 million spectators saw it in France in the first nine months, and, by 1958, it had drawn a total of 12.2 million entries, by far Duvivier's most successful film.[40] The film achieved the same levels of success in Italy, partly because of its continuation of the 'pink neo-realism' style and partly because, in a highly politicised environment, a gap existed for popular cinema to deal with contemporary issues in an irreverent manner. When producers approached Duvivier to direct the sequel, he agreed, on the proviso that he could kill Don Camillo off at the end of the second film. Fernandel and Duvivier returned a year later with *Le Retour de Don Camillo* (1953).[41] The sequel is divided into two parts – Don Camillo's exile and then his return to the village. It begins at the exact moment the first film ends, with Don Camillo forced into retreat on a train. This first half allows Duvivier the opportunity to inject some trademark darker, more pessimistic tones (something he had not been fully able to do in *Le Petit monde*). Don Camillo arrives at a new mountainside parish surrounded by fog, mist, and snow. The cheering crowd on the train platform is there to greet a returning sportsman, not the new priest. The church has fallen into rack and ruin, and his lodgings are meagre. The crucifix of

---

40 Its final total stands at 12.8 million. Even in 2017, it remains the seventeenth highest-grossing film of all time in France (and the sixth highest French film). Duvivier became incredibly wealthy after he opted for a percentage of the film's profits rather than an upfront fee.

41 It seems that the sequel was inevitable – in May 1952, a full month before the French release of *Le Petit monde*, *Les Lettres françaises* had already announced the follow-up was entering production.

Jesus, so loquacious in *Le Petit monde*, has fallen silent. To compound this air of despondency and despair, Duvivier gives Don Camillo a scene where he climbs the side of a mountain, holding a wooden cross through a snowstorm. Back in Bassa, 'les vieillards refusent de mourir et les enfants de naître',[42] the rising waters of the Po threaten to flood the village, and an obstructive landlord refuses to builds a dyke. It is against this backdrop that Don Camillo returns to the village to be reunited with Peppone. Box-office figures for *Le Retour* were almost as impressive as those for the first film, with audience numbers of nearly 7.5 million.

The success of the two Don Camillo films demonstrates an often overlooked aspect of Duvivier's career, namely his willingness to tack and jibe between popular cinema and auteur cinema. Sometimes this move was due to a contractual obligation; other times it fitted with the 'rotation' model of a career professional like Duvivier (i.e. a 'one for them, one for me' compromise that allows future personal projects to be greenlit on the back of more commercial assignments). The sheer diversity of genre and subject matter in Duvivier's work suggests a supple interfacing with both popular and auteur modes of French cinema and a blending together of some of their different properties in the same film. *Le Retour*, despite its box-office success, is frequently anti-comedic and anti-popular, in terms of both its visual style and its thematic treatment. Critics looking for the 'lightness' of *Le Petit monde* or the playfulness of *La Fête à Henriette* were disappointed; words such as 'melancholic', 'gloomy', and 'sad' were commonplace in the film's reception. This suggests Duvivier, as he had done in *Tales of Manhattan*, was smuggling into a mainstream film particular personal preoccupations, using the 'comedy film' as a vehicle to critique weightier issues of exile and the clash between politics and religion.

Tonal swerves: *L'Affaire Maurizius* (1954) and *Marianne de ma jeunesse* (1955)

It seems typical of Duvivier that, so soon after the commercial success of the Don Camillo films and following the ludic transgressions

---

42 'the elderly refuse to die, children refuse to be born'.

of *La Fête à Henriette*, he would once again shift direction abruptly and make *L'Affaire Maurizius* (1954). Jammed alongside his lighter and more accessible work, it remains one of Duvivier's most depressing films, notable for its austere *mise en scène* and its deep distrust of family relationships. It is not hard to see why Duvivier was so attracted to the material: for Aurélien Ferenczi (2000: 189), the film 'véhicule une implacable misanthropie' ('conveys an implacable misanthropy'). Etzel Andergast (Jacques Chabassol) realises that his father, Wolf (Charles Vanel), has sent an innocent man, Maurizius (Daniel Gélin), to prison for the murder of his wife eighteen years earlier. Etzel sets out to uncover the truth, and, via a series of flashbacks and parallel storylines, the facts about the real criminal emerge. Grégoire Waremme (Anton Walbrook) gave a false witness statement during the investigation, thus condemning Maurizius. In a bitter ending, Maurizius is released, but he commits suicide. Duvivier had long hankered after adapting the novel, written by German novelist Jakob Wassermann in 1928, and he wrote both the adaptation and the dialogue himself. In transposing the action from Germany to Switzerland, Duvivier spent two months on location in Bern. Another interesting aspect of this French-Italian co-production was the casting. Vanel, with whom Duvivier had already worked on *La Belle équipe*, starred alongside two non-French actors, Anton Walbrook and Eleonora Rossi-Drago. The latter two actors' 'foreignness' adds to the film's mysterious, out-of-joint allure.

At first glance, it seems that Duvivier is following in the footsteps of fellow director André Cayatte, championing a *cause célèbre* and focusing on miscarriages of justice.[43] But, whereas Cayatte's films usually featured some form of restorative resolution (René is granted a pardon in *Nous sommes tous des assassins* [1952] and the schoolteacher is rehabilitated in *Les Risques du métier* [1967]), Duvivier is much more pessimistic. By the end of *L'Affaire Maurizius*, a judge is rejected by his son, a son is ashamed of his father, and an innocent man has committed suicide. In a narrative swerve similar to that in *La Tête d'un homme*, Duvivier takes little interest in engineering suspense or leading the audience towards the final revelations. Instead, the film wishes to portray a dysfunctional family through the inhumanity of the judicial system and a large part of the film is devoted to charting

---

43 Chabassol had a key role in Cayatte's *Avant le déluge* (1954).

a generational clash between Etzel and Wolf. While the father–son dynamic in Duvivier's earlier work was freighted with hope and reconciliation, most notably in *L'Agonie de Jérusalem* (1927) and the two versions of *Poil de carotte* (1925, 1932), here, the dynamic is far more fraught, and, placed alongside the equally disturbing father–daughter power struggles of *Voici le temps des assassins* (1956), suggests that Duvivier's misanthropic outlook had hardened considerably.

As in *Sous le ciel de Paris* and *La Fête à Henriette*, Duvivier recounts the story episodically, allowing it to fold in on itself as various perspectives are articulated. But, while those earlier films used a fragmented narrative form to offer a fresco of Parisian life and a meta-commentary on artistic creation, Duvivier incorporates a complex series of flashbacks in *L'Affaire Maurizius* that pull us backwards and forwards across time. These multiple viewpoints bring to the fore the film's insistence on the clash between a troubled past and an uncertain present. Maurizius' exoneration does not bring peace and justice but rather provokes madness and death. Anna's death in *Anna Karenina* is replicated here, as Maurizius throws himself from a train. Suicide, from *Poil de carotte* to *Un Carnet de bal* to *David Golder* (1930), is an integral part of Duvivier's world.

The fluidity of this complicated narrative structure is matched by the rigour of Duvivier's visual composition. The neo-expressionistic, sombre design scheme is a perfect fit for this universe of secrets and hidden truths. Some of Max Douy's sets are reminiscent of Alexandre Trauner's misty poetic realist décor in *Les Portes de la nuit* and look ahead to the crepuscular strangeness of other Duvivier works such as *Marianne de ma jeunesse* and *La Chambre ardente*. Often, scenes set in the past are filmed inside bare rooms, symbolising not just the inner mood of the protagonists but also their purposeless, futile existence. The film is highly critical of what it sees as a complacent and corrupt legal system. As the bourgeois judge, Vanel, is unmoved by his son's attempts to address a miscarriage of justice, and when Waremme explains to Etzel that society mocks the law, two dancers appear as shadowgraphs on the window.[44] It transpires that Waremme is a false witness, like the adulterous couple in *Panique*, who bring about the death of a man by shifting the blame – and the crowd's murderously suspicious gaze – onto him. At the time of its release, critics were

44 Duvivier employed the same visual trick in *Le Mystère de la Tour Eiffel* (1927).

generally disappointed by the film's coldness, jumbled narration, and miscasting of actors; yet Robert Chazal in *Paris-Presse* applauded how Duvivier's camera 'a l'éclat et la vigueur du scalpel' ('has the flash and forcefulness of a scalpel'). Desrichard (2001) and Bonnefille (2002) also regard *L'Affaire Maurizius* as a return to form for Duvivier after his 'touch' had been diluted in the Don Camillo films. His 'implacable misanthropy' remained unblunted.

In a world as bleak and sardonic as Duvivier's, the director's next move seemed an odd one. *Marianne de ma jeunesse* (1955) remains an anomaly. This romantic fable, inflected with the spirit of Charles Perrault and Edgar Allen Poe, and sandwiched between the *noir* of *L'Affaire Maurizius* and *Voici le temps des assassins*, seemed to offer a corrective to the vitriol of these works. It is a late addition to a particular genre of French cinema that flourished in the 1940s and 1950s – the *fantastique poétique*. With its folkloric tone and unalloyed atmosphere of innocence and purity, it shares similarities with Carné's *Les Visiteurs du soir* (1942) and *Juliette, ou la clé des songes* (1951) and Jean Delannoy's *L'Eternel retour* (1943). Most of all, its haunted-house setting, mirrors and walls that are not what they seem, and the mysterious woman and her keeper strongly evoke *La Belle et la bête*.

In 1954, Duvivier's friend and producer André Daven suggested he adapt Alain-Fournier's *Le Grand Meaulnes*. When their plans to adapt the novel failed because of the opposition of Alain-Fournier's sister, Duvivier turned to German novelist Peter de Mendelssohn's 1932 Bildungsroman *Sorrowful Arcadia* (1932). Pierre Vaneck plays Vincent (also known as 'L'Argentin'), a young romantic student at a Bavarian boarding school at a remote castle on the misty banks of a lake. Across the lake resides Marianne (Marianne Hold), who appears to be held captive by a man she calls 'the Knight' (Jean Yonnel). Vincent visits the castle and meets Marianne. She tells him that she has been expecting him for a long time, but the Knight explains to Vincent that Marianne is suffering from a mental disease that began after her lover abandoned her on her wedding day. The forthcoming marriage between the Knight and Marianne is a form of shock therapy that will hopefully cure her. The Knight tells Vincent that, when Marianne is healed, she will meet him again. There are strong Freudian undertones: Vincent seeks to liberate himself from his mother fixation and replace her with the beautiful woman who lives in the castle across the lake. Vincent's efforts to possess the elusive Marianne are ultimately thwarted by an older man who means to marry her.

With echoes of the flashbacks and alternate storylines in *L'Affaire Maurizius*, the film evolves via a series of frames within frames that focus on the haziness of memory and the tricks it can play. While Vincent is the nominal hero – he has by far the most screen time – the narrator of *Marianne de ma jeunesse* is Manfred (Gil Vidal), who gives an account of the story in flashback. As Manfred speaks, Duvivier includes a series of oneiric, woozy images – a castle on a hill, deer in a misty courtyard, shafts of light penetrating the gloom of a forest – that are both unsettling and captivating. Léonce-Henri Burel's cinematography envelops the film in dense layers of fog, mist, and mountains. The flair for mysterious dream-like atmospheres Duvivier had shown in *La Charrette fantôme* (1939) and *Flesh and Fantasy* (1943) returns here. This is a land of fairy-tales, and the camera is alive to the energy of the story as it tracks characters racing through the forest and reveals the approaching dawn through an eerie mist.[45]

When Vincent and Marianne meet for the first time, the décor is beautifully rendered. Numerous *plans américain* carve up the screen and create sharp lines that separate the darkness of Vincent's clothes from Marianne's luscious white gowns. Duvivier's roaming camera draws us deeper into the house's fantasy realm, which may actually only exist in Vincent's fevered imagination. All the scenes in the house exude an unsettling atmosphere that calls into question reality itself. Margaret Butler (2004: 180) describes female characters in French films of the mid-1950s as 'innocuous objects of desire, alluring and unthreatening, yet somehow still undefinable'. Marianne fits squarely into this category. So stylised are the encounters between her and Vincent that the boundary between dream and real life is blurred.

At the same time, Duvivier shot a German-language version of the film, entitled *Marianne, meine Jugendliebe**. As he had done in 1931 with *Les Cinq gentlemen maudits*, Duvivier used the same locations, sets, and technical crew (including future director Marcel Ophuls as an assistant), but only Marianne Hold from the original

---

45 Principal exterior filming took place at Hohenschwangau castle in Germany and Fuschl am See in Austria.

cast was retained. This time, Horst Buchholz played Vincent. Despite the film's ambitious launches in Paris (18 March 1955) and Cologne (8 April 1955), neither version was successful. Critics rejected its formal and visual innovations, with some comparing it unfavourably to Max Ophuls' *Lola Montès* (1955). Its reputation improved in the 1970s, when new critics rediscovered Duvivier; Patrick Brion (1971: 423) called it Duvivier's most personal film.

Other than the Don Camillo films, few of Duvivier's films of the post-war decade were a commercial success. With remarkable consistency, his audience numbers were stable but very low: *Anna Karenina* (1.7 million spectators), *Black Jack* (1 million), *Sous le ciel de Paris* (1.4 million), *La Fête à Henriette* (1.3 million), *L'Affaire Maurizius* (1.6 million), and *Marianne de ma jeunesse* (1.5 million) (Simsi 2000).[46] But, with hindsight, the repeated tonal lurches and audience-distancing effects post-*Panique* can be seen as deliberate attempts by Duvivier to prove his versatility, his *savoir-faire*, and his enduring professionalism. Here is a director who moves deftly from proto-modernist episode film to blockbuster comedy to atmospheric fairy tale, while at the same time applying versions of the same consistent visual, formal, and thematic styles that had been established three decades earlier. Even though Duvivier was shooting on average one film per year from 1946 to 1956, he cannot stand accused of being a hack director producing anonymous works. His work epitomises a 'cinema of quality', not in a negative sense but as part of a dynamic, perpetually evolving style that straddled original screenplays and European literature, star actors and unknowns, Arcadian forests and nocturnal cities. As with so many other directors from this period, Duvivier would be engulfed by the first surges of the New Wave. But not before he made one film in particular.

'Surrounded by monsters': *Voici le temps des assassins* (1956)

The camera tracks down a Paris street alongside a young woman. She has just rejected an old lover, telling him that their relationship

---

46 Paradoxically, Duvivier's more modest successes came with *The Impostor* (2.2 million), *Untel père et fils* (2.1 million), and *Panique* (2.5 million), films that had all received highly negative reviews.

is over. His response is to run into the path of an oncoming truck, killing himself instantly. We hear the screams of passers-by, but the camera follows the woman as she walks dispassionately past the off-screen body and further on down the street. She climbs the staircase of a run-down hotel and enters the room of a drug-addled woman. Both women look out of the window at the dead man below. Almost absent-mindedly, one says, 'les morts, ça ne raconte pas d'histoires'; the other simply replies, 't'es un monstre'.[47] The two then proceed to make plans to seduce an ageing *restaurateur* and divide up his money. Welcome to *Voici le temps des assassins* (1956). This traumatic scene, more than any other in Duvivier's films, encapsulates his worldview. The young woman is Catherine (Danièle Delorme), the other her mother, Gabrielle (Lucienne Bogaert), who used to be married to André Chatelin (Jean Gabin). Chatelin is the respected restaurant boss who accepts Catherine first as his adopted daughter and then as his wife. We eventually realise that Catherine's motives are profoundly sinister, and her coquettish deception eventually leads to murder. Catherine's machinations are controlled by Gabrielle, who encourages her daughter to marry Chatelin so that they will inherit his wealth. To fulfil the plan, the women need to ensure that Chatelin's adopted son, medical student Gérard (Gérard Blain), distances himself from his father.

Voici le temps des assassins is Duvivier's finest film; it's exhibit A when making the case for Duvivier as an auteur. It is a harrowing drama that offers definitive proof that Duvivier's brand of 'quality' cinema was alive and well in the 1950s. It is a dense network of favoured Duvivier themes and techniques: bitterness, cynicism, the bleakness of human nature, the crushing of anything bright or optimistic. This is a Paris where the sun does not shine. After *Panique*, women in Duvivier's films had been a mixture of the haughty, the unattainable, the dream-like, and the naïve. The arrival of Catherine here marks the return of the *garce*. Everything about *Voici le temps des assassins*, from its depraved climate and its fluid cinematography to the modulated acting and the sustained claustral tone, points to a director in complete command of his craft. It is little wonder that

---

47 'dead men don't talk'; 'you are a monster'.

Jacques Siclier (1986) would later describe it as 'le film le plus naturaliste, le plus noir, le plus pessimiste de Duvivier'.⁴⁸

It was co-written by Maurice Bessy and Charles Dorat, and takes its title from the final line of Arthur Rimbaud's poem 'Matinée d'ivresse'.⁴⁹ The first half of the film traces in vivid and extensive detail the inner workings of a Parisian restaurant. Location footage of the food markets of Les Halles opens the film, as Catherine emerges from the metro station to make her way to Chatelin's restaurant. Moving into the studio, Robert Gys' highly detailed reconstructed sets capture the evocative, lively nature of this area in ways that recalls the Montparnasse in *La Tête d'un homme* and the Algiers Casbah in *Pépé le Moko*. The restaurant – ironically called Au Rendez-Vous des Innocents⁵⁰ – is a hive of activity, and Armand Thirard's tracking shots follow waiters, cooks, and customers as they move through and across the restaurant. The camera work becomes progressively more static as the film develops, with Duvivier favouring tight close-ups and *plans américain* as the emotional stakes are raised.

The role of Chatelin was written specifically for Gabin, in the last of the seven roles he played for Duvivier. The director had told *Cinémonde* (Duvivier 1947a) that current French directors were not using Gabin properly as an actor, offering up Georges Lacombe's *Martin Roumagnac* (1946) as an example that had left the audience cold because 'la grande vedette n'est plus qu'un acteur ordinaire'.⁵¹ In *Voici le temps des assassins*, Duvivier proceeds to demolish the 'Gabin myth' that he himself established two decades earlier. Gabin's role as the solid, bourgeois Chatelin is a knight's move away from his virile, hyper-masculinised *bon gars* of the 1930s; here, he plays a man deceived and destroyed by his 'wife'. The film also marked Gabin's career move into playing middle-class patriarchs and gangsters. Post-*Pépé*, his heavier, bulkier physique in *Voici le temps des assassins* and *Touchez pas au grisbi* (Jacques Becker, 1954) indicates the transformative process of ageing that Nicholas Hewitt (2004: 68) sees as the

---

48 'Duvivier's most naturalistic, blackest, most pessimistic film'.
49 'Nous avons foi au poison. Nous savons donner notre vie tout entière tous les jours. Voici le temps des Assassins' ('We have faith in the poison. We know how to give our whole life every day. Now is the time of the Assassins').
50 It is as ironic as the name of the building into which Hire flees at the end of *Panique*: Lavoir de la Fraternité.
51 'the great star is now no more than an ordinary actor'.

incarnation of a 'lost' France under threat from historical, political, and sociological processes. Many critics have regarded *Voici le temps des assassins* as a semi-sequel to *La Belle équipe*, with Gabrielle as a version of Gina's rejected *garce*. Chatelin's mother runs a *guinguette* on the edge of the Marne, and there is a brief scene when Chatelin sings and dances with her clientele. In the twenty years since the *printemps glorieux* of the Popular Front and *La Belle équipe*, Gabin, Duvivier, and France had all changed.

Voici le temps des assassins serves up another version of the 'diabolical female' that Burch and Sellier (1996: 36) argue defined a large part of French post-war cinema.[52] This model involved an ageing woman who is no longer sexually attractive but whose 'cupidité et [...] mesquinerie sont telles qu'elles sont perçues comme pur sadisme'.[53] Burch and Sellier also note that the father–daughter relationship between Chatelin and Catherine is representative of a particular kind of affiliation in much of post-war French cinema. When she dances with Chatelin after having just danced with Gérard, she tells him that 'Je n'aime pas les jeunes gens' ('I don't care much for young people'). Duvivier fades to black after this remark, giving the scene a transgressive, semi-incestuous afterglow. Later, discussing marriage, Gabin asks a non-rhetorical question: 'Tu connais une femme qui me donne la main, toi?' Catherine's response – 'Au moins une' – is delivered in a flirtatious, provocative manner.[54] This suggestive blurring of parent–child roles is one of the unsettling plot points of the film, not least because Chatelin's developing relationship with Catherine throws into sharp relief the gradual decline of the father–son bond between Chatelin and Gérard. It remains the great unanswered question in the film: is Catherine Chatelin's daughter? She mentions a father, but can we believe her?

When it comes to the quadrangular relationship of which Chatelin is a part, Susan Hayward's (2005: 178) observation on the general representation of the woman in 1950s French cinema is apt: she is 'either fallen (or about to fall), adulterous, ensnaring or scheming'. At the three other points of this quadrangle are Chatelin's 'daughter'-wife, his ex-wife, and his mother. Each one of these women is

---

52 They include Yves Allégret's *Manèges* (1949) as another example.
53 'greed and [...] pettiness are such that they are perceived to be purely sadistic'.
54 'Do you know a woman who would have me?'; 'At least one.'

degenerate or depraved – Catherine is murderous, Gabrielle drug-addled, and the mother jealously possessive. Critics have voiced reservations about the film's depiction of women, but, in truth, this is not so much a misogynistic tract as a condensing of Duvivier's outlook on life. Human relations are cruel and the fissures in the family unit run deep. In Duvivier's world, we have limitless capability to hurt – either psychologically (a mother who weaponises her daughter) or physically (Chatelin's mother whips and decapitates chickens at her riverside *guinguette*). This interplay is supplemented by a fourth female character – Chatelin's housekeeper Madame Jules (Gabrielle Fontan), a spinster who listens behinds doors and who is immediately jealous of the young and beautiful Catherine.

In her essay *Powers of Horror*, Julia Kristeva (1982: 4) conceptualises the abject as that which 'disturbs identity, system, order. What does not respect borders, positions, rules. The in-between, the ambiguous.' Catherine and Gabrielle present a clear threat to the stability of Chatelin's symbolic order, crossing the border into a clearly defined patriarchal space and then undermining its integrity from within. Gabrielle is a version of the 'monstrous feminine' that shocks and horrifies us with her abject behaviour. Ravaged by substance abuse and bed-ridden in a decaying hotel room, she plots to murder the patriarch. No less unsettling is Germaine Kerjean as Chatelin's mother. While the film only implies that she was the cause of the collapse of her son's first marriage ('Ce que j'ai fait j'ai fait pour ton bien,'[55] she discloses), Duvivier demonstrates how she continues to dominate Chatelin's life. At one point, Chatelin tells his mother, 'Je suis plus un gamin, t'occupes pas de mes affaires!'[56] After the mother has been introduced to Catherine, she replies that 'elle me glace' ('she gives me a chill'). Catherine 'disturbs' and does not 'respect rules'. Duvivier repeatedly films other (female) characters both young and old eyeing her suspiciously, looking her up and down, sizing her up, and questioning her motivations. The irony is that neither André nor Gérard ever stop to do the same.

Voici le temps des assassins contains a number of paroxystic moments that act as safety valves to counter the increasing build-up of pressure. Catherine calls Chatelin's mother 'peau de vache' ('cowhide')

---

55 'What I did I did for you.'
56 'I'm not a kid anymore, leave me alone!'

and receives a slapped face in return, and, in one extraordinary scene, the mother whips Catherine in a prolonged scene of cathartic violence, yelling 'je te dresserai, ma fille' ('I'll break you in, my child') while a train whistle screeches in the background. The film's visual language becomes progressively circumscribed: the bustling restaurant, with its graceful tracking shots, is replaced by unyielding close-ups of faces in dingy hotel rooms and the gloomy *guinguette*. As the film draws to a close, the tension becomes stifling: Catherine murders Gérard in his car, then pushes it into the river while his dog barks incessantly; André nearly strangles Catherine (offering Gabin the chance to perform his trademark 'explosion of violence'); then finally Catherine is mauled to death by Gérard's dog. When André discovers her body, Catherine's hand protrudes at the exact same angle as Radek's, crushed under a wheel in *La Tête d'un homme*.

Duvivier explained his reasons for making *Voici le temps des assassins* thus:

> Je crois que nous sommes entourés de monstres comme ça. On n'a qu'à lire les journaux, c'est quelque chose d'effrayant. Je crois que nous sommes comme ça depuis vingt ans, nous sommes au temps des assassins. Nous sommes absolument entourés de monstres et je connais, moi, des jeunes filles qui sont exactement pareilles au personnage de Catherine, je crois avoir fait quelque chose de violent, mais tout à fait logique.[57]

As in his earlier comments about the origins of *Panique*, Duvivier was here reiterating his worldview and articulating his perception of the zeitgeist. Order is putatively restored at the end of the film, but, in a final ironic touch, it is Gérard's dog that mauls Catherine to death. Yet, while the depravity of Catherine and Gabrielle and their threats to jeopardise the reinstatement of patriarchal control have been momentarily contained, this has been achieved only at the expense of the younger man. Gérard has been destroyed so that the older man might live. The patriarchal order has been contested, but, in Duvivier's eyes, the younger generation have had to be sacrificed

---

57 'I think that we are surrounded by monsters like that. You only have to read the papers to see how frightening it is. I think that we've been like this for twenty years; we are in the time of assassins. We are absolutely surrounded by monsters and I've come across young women who are exactly like Catherine. I think I've made a violent film. But I've also made a logical film.'

to save it. Yet, in a fascinating turn by Duvivier, Chatelin leaves Catherine with his mother to return to Paris, telling her: 'garde-la et surveille-la' ('keep an eye on her'). André, rather than dealing with the situation forcefully, flees, ceding patriarchal control of Catherine to his mother. If post-Liberation cinema, with its frequent demonisation of women, marked the reassertion of male dominance and patriarchal authority, then this altered scenario of *Voici le temps des assassins* offered a counterpunch. It presents Gabin as the impotent 'father', unable to tame the excesses of the 'daughter', and instead positions the ageing 'mother' as the agent of retribution against the bad daughter. Eventually, it is a dog who restores order, not André, who struggles to open the hotel room door and arrives at the scene too late.

When the film was released in April 1956, audiences under the age of sixteen were prohibited from attending. The decision probably did not affect the film's tepid final box-office figures: only 1.5 million tickets were sold, making it one of Duvivier's least successful films in the period 1946–56. Its commercial run was undoubtedly hampered by yet more scathing reviews. *Rivarol* (Martain 1956) called it a 'faux chef-d'œuvre' ('a false masterpiece') and *Franc-tireur* (Anon. 1956) saw it as a retrograde step for Duvivier. Here was 'un film paralysé' because its director remained 'fidèle à l'esthétique périmée qui fit le succès du cinéma français en 1935'.[58] Others regarded *Voici le temps des assassins* far more favourably, seeing it as a welcome return to form for Duvivier after the perceived unevenness of his output since his return from America. Jacques Doniol-Valcroze (1956), no fan of Duvivier in the past, called it 'puissante, sobre, dense' ('powerful, simple, concise'), with a depth and intelligence worthy of Balzac or Tolstoy.

Conclusion

Marc-Edouard Nabé (2010: 40) calls Duvivier's post-war films 'foisonnants, complexes, hyperconstruits' ('prolific, complex, hyperconstructed'). Despite a tricky homecoming, Duvivier's ease with

---

58 'a paralysed film'; 'faithful to a visual style that went out of date in French cinema in 1935'.

complex narrative structure, coupled with a deft visual language and a canny incorporation of star actors, firmly positioned him at the interface between auteur and popular cinema in the 1950s. One of the warmest endorsements of any of his films from this period came from François Truffaut (1956: 5), who praised *Voici le temps des assassins* to the skies:

> Julien Duvivier a tourné cinquante-sept films. J'en ai vu vingt-trois et j'en ai aimé huit. De tous, *Voici le temps des assassins* me semble le meilleur, celui dans lequel on peut sentir sur tous les éléments: scénario, mise en scène, jeu, photo, musique, etc. un contrôle qui est celui d'un cinéaste parvenu à une totale sûreté de lui-même, et de son métier. Le scénario de *Voici le temps des assassins* [...] est pratiquement irréprochable dans sa construction comme dans sa conception.[59]

Truffaut's focus on 'control' and 'confidence' in terms of the film's acting, writing, and *mise en scène* endorses Duvivier's ongoing technical skill and his endurance in a fast-changing industry. Yet, as we shall see in Chapter 6, Duvivier's relationship with Truffaut in the last ten years of his career would develop into something far rockier and more fraught.

References

Anon. (1945), 'Duvivier rentre en Europe', *Le Film français*, 24, 18 May, p. 3.
Anon. (1956), '*Voici le temps des assassins*', *Le Franc-tireur*, 21 April, np.
Billard, P. (1995), *L'Age classique du cinéma français: Du cinéma parlant à la Nouvelle Vague*, Paris, Flammarion.
Billard, P. (1998), *Le mystère René Clair*, Paris, Plon.
Bonnefille, E. (2002b), *Julien Duvivier: Le Mal aimant du cinéma français*, vol. 2, Paris, Harmattan.
Brion, P. (1971), 'Julien Duvivier', in *Dossiers du cinéma: Cinéastes*, ed. J.-L. Bory and C. M. Cluny, Tournai, Casterman, pp. 420–4.
Burch N. and G. Sellier (1996), *La Drôle de guerre des sexes du cinéma français (1930–1956)*, Paris, Nathan.

---

59 'Julien Duvivier has made fifty-seven films. I've seen twenty-three, and liked eight. Of them all, *Voici le temps des assassins* seems to me the best, where one can sense the control over every aspect (script, *mise en scène*, acting, image, music, etc.) – control by a filmmaker who has arrived at total confidence in himself and his vocation. The script of *Voici le temps des assassins* [...] is practically flawless in its construction as in its design.'

Butler, M. (2003), '*Paysan, paysage, patrie*: French Films and Rural Life', *Rural History*, 14:2, pp. 219–37.

Butler, M. (2004), *Film and Community in Britain and France: From* La Règle du jeu *to* Room at the Top, London, I. B. Tauris.

Crisp, C. (2015), *French Cinema: A Critical Filmography*, vol. 2, *1940–1958*, Indiana, Indiana University Press.

Crowther, B. (1948), '*Anna Karenina*', *New York Times*, 28 April, available at http://www.nytimes.com/movie/review?res=9E03E2DA1F3EE53ABC4051 DFB2668383659EDE, accessed 16 September 2016.

Crowther, B. (1953), '*The Little World of Don Camillo* [i.e. *Le Petit monde de Don Camillo*]', *New York Times*, 14 January, available at http://www.nytimes.com/movie/review?res=9E00E6D91F3CE23BBC4C52DFB7668388649 EDE, accessed 16 September 2016.

Desrichard, Y. (2001), *Julien Duvivier: Cinquante ans de noirs destins*, Paris, BiFi/Durante.

Doniol-Valcroze, J. (1956), '*Voici le temps des assassins*', *France-observateur*, 26 April, np.

Duca, J.-M. L. (1946), '*Panique*', *Cinémonde*, 648, 31 December, p. 6.

Duvivier, J. (1946a), 'Julien Duvivier fête ses 30 ans de cinéma: Interview with Marcel Idzkowski', *Cinémonde*, 639, 29 October, pp. 10–11.

Duvivier, J. (1946b), 'Les libres propos de Monsieur Platon', *Cinémonde*, 645, 10 December, p. 5.

Duvivier, J. (1946c), 'Les libres propos de Monsieur Platon', *Cinémonde*, 648, 31 December, p. 6.

Duvivier, J. (1946d), 'De la création à la mise en scène', *Cinémonde*, special issue, December, p. 18.

Duvivier, J. (1947a), 'Les libres propos de Monsieur Platon', *Cinémonde*, 649, 7 January, p. 6.

Duvivier, J. (1947b), 'Les libres propos de Monsieur Platon', *Cinémonde*, 650, 14 January, p. 16.

Duvivier, J. (1947c), '*Anna Karenine*: Interview with Marcel Idzkowski', *Cinémonde*, 671, 10 June, p. 14.

Duvivier, J. (1959), 'J'ai la chance de n'avoir pas de mémoire', Interview with Julien Duvivier by Pierre des Vallières and Hervé Le Boterf, *Cinémonde*, 1310, 15 September, pp. 14–16.

Edwards, A. (1977), *Vivien Leigh*, New York: Simon and Schuster.

Fayard, J. (1947), '*Panique*', *Opéra*, 22 January, np.

Ferenczi, A. (2000), '*L'Affaire Maurizius*', *Télérama*, 2656, 6 December, p. 189.

Gaillard, P. (1947), '*Panique*', *L'Humanité*, 17 January, np.

Harper, S. (1992), 'The Representation of Women in British Feature Film, 1945–1950', *Historical Journal of Film, Radio and Television*, 12:3, pp. 217–30.

Hayward, S. (2005), *French National Cinema*, 2nd edn, London and New York, Routledge.

Hewitt, N. (2004), 'Gabin, *Grisbi* and 1950s France', *Studies in French Cinema*, 4:1, pp. 65–75.

Huret, M. (1952), '*La Fête à Henriette*', *Radio cinéma*, 28 December, np.

Idzkowski, M. (1945), 'Julien Duvivier évoque les problèmes internationaux du cinéma', *Le Film français*, 28, 15 June, p. 1.
Jeanson, H. (2000), *Jeanson par Jeanson*, Paris, Éditions René Château.
Kristeva, J. (1982), *Powers of Horror: An Essay on Abjection*, trans. Leon S. Roudiez, New York, Columbia University Press.
Lanzoni, R. F. (2008), *Comedy Italian Style: The Golden Age of Italian Film Comedies*, New York and London, Continuum.
Le Forestier, L. (2004), 'L'accueil en France des films américains de réalisateurs français à l'époque des accords Blum-Byrnes', *Revue d'histoire moderne et contemporaine*, 4:51, pp. 78–97.
Leprohon, P. (1968), *Julien Duvivier*, Paris, Avant-Scène/Collection Anthologie du Cinéma.
Makoveeva, I. (2001), 'Cinematic Adaptations of *Anna Karenina*', *Studies in Slavic Cultures*, 2, pp. 111–33.
Martain, G. (1956), '*Voici le temps des assassins*', *Rivarol*, 19 April, np.
Nabé, M.-E. (2010), 'Le cauchemar Duvivier', programme notes for Cinémathèque Française, March–May, Paris, La Cinémathèque Française, pp. 38–42, available at http://www.cinematheque.fr/cycle/julien-duvivier-45.html, accessed 13 September 2016.
Néry, J. (1949), '*Anna Karénine*', *Franc-tireur*, 28 May, np.
Niogret, H. (2010), *Julien Duvivier: 50 ans de cinéma*, Paris, Bazaar and Co.
Nissen, A. (2013), *The Films of Agnes Moorehead*, Plymouth, Scarecrow Press.
Ousselin, E. (2007), 'La Panique de M. Hire', *Cincinnati Romance Review*, 26, pp. 63–78.
Phillips, A. (2004). 'Migration and Exile in the Classical Period', in *The French Cinema Book*, eds M. Temple and M. Witt, London, BFI, pp. 103–17.
Siclier, J. (1986), '*Voici le temps des assassins*', *Télérama*, 2445, 2 March, np.
Simsi, S. (2000), *Ciné-passions, 7eme art et industrie de 1945 à 2000*, Paris, Dixit.
Truffaut, F. (1956), 'Débat sur Duvivier', *Arts*, 564, 18 April, p. 5.
Vidal, J. (1947), '*Panique*', *L'Ecran français*, 82, 21 January, p. 5.
Wild, F. (1996), 'L'Histoire resuscitée: Jewishness and Scapegoating in Julien Duvivier's *Panique*', in *Identity Papers: Contested Nationhood in Twentieth-Century France*, eds S. Ungar and T. Conley, Minneapolis, University of Minnesota Press, pp. 178–92.

6

Late style

Le cinéma français est mort.[1]

(Duvivier 1965: 31)

Il faut tuer le père, mais on ne peut pas tuer Renoir.[2]

(Garnier 1996)

The films Duvivier made after *Voici le temps des assassins* (1956) have generally been dismissed as anonymous hack works. Borger (1998: 30) notes how critics classify Duvivier's late period, from *L'Homme à l'imperméable* (1957) to *Diaboliquement vôtre* (1967), as his 'definitive decline into rank commercialism'. In his review for *Boulevard* (1960), Robin Bean (1961: 27) laments that 'Julien Duvivier's gradual artistic degradation over the past decade [...] has been sad to watch.' In actual fact, these 'lesser' films provide a visual consistency with Duvivier's earlier career and cement his auteur status. The classicism of the *mise en scène*, evocative location shooting, and core thematic concerns – deception, misanthropy, the fragility of the (male) group, the dangerous woman – remain largely intact in these later works. I noted earlier that Duvivier's post-war films signalled the emergence of several distinct tendencies: works that highlighted their own construction (*Sous le ciel de Paris* [1951], *La Fête à Henriette* [1952]), that reflected the destabilisation of gender relations in French society (*Panique* [1946], *Au royaume des cieux* [1949]), or that interfaced between the commercial and the art-house (the Don Camillo series [1952, 1953], *L'Affaire Maurizius* [1954]).

1 'French cinema is dead.'
2 'You must kill the father, but you cannot kill Renoir.'

Now, towards the end of his career, Duvivier continued to return to source texts (*Pot-Bouille* [1957], *Chair de poule* [1963]) and made minor films with New Wave inflections (*La Grande vie* [1960], *Boulevard* [1960]), chamber pieces (*Marie-Octobre* [1959], *Diaboliquement vôtre* [1967]), and Gothic *noir* (*La Chambre ardente* [1962]). This period also saw Duvivier re-imagine the coordinates of French *noir* and the fantasy film, two genres generally overlooked by most critics at the time. *Voici le temps des assassins* was not the final highpoint in his career, as most critics make out. Instead, post-1956, Duvivier continued to push at the rigid boundaries between commercial and auteur projects, working with significant stars (Bardot, Darrieux, Delon, Léaud) and creating a diverse body of 'late style' work that is a rich storehouse of themes and ideas about the future of French cinema.

Duvivier, the tradition of quality, and François Truffaut

Nine of the ten films discussed in this chapter (plus eight of the eleven in Chapter 5) are adaptations by Duvivier of extant literature. It is for this reason, among others, that Duvivier has often been labelled a director working at the coalface of the 'tradition of quality'. This was a style of mainstream film-making that predominated in the 1940s and 1950s in France, displaying 'a preference for high production values, studio-based filming, stars, literary adaptations and high budgets supported by significant levels of government funding' (Esposito 2001: 25). Despite their immense commercial popularity, and their often incisive critiques of gender and social norms, films such as *La Reine Margot* (Jean Dréville, 1954) and *Le Rouge et le noir* (Claude Autant-Lara, 1954), as well as Duvivier's own work, have been encumbered with the negative reputation of being retrograde, aesthetically bland, and formally unambitious. Much of this damage was done by François Truffaut's condemnation of the tradition of quality in his infamous 1954 article 'Une certaine tendance du cinéma français' ('A Certain Tendency in French Cinema') (Truffaut 1954). Labelling those films that made up the commercial mainstream of the 1950s *le cinéma de papa* (daddy's cinema), Truffaut (1954: 23) criticised directors for their version of psychological realism that was 'ni réel, ni psychologique' ('neither real nor psychological'). Truffaut's argument, and its seismic ramifications, are well known and need not be repeated here. Suffice to say, since the article's appearance, critics and scholars have tended to march in lockstep behind Truffaut, systematically ignoring Duvivier's post-war films (the great irony being that Duvivier's name is never mentioned in Truffaut's article).[3]

Complicating matters further is the rather ambivalent relationship that existed between Duvivier and Truffaut at this time. Some of Truffaut's reviews, in particular of *Voici le temps des assassins*, were full of warmth and respect for Duvivier. Truffaut recounts in *Les films de ma vie* (1975: 25) that he met with Duvivier a few weeks before his death and told him 'qu'il avait eu une belle carrière, variée et complète, et que, somme toute, il avait bien réussi sa vie et devait se sentir heureux'.[4] Duvivier was also a jury member at the 1959 Cannes Film Festival, which had awarded Truffaut the Best Director prize for *Les 400 coups*. He even wrote Truffaut a touching letter in August 1956, recounting a dream in which they both boarded an ocean liner bound for America. Duvivier signed off by expressing the hope that the two might work together on a film in the future: 'Vous avez en moi un ami qui vous estime et qui vous apprécie' (Duvivier 1996: 96).[5]

'Une certaine tendance' precipitated Duvivier's downfall, but it did not trigger it. The decline in his reputation had begun much earlier. As early as 1933, Henri Langlois (2014: 411) wrote that 'Duvivier n'a aucun génie, à peine du talent'.[6] Two years later, François Vinneuil (1935: 332) described Duvivier as an important director but not a particularly good one; this was the same year that Roger Leenhardt (1935) called him a 'workhorse'. As noted in Chapter 5, the French critical response to *Panique* was savage, and the reaction to Duvivier's films thereafter often ranged from the indifferent to the outraged.

---

3 Duvivier is hinted at but not name-checked. In the opening paragraph, Truffaut (1954: 15) writes, 'Sous l'influence de *Scarface* [1932], nous faisions l'amusant *Pépé le Moko*' ('Under the influence of *Scarface*, we made the amusing *Pépé le Moko*').

4 'he had had a fine career, varied and full, and that all things considered he had achieved great success and ought to be contented'. Duvivier's response to Truffaut (1975: 25) tells us much about the older director: 'Sûrement je me serais senti heureux...s'il n'y avait pas eu la critique' ('Sure, I would feel contented...if there hadn't been any reviews').

5 'You have in me a friend who thinks highly of you and likes you.' The two met at Cannes in May 1956 and discussed doing a project together called *Grand amour*.

6 'Duvivier is no genius, and is barely talented.'

His films of the early and mid-1950s in particular were relentlessly criticised by *Cahiers du cinéma*. Critic-turned-director Jacques Rivette ranked every Duvivier film released during his time at *Cahiers* (April 1959 to January 1964) with a 'bullet point'.[7] *Positif* was equally brutal. Between 1952, when it published a review of *Le Petit monde de Don Camillo*, and 1968, when it published a posthumous review of *Diaboliquement vôtre*, *Positif* did not review a single Duvivier film.[8] Jean-Paul Marquet (1952: 57) wrote perhaps the most scathing of all pieces about Duvivier, castigating *Un Carnet de bal* (1937) and *The Great Waltz* (1938) for their aesthetic and formal pretentiousness; 'ses personnages n'ont pas d'âme. Mais Julien Duvivier en a-t-il une? C'est là tout le problème.'[9]

This was a generational conflict not just with Duvivier but with other established directors and their modes of narration. Jonathan Driskell (2012: 131–49) notes how Marcel Carné's career suffered the same critical hostility over issues of authorship and aesthetics. The careers of Yves Allégret, Claude Autant-Lara, Jean Dréville, Christian-Jaque, and others stagnated due to the adverse critical reaction of *Cahiers* and the 'bullets' of the *conseil des dix*. Even if we bear in mind that *Cahiers*' readership in the 1950s was relatively low, and therefore that we need to be careful in ascribing Duvivier's marginalised status to a small but dedicated group of non-believers herding towards a majority opinion, it is clear that his reputation suffered at the hands of the high-brow French film press. Yet Duvivier's contributions to the look and logic of the 1950s and 1960s tradition of quality cinema are vital, and require a more balanced judgement. In the films that follow, a tension between the auteur and the *metteur en scène* reveals itself. Let us turn to that.

7 The November 1955 issue of *Cahiers du cinéma* saw the introduction of a new rating scheme, 'Le conseil des dix', whereby ten critics rated the films released in the preceding month. Films were ranked as follows: a bullet point ('inutile de se déranger' / 'don't bother going'), 1 star ('à voir à la rigueur' / 'if one likes that sort of thing'), 2 stars ('à voir' / 'merits being seen'), 3 stars ('à voir absolument' / 'absolutely has to be seen'), 4 stars ('chef-d'oeuvre' / 'a masterpiece').

8 I am grateful to J. D. Copp's blog *My Gleanings* and a post entitled 'Julien Duvivier, the "young turcs" against the Parisian press: the Bonnefille connection' for alerting me to this. See http://jdcopp.blogspot.com.au/2007/02/julien-duvivierfrancois-truffaut.html, accessed 12 March 2015.

9 'his characters are soulless. But does Duvivier even possess a soul? That's really where the problem lies.'

Working with stars: *L'Homme à l'imperméable* (1957), *Pot-Bouille* (1957), and *La Femme et le pantin* (1959)

L'Homme à l'imperméable was a Franco-Italian co-production, adapted by Duvivier and René Barjavel from British author James Hadley Chase's novel *Tiger by the Tail*. Chase was heavily influenced by American pulp fiction and sought to emulate the style of James M. Cain (Duvivier's second Chase adaptation, *Chair de poule* [1963], would be heavily indebted to Cain's *The Postman Always Rings Twice*).

When the wife of Albert Constantin, a clarinettist at the Théâtre du Châtelet, leaves to visit her uncle, Albert is left behind in Paris. He struggles to adapt to his wife's absence, and one night is recommended by a friend to visit a prostitute, Eva. When Eva is found murdered, Albert becomes the prime suspect (reports emerge of a man fleeing the crime scene in a raincoat similar to the one Albert was wearing that evening). To clear his name, he must deal with blackmailers and professional assassins and all the while prevent his returning wife from discovering the truth. Duvivier cast Fernandel as Albert, reuniting with him a fourth time, after *Un Carnet de bal* and the Don Camillo diptych. For the role of Raphaël, a neighbour of the dead woman who begins to extort Albert, Duvivier turned to Bernard Blier.

Like *Voici le temps des assassins*, *L'Homme à l'imperméable* was released during the peak of French *noir*. But this is not *Voici*, nor the domestic *noir* of *Touchez pas au grisbi* (Jacques Becker, 1954) and *Du rififi chez les hommes* (Jules Dassin, 1955); this is comedy *noir*. By casting Fernandel, Duvivier and Barjavel significantly altered the hard-boiled tone of Chase's original text, so that *L'Homme à l'imperméable* plays out instead like an Ealing comedy, a sort of French version of *The Ladykillers* (1955), with its musical backdrop, crepuscular setting, and rich vein of louche supporting players. The film found favour with the public – with 2.8 million entries, it ranked twentieth in that year's national viewing figures and was Duvivier's third-highest grossing film of his career.

Thematically, the film continues Duvivier's fascination with the theatrical. The opening credits play out over a theatre curtain and the sound of an orchestra warming up for a rehearsal. The film then begins with a graceful crane shot from the back of Théâtre du Châtelet to the orchestra pit, followed by a close-up of a small model of Venice.

The actors are berated by an impatient director (we may presume this to be a version of Duvivier poking fun at his irascible image). The film's gender politics is also interesting. Albert's friend Emil describes Eva as a piece of architecture designed by Le Corbusier, and, as he hands him her business card, declares that marriage is like chewing gum – the more you chew, the less it tastes. Albert himself is henpecked. In her absence, his wife has left chalked instructions on a blackboard, and he has to walk around their flat wearing slippers. He reads his wife's fashion magazines, full of advertisements for nylon tights and breast-enhancement pills. Eva has a Cubist-style picture of herself hanging in her apartment, with one half of the face painted black, the other white. It is tempting to read this as a visual representation of Duvivier's view of women, similar to Mathias' deformed female sculptures in *Sous le ciel de Paris*. Finally, the portrayal of a man struck down by paranoia and the perceived accusatory glances of the crowd recalls, obliquely, Hire in *Panique*.

What makes this such a fascinating film is the way Duvivier shifts the fixed genre coordinates of *noir* to create an atmosphere that constantly switches between suspense and slapstick. The scene in which Albert visits Eva is a case in point. An over-excited barking dog greets him on the staircase and Albert's generous swig of alcohol causes a coughing fit. When Eva tumbles through her bathroom door and into Albert's arms with a dagger planted between her shoulders, Duvivier films the scene from above, with the action reflected in a large ceiling mirror above the bed. Albert's shock as he realises Eva has been stabbed is accentuated by a band of light across his eyes, reminiscent of the *noir* effects used to capture Gabin's allure in *Pépé le Moko* and *La Bandera*. If we recall how Duvivier filmed the aftermath of a murder scene in *La Tête d'un homme*, he focused there on bloodied handprints and footprints, generating tension with a barking dog, a slowly opening door, and a beam of torchlight. Here, the aftermath is very different. Albert tries to put a goldfish back into its upset bowl and frantically tries to wipe off his fingerprints. This is murder as pantomime.

Albert's anxiety increases as the days go by. He tries to get rid of the clothes he was wearing at the murder scene by throwing them out of a car window, but they are picked up by a nun and returned to him. Each time he tries to throw away the package, he is either stopped by the police, spotted by a passer-by, or interrupted by an amorous couple. When the package is eventually stolen by a tramp, Albert's relief is cut short when the tramp is forced to return the clothes. This collision between comic and dark tones is exemplified in a scene in a restaurant, when one of the extras in the musical reads out the police report of the murder from the newspaper. As she reads that the murderer had big hands, Albert slowly moves his hands underneath the table. When the waiter asks him if he wants to order fish, he spits out his drink, presumably as a reaction to the goldfish mishap from the previous night. Thomas Pillard (2015: 83) notes how these scenes all play off Fernandel's physical uniqueness, removing him from the heavily prescribed *noir* codes of Chase's original novel into world of 'jovial nonchalance' in which the actor's recognisable face is a far cry from the usual blank anonymity of the *noir* protagonist. Chase depicts the American protagonist of *Tiger by the Tail*, Ken Holland, as physically anonymous, blending into the Californian suburbs like so many other *noir* types. Fernandel's physical 'to-be-looked-at-ness', however, effaces any trace of Albert's indistinctness and thus increases the comic tension.

Duvivier is aided throughout these scenes by Fernandel's exquisite corporeal dexterity. His deliberately enlarged facial features, vocal mannerisms, and shifts in body language embody at various points in the film confusion, fear, or anxiety. Such fluidity was vital to the commercial success and international exportability of Don Camillo, but *L'Homme à l'imperméable* develops this further. The film's finest scene is a short one: early on, Albert arrives home after a rehearsal to an empty house, and turns on the radio. He removes two eggs from the refrigerator and leaves them on the kitchen table. One of the eggs rolls off and breaks. He cleans it up but then slips, falls back onto the floor, and drops the egg on his trousers. He moves to the cooker, turns on the gas, and tries to light it with an electric lighter. When that doesn't work, he tries a match, but he burns himself, falling back into the table with the unbroken egg on it. He manages to catch the egg before it falls, returns to the cooker, cracks the egg, and drops it onto the floor. He then cleans the parquet floor with a brush attached to his foot, moving his legs backwards and forwards in time with the music coming from the radio. Fernandel makes his performance 'fit' with the music, rhythmically swinging his legs backwards and forwards. This three-minute sequence showcases his talent; it's part Chaplin-esque in its balletic energy and foreshadows

Jacques Tati's perplexed encounter with kitchen gadgets in *Mon Oncle* (1958).

The clean, white surfaces of the kitchen and the polished parquet floors of the salon mark the beginnings of the 1950s buying power and consumerism in France and herald the nation's evolution from post-war austerity towards a culture of affluent residential suburbs, white goods, and fashion magazines. Kristin Ross (1995: 81) notes how women's magazines in the 1950s offered up this daily narrative of routines, chores, and beautification via a 'ready-made model of accomplishment, fulfilment and satisfaction'. This shift towards a ritualistic attention to cleaning and purification across French society is neatly mirrored in the scene when Albert cleans the apartment: he puts on an apron, listens to the radio, sweeps the floors, and browses his wife's magazines. For a brief moment, Albert/Fernandel 'becomes' the modern woman: house-proud, upwardly mobile, aspirational. Pillard (2015: 84) reads this scene as Duvivier's mocking take on the new domestic spaces of the 1950s, with their blandness and excessive emphasis on femininity. It is no coincidence that Albert eventually decides to call Eva, the prostitute, out of boredom and a spoiled dinner rather than due to any carnal motives. Albert's desire to escape from this antiseptic bourgeois setting (in the commune of Le Vésinet, in western Paris) to a grimier, *noir*-inflected Montmartre suggests a conscious turning away from the cosy and the superficial.

The closing scenes graft Clouzot-like *noir* flourishes (expressionistic shadows, footsteps in the dark, settling of scores) onto a Feydeau-esque farce (characters moving in and out of doors, bodies falling out of wardrobes, Fernandel hiding in the shower). *L'Homme à l'imperméable* concludes back at the theatre. Albert's wife has returned and sits on the front row listening to her husband finally play his clarinet solo. The last thing we see is Raphaël's dog barking in a basket. Here, the clash between Albert's and Duvivier's two worlds – domestic containment versus double-crossing murder – comes into sharp focus.

The critical response to the film was decidedly mixed. Jean-Louis Caussou (1957) wrote that it was perhaps Duvivier's best film. For Truffaut (1957a), one single element spoiled his enjoyment: 'Je ne puis plus supporter Fernandel, il m'agace, m'insupporte', but despite this, he (faintly) praised Duvivier for 'le travail [...] laborieux mais impeccable, soigné avec un amour qui dépasse la simple conscience professionnelle'.¹⁰ Other critics were put off by the disjunctive style of the film. While it showed for some the ease with which Duvivier could negotiate and interweave the comedy and the *noir* elements, the likes of Jacques Doniol-Valcroze (1957) disapproved of the tonal shifts: 'nous oscillons sans cesse entre réalisme minutieux [...] et une sorte de fantaisie burlesque [...] et cela ne valait pas la peine.'¹¹

If the star power of Fernandel threatened to overwhelm the original source material of *L'Homme à l'imperméable*, then Duvivier's next film would deploy stars in a similarly destabilising way. *Pot-Bouille* (1957) was Duvivier's second film based on a novel in Emile Zola's Rougon-Macquart series, after *Au bonheur des dames* in 1930, and returns once more to the story of Octave Mouret. Whereas Mouret was already well established in Paris' mercantile élite in *Au bonheur de dames*, *Pot-Bouille* charts Mouret's first arrival in the capital during the Second Empire, his various romantic entanglements, and his rise through the city's textile trade to become the powerful Mouret whom audiences had met in Duvivier's last silent film. As had been the case in the late 1920s, the 1950s was a fruitful period for Zola adaptations. Along with highly successful versions of *Thérèse Raquin* (Marcel Carné 1953), *Nana* (Christian-Jaque, 1955), and *Gervaise* (René Clément, 1956), Duvivier's *Pot-Bouille*, described by Bosley Crowther (1958) as 'a frothy surface-skimming of the manners and morals', was one of the most popular French films of 1957. As they had done with *Pépé le Moko*, the film was financed by the Hakim brothers, who were by now known for their star-driven melodramas. With its caustic, incisive dialogue by Henri Jeanson and impressive roster of star actors (Gérard Philipe, Danielle Darrieux, Dany Carrel, Anouk Aimée), *Pot-Bouille* targets the hypocrisies of the fin-de-siècle Parisian petite bourgeoisie. Much of the action takes place in an opulent Hausmannian apartment building, the 'melting pot' of the film's title. Within the context of the 'tradition of quality', *Pot-Bouille* exhibits the usual technical and visual touches that one expects from Duvivier. The look is beautiful: the costumes, décor, lighting, and

---

10 'I cannot stand Fernandel any longer, he annoys me, I find him intolerable'; 'the laboured [...] but impeccable work, cared for with a love that goes beyond simple professionalism'.

11 'we are forever to-ing and fro-ing between a meticulous realism [...] and a kind of burlesque fantasy [...], and it's not worth it'.

fluid, unbroken camera movements as people walk upstairs or along corridors all serve to exemplify Duvivier's classicism.

Zola's intention in *Pot-Bouille* was to reveal the discrepancy in the bourgeoisie between outward decorum and inward sordidness. Such a theme would undoubtedly have interested Duvivier, who had already explored the conflict between external respectability and inner deceit in *David Golder* (1930) and *L'Affaire Maurizius*. Yet Duvivier's rendering assuages the novel's harshness in favour of a more humorously satirical gaze at the transgressions of Zola's middle classes. Duvivier had recently shown his versatility in *L'Homme à l'impérmeable*, butting the comic and the *noir* against each other. A similar clash occurs in *Pot-Bouille*, where on the one hand we are exposed to the degeneracy of the Parisian bourgeoisie and on the other are immersed in a light-hearted satire of their lives and loves. As he had done with *Anna Karenina* (1948), Duvivier significantly streamlined Zola's novel, removing secondary characters, focusing on romantic misadventures, and occluding Zola's more savage indictments of the squalid promiscuity of the bourgeoisie.

Duvivier (1957: 8) explained his choices to *Les Lettres françaises*: 'J'ai trahi Zola dans la mesure où la lecture de *Pot-Bouille*, avec son univers sordide, sa cruauté et les vices des bourgeois décrits avec un naturalisme souvent outrancier, laisse une impression désespérée. Pourtant, je ne crois pas avoir trahi l'esprit du livre. J'ai traité *Pot-Bouille* en comédie.'[12] For Duvivier, the arch-pessimist and hitherto faithful adaptor of classic French literature, to suggest that he had toned down Zola's bleaker, more cynical view of human nature is significant. Russell Cousins (1989: 142–8) suggests that a major factor behind Duvivier's refocusing of the novel was economic; namely, that mid-1950s audiences were gravitating towards more broadly optimistic, less class-conscious, depictions of France's historical past. Morever, the casting of Philipe – already a huge box-office romantic lead after roles in *Fanfan la Tulipe* (1951) and *Le Rouge et le noir* (1954) – as Zola's Mouret mollified the corrosive aspects of the character precisely because Philipe's pre-programmed star status required a

---

12 'I have betrayed Zola in the respect that *Pot-Bouille*, with its cruel, sordid world of bourgeois vices, frequently described in excessive narrative details, leaves the reader with feelings of despair. I have treated *Pot-Bouille* as a comedy.'

continuation of his dashing romantic hero persona from those earlier films. In the novel, Mouret takes anyone he pleases by force – Zola (1961: 308) refers to his 'brutalité' and 'le dédain féroce qu'il [a] de la femme, sous son air d'adoration câline'.[13] Duvivier now makes him a charming and far less threatening seducer (his chaste, compassionate relationship with Marie Pichon is a case in point; in Zola's *Pot-Bouille*, Mouret rapes her and makes her pregnant) and, as with the rest of the characters, invites us to sympathise with him rather than be repelled by him. Philipe is positioned at the centre of the story in a way not dissimilar to the placement of Gabin in the actor's 1930s films with Duvivier. He coordinates the main plot points and carries the audience with him through the story. Wherever he goes, Mouret is figured as an object of desire (Mme. Josserand whispers 'C'est votre fameux jeune homme' ['So this is your famous young man'] to Campardon in the opening moments) and throughout *Pot-Bouille* gains increasingly in stature, 'to become even more elegant, more energetic, more decisive, more imaginative' (Cousins 1989: 147). The result is that we laugh at the hypocrisy in the film rather than recoil from it, as was Zola's original intention.

Yet, despite this softening of the edges, *Pot-Bouille* remains a highly effective synthesis of Zola's and Duvivier's cynicism. The unflattering portrayal of virtually all of the characters as a group of schemers, parasites, and amoral social climbers fits perfectly with a worldview that had grown increasingly more sceptical of human nature since *Panique*. Despite the reading of the film that Philipe's star presence pre-ordains, Mouret, the film's 'hero', is still depicted as a womanising scoundrel who ruthlessly exploits the people around him for the purposes of career advancement and financial betterment. In typical Duvivier fashion, we do not necessarily sympathise with Mouret's 'victims' because they too are framed in a negative light. None of the couples are happy. They cheat on each other (the Vabres), take mistresses (the Duveyriers, the Campardons), or simply go through the motions (the Pichons). Mme. Josserand's continual criticism of her husband for his lack of ambition in particular forms a direct line back to the mutual loathing of the Lepics in *Poil de carotte*.

---

13 'brutality'; 'the ferocious disdain in which he held woman, beneath his air of amorous adoration'.

Audiences approved of the treatment of bourgeois infidelity and the star qualities of Darrieux and Philipe. The film ranked eighth in 1957 for tickets sold in France (over 2.6 million) and was warmly received in New York (where it was retitled *The Lovers of Paris*). Critics were less forgiving and admonished Duvivier for his tonal shifts and repositioning: 'Zola sans Zola' ('Zola without Zola'), wrote Martine Monod (1957: 6). Truffaut's (1957b: 58) rather condescending review for *Cahiers du cinéma* began by dismissing Duvivier's authorial intentions: '*Pot Bouille* n'est pas un film d'auteur; c'est même tout le contraire!'[14] Nevertheless, Truffaut admired the film for its move away from academicism, its unusual qualities, and the ferocity of Jeanson's portrayals. Pierre Leprohon (1968: 240) noted how Duvivier's cinema had become increasingly 'excessif' by the mid-1950s, and how he seemed to want to show everything; in *Pot-Bouille*, for example, the director 'ne peut évoquer une mort sans montrer l'enterrement, relater un mariage sans filmer la cérémonie'.[15] While Duvivier's desire to 'show' may in part be attributed to a deference to Zola's naturalistic tendencies, Leprohon's observation is instructive, for it suggests Duvivier was a director who had by now become too closely implicated in adaptation practices.

The final film in this 'star section' took place in 1959, a vital date in French cinema. 1959 is the year commonly held to have heralded the start of the French New Wave.[16] And it was the year Duvivier would work with Brigitte Bardot. *La Femme et le pantin* was an adaptation of Pierre Louÿs' 1898 melodramatic novel about rich, married bullbreeder Don Matteo Diaz (António Vilar), who falls obsessively in love with a young flamenco student, Eva (Brigitte Bardot). Louÿs' novel had already been adapted three times, including a 1935 version, *The Devil is a Woman*, directed by Josef von Sternberg and starring Marlene Dietrich.[17] Duvivier was offered the contract while working on *Pot-Bouille*, though he was not first choice. The producer,

14 '*Pot-Bouille* is not a *film d'auteur*; on the contrary!'
15 'cannot allude to a death without showing us the funeral, recount a wedding without filming the ceremony'.
16 This was the year of *Les 400 coups* (François Truffaut), *Hiroshima mon amour* (Alain Resnais), and *Le beau Serge* (Claude Chabrol).
17 The novel would also form the basis of Luis Buñuel's *Cet obscur objet du désir* (*That Obscure Object of Desire* [1977]), adapted by Jean-Claude Carrière and starring Fernando Rey and Carole Bouquet.

Christine Gouze-Rénal, and the star, Brigitte Bardot, both wanted Roger Vadim (to capitalise on the success of *Et Dieu...créa la femme* [1956]). From the start, then, Duvivier's engagment with the material and his relationship with Bardot feel compromised. *La Femme et le pantin* is one of Duvivier's weakest films, containing little of the thematic consistency of his other work. *Cahiers du cinéma* (Marcorelles 1959: 56) wrote dismissively that *La Femme et le pantin* was not a Duvivier film, but rather 'un film de Bardot par Duvivier' ('a Bardot film by Duvivier').

Nonetheless, it remains an interesting work. Firstly, it is Duvivier's first colour film, and was filmed during Seville's cultural festival (*feria*). In her autobiography, Bardot (1996: 187) hints at the Bakhtinian context of the *feria*, describing it as a post-Lent 'défoulement collectif' ('collective release'). As with *Credo*, *Les Cinq gentlemen maudits*, and *Black Jack*, Duvivier is most at ease when documenting a culture and an ambience: here, the songs, dances, costume balls, horse races, and bull fights of the *feria* are lovingly shot. He depicts the festival's communal atmosphere and its attendant music, colour, dancing, and wild movements of the crowd. Roger Hubert's luscious Technicolor cinematography also captures Bardot's golden hair and her numerous costumes of reds, greens, yellows, and blacks.

Throughout *La Femme et le pantin*, Duvivier makes Bardot the object of both the male and female gaze wherever she goes. Women fear her and men are drawn to her. Ginette Vincendeau (2013: 330) notes that a crucial element of Bardot's stardom has always been her projection of a radically modern form of sexuality: 'captivating, yet devoid of mystery, active, yet not aggressive, young, open, erotic, sex without guilt or shame'. These multiple aspects are displayed throughout the film. Duvivier makes a telling choice right at the start. He begins with a three-quarters shot of Bardot before proceeding to slowly pan down to her legs. Throughout, she is either barefoot or wears tiny slippers, and Duvivier often films her trademark dancer's walk in a long shot. In one scene, American tourists pay for a private dance from Eva in the back room of a bar. She is almost naked (we only see her buttocks) and Diaz spies the scene through a curtain. When he interrupts the dance, pushing out the tourists, Eva tells him that 'J'ai dansé, ce n'est pas un péché' ('I only danced, it's not a sin'). Vincendeau (2013: 71) states that Eva is not a *femme fatale* in the traditional *noir* sense, as she is not 'opaque, unpredictable, manipulative'.

Nonetheless, her retort to Diaz here suggests a profoundly ambiguous figure who can deploy both a coy sexuality and a more knowing awareness that she can use her body as a means to seduce, tease, and make men jealous. Just as she had been in *Et Dieu...créa la femme*, Bardot is both vamp *and* gamine at the same time.

Scenes of Bardot dancing in her films are among the most pleasurable to watch, in part because the spectator is able to collude with her dancing body in its transgressive nature and admire Bardot's display of erotic spectacle (Leahy 2002: 49). In *La Femme et le pantin*, there are four dancing scenes: two that awaken desire and then two that awaken jealousy. Spectator identification during the dancing is strengthened by Duvivier's camerawork and *mise en scène*. He films most of the dances from the waist up, often pulling into Bardot's tousled hair and around her frenetic dancing body. Alongside the rapid cuts and multiple camera angles, such strategies allow the spectator to identify with the dancing body and doubly position us as subject and object of our own desire, dancing with Bardot, and with our own ego ideal (Leahy 2002: 57).

If we are looking for thematic throughlines in the film, what is particularly noteworthy is how Bardot represents the epitome of the modern woman: confident, sensual, sexually liberated, and a threat to patriarchal authority. Duvivier presented this archetype on numerous occasions – from *Maman Colibri* to *Panique* to *Voici le temps des assassins* – and Bardot here functions as a modern extension of the dangerous woman who threatens to send the male protagonist spiralling into existential despair. Driven by jealousy, Diaz grabs her from the stage, slaps her, and fights with everyone in a seedy bar.[18] In his efforts to contain Eva's disruptive force, Diaz must resort to physical violence. He beats her into submission, and only then does she agree to sleep with him. Eva is not 'punished' but in fact ends up getting what she wants: Diaz, cowed, and obedient. Here, the younger 'force of nature' has tamed the older patriarch.

With entries of nearly 2.5 million (Duvivier's sixth-highest box-office score), *La Femme et le pantin* found some degree of favour with Bardot fans. Yet critics were highly dismissive of Duvivier's

---

18 This scene contains one of the more audacious camera movements in a Duvivier film – the camera is very close up to the fighting and captures the chaos and the violence inside the dance hall.

attempts to modernise and commercialise his style by working with Bardot; he received some of the worst reviews of his career (*Libération* [Jeander 1959] called it 'cinéma sénile' ['senile cinema']). For Louis Marcorelles (1959: 56), part of the problem was the generational gulf between Duvivier (born in 1896) and Bardot (born in 1934); he argued that 'le scénario est ridicule [et] aucun personnage n'est psychologiquement vraisemblable' (Truffaut 1957b: 58).[19] Duvivier certainly had no time for the film. After a rare favourable review in *Paris-presse*, he wrote to the critic in question, Michel Aubriant: 'Je vous remercie, mais mon film est totalement idiot' (Leprohon 1968: 243).[20]

Marie-Octobre (1959)

Marie-Octobre remains one of Duvivier's most formally interesting films. It was shot between *La Femme et le pantin* and *La Grande vie*, and ranks as one of Duvivier's most underrated achievements, in part because of its adroit visual style and its willingness to confront a still raw process of France coming to terms with its past. This adaptation of Jacques Robert's eponymous novel[21] is nestled partway between *policier* and psychological drama. It takes place in a grand French country house, where the eleven remaining members of a former Resistance network known as 'Vaillance' gather under the same roof. Danielle Darrieux plays former Resistance fighter Marie-Hélène Dumoulin (known also by her old code name: Marie-Octobre), who suspects that there is a traitor among their members who betrayed one of them to the Gestapo back in 1944. With its classical dramatic structure (the three unities of time, place, and action), *Marie-Octobre* asks two questions: who is the traitor, and what will happen to them? Some of the biggest stars of the era were cast; aside from Darrieux, Duvivier chose Lino Ventura, Paul Meurisse, Bernard Blier, Noël Roquevert, Robert Dalban, and Serge Reggiani. *Marie-Octobre* alludes to Henri-Georges Clouzot's *Le Corbeau* (1943) in its exploration of

---

19 'the screenplay was ridiculous and no figure psychologically convincing'.
20 'Thank you, but my film is totally idiotic.'
21 Duvivier worked closely with Robert on the treatment and teamed up once more with Henri Jeanson. The latter's fingerprints are all over the film: the nickname of a former *résistant* is 'Au Bonheur des Dames'.

war-time denunciation and complicity. The surname 'Dumoulin' is a clear reference to real-life Resistance hero Jean Moulin, who died at the hands of the Nazis in 1943 (and was possibly betrayed by one of his network members). Each of the characters' past lives is explored, and so, ideologically, our sympathy for each character is carefully modulated as the former bonds of solidarity between the men are gradually stress-tested.

Despite its Resistance backdrop, there are no flashbacks that reconstruct an Occupation past. The war finished fifteen years ago, but Duvivier is more interested in resurrecting the buried past. He never shows us Castille, the murdered *résistant*, and yet his presence looms large in the photograph to which the reunited members propose a toast. The reunion is thus a pretext for the reconstruction of war as a memory in the present day. Charles de Gaulle, who had become president of France in 1958, had called on France to promote national reconciliation, to paper over the collaborationist elements of France's war-time past, and to perpetuate a Gaullist 'myth of resistance'. By the end of the 1950s in France, it seems that the obsession with vengeance for war-time collaboration had waned.

Duvivier and Jeanson problematise this ideological conviction. For instance, not all of the members of the Vaillance network joined out of patriotic duty; some joined out of love, others to prove their masculinity. Others passively collaborated with the Germans in an effort to secure a safe and stable existence. The butcher Marinval (Paul Frankeur) dabbled in the black market, while the lawyer Simoneau (Blier) later asks, rhetorically, 'Pendant l'Occupation, quel est le Français qui n'a pas eu de relation avec les occupants?'[22] By the close of *Marie-Octobre*, characters who at the outset appeared to possess outstanding moral and personal traits have turned against each other, questioning each other's every word, parsing it for potential treachery and admission of guilt.

Duvivier explores some of his favoured topics – principles of personal justice and vengeance, how individuals dissimulate to avoid suspicion, how events from the past can weigh heavily on the present, and above all how collective fraternity and shared group cohesion

---

22 'During the Occupation, which Frenchman didn't have some kind of relationship with the occupiers?'

can be eroded from within. Throughout, memory and truth are intermingled. Scenes are misremembered or mixed up, traumatic events forgotten and falsely reconstituted. Duvivier is returning to similar philosophical questions about the nature of memory – where the stakes were far lower – that were posed in *Un Carnet de bal* and *Lydia*. Here, suspicions about the past emerge once the convivial façade of the group starts to crumble. We observe an intense depiction of a community toxified by suspicion, full of differing opinions about what course of action to follow. Some advocate vengeance and the settling of scores; others wish to forget the past and move on. The film plays out like a cruel experiment – eleven characters, placed into a petri dish of mistrust and misgiving, slowly decomposing.

Duvivier and Jeanson amplify Robert's original novel and introduce a cross-section of French post-war society that encompasses lawyers and locksmiths, printers and priests. By far the most chilling aspect of their adaptation is the suggestion that anyone could have collaborated, and often the choice to do so was an arbitrary one. Fifteen years before Louis Malle would address similar issues in *Lacombe Lucien* (1974), Duvivier posits that the Occupation often meant taking sides and weighing up agonising dilemmas.

The term often used to describe the visual style of *Marie-Octobre* is 'huis clos' (literally, 'closed door', but figuratively, a work of fiction that takes place within a confined, enclosed space).[23] The required claustrophobia was generated from a series of innovative technical achievements. Firstly, the film was shot in twenty-three days, with Duvivier shooting scenes in the order laid down in the filming script, storyboarding every shot in advance with the aid of models and stick figures. Secondly, it is ninety-five minutes long and is shot in real time (i.e. the length of the film is identical to the length of time it takes for the film's narrative to unfold). This was the first time that this had been done in a French film (Marcel Carné's *Le Jour se lève* [1939] had come close, containing long sequences that followed its barricaded-in-a-room protagonist in real time). Such a singular narrative construction was not without its challenges. Jeanson and Robert needed to precisely time their dialogue with the aid of stopwatches, but the

---

23 Thibault Schilt (2011: 67–8), in his study of François Ozon, notes that Darrieux's casting in Ozon's *8 Femmes* (2002) is a nod to *Marie-Octobre* and its 'huis-clos, gender-imbalanced format'.

resulting precision means that no shot or line of dialogue is wasted. Everything is calibrated to extract maximum tension and a creeping sense of paranoia. Thirdly, set design became a crucial component in the film's taut visual style. Because the only set of the film was the main salon of the house, Duvivier and production designer Georges Wakhévitch needed to find ways of prolonging pressure while not losing sight of character development. Marie Epstein (1958: 328), who visited the set, noted that Duvivier and Wakhévitch were both technically astute and aesthetically adept: 'ces pions sont humains: ce n'est pas seulement un jeu de précision mathématique, mais un jeu dramatique'.[24] One way this 'drama' was achieved was through the unusual decision by Wakhévitch to place a ceiling on top of the sound stage that Duvivier would then periodically film to remind audiences of *Marie-Octobre*'s oppressive, relentless momentum.

Critics derided the film as an example of *théâtre filmé* (filmed theatre). Jean de Baroncelli's review in *Le Monde* is a case in point: Duvivier's *mise en scène* was 'trop précise, trop parfaitement agencée, trop mécanique' ('too precise, too perfectly laid out, too mechanical'). Yet I would argue that *Marie-Octobre* is quintessential Duvivier in the way various theatrical and cinematic devices are deployed to achieve maximum results: the facial reactions of different characters as they each in turn come under suspicion, the raft of film techniques (chiaroscuro lighting, depth of field, tracking shots, high- and low-angle shots, *plans rapprochés*), and the single-set goldfish bowl.

Darrieux, like Gabin, Fernandel, Philipe, and Bardot, brought a 'name-above-the-title' status to *Marie-Octobre*. Like those other stars, she functions ideologically. As the only female *résistante*, she is on the outside. She, unlike the other characters, remains frozen in 1944. She has never married, nor forgotten the previous treacherous events. It is at her insistence that the former network members have been summoned for this climactic day of reckoning. She stands in stark contrast to the men in the room, who exhibit a combination of indifference and willed amnesia. This is reflected most clearly when Marinval insists on breaking away from the investigation to watch a wrestling match on the television. His attempt to turn up the volume

---

24 'these pawns are human after all: it is not just a game of mathematical precision; it's also a drama'.

to drown out the recriminations taking place behind him is a deft metaphor for France's inability to confront its past. The traitor is eventually revealed to be Rougier (Serge Reggiani), who is then forced to write a confession/suicide note. As he tries to escape, Marie-Octobre shoots and kills him. The archetypal 'dangerous woman' (Burch and Sellier 1996: 268) was still on show in 1950s French cinema, resuscitated by Duvivier.

Embracing the New Wave? The case of *La Grande vie* (1960) and *Boulevard* (1960)

Duvivier's next two films featured two different kind of 'stars': Giulietta Masina, the Italian actress, and Jean-Pierre Léaud, the avatar of the French New Wave. Filmed on location in Berlin with a largely German cast and crew, *La Grande vie* (1960) remains a minor film in Duvivier's career that is rarely shown today. Duvivier and René Barjavel adapted Irmgard Keun's 1932 novel *Das kunstseidene Mädchen* (The Artificial Silk Girl), which traced the life of a young woman (Doris) who moves through a succession of relationships with men without ever finding happiness or the stability she craves. While Duvivier admitted during pre-production that he was drawn to the novel's ironic tone, the end result is a muddled film. What could have been a satirical, scathing look at the position of women in post-war Europe is reduced to a more mundane depiction of one woman's unluckiness in love. Bonnefille (2002: 176) sees Duvivier 'dans un creux de la carrière' ('in a career trough'), pointing at both *La Grande vie* and *La Femme et le pantin* as by-the-number assignments. The most notable aspect of *La Grande vie* was its casting of Masina as Doris, who had just starred in *Nights of Cabiria* (1957), directed by her husband, Federico Fellini. Duvivier channels the spirit and some of the plot points of *Cabiria* throughout *La Grande vie*, and also incorporates a series of typical melancholic motifs: Doris' crushed dreams, pimping, wife-beating, suicide, and mistreatment of an invalid are all woven into the screenplay, which makes the film's English-language title – *The High Life* – particularly ironic.

Masina is Doris, a working-class Berliner who seeks a man who can provide her with the material trappings she needs to live a successful life. The ensuing film is a collection of anecdotes and picaresque episodes in which Doris works as a secretary for Dr. Kölling (Gert Fröbe) and as a maid for an upper-class household (and has a relationship with the elderly owner and his son), and takes a one-line role in a theatre production. In a move that recalls Gloria and Joyce in *David Golder*, Duvivier initially presents Doris as a cynical gold-digger. She dreams of living in a huge house, sleeping in a beautiful silk white bed, having servants and three-hour baths, and being massaged and wearing beautiful clothes. In the opening scene, Doris allows herself to be wined and dined in the hope of some remuneration and receives a gold watch for spending a platonic evening with a stranger. Midway through, she finds Ernst (Hannes Messemer), an apparently dependable partner who can guarantee emotional stability. Masina's romantic attachment is fleeting, however, as Ernst is still in love with a previous girlfriend. In Duvivier's universe, love and lasting happiness remain elusive. Doris joins a line behind Pépé, Lydia, and Mike Alexander.

La Grande vie nonetheless tells us about Duvivier's thematic and formal preoccupations at this time. In Keun's original novel, Doris keeps a diary; here, Duvivier uses an interior monologue to allow access to Doris' inner thoughts. She records her romantic daydreams onto a record that her blind flatmate listens to while Doris is out. By the end of the film, the social climber Doris is reduced to walking the streets alone, approaching men to see whether they will give her board and lodgings. After Ernst leaves her, she resigns herself once more to continuing to look for a partner. The final line of the film is a voiceover from Doris – 'faites que c'est celui-là qui est le bon' ('make him the right one') – as she looks across at the man with whom she is about to spend the evening. Doris may have been unlucky in love, but she positions herself as a new kind of Duvivier heroine – resourceful, resilient, and irrepressible. After the incarnations of covetous women in Duvivier's recent films, she is a welcome recalibration, and she takes us back to the exuberance of Lily in *Allô Berlin? Ici Paris!* and the decency of Maria Chapdelaine. Barjavel and Duvivier include a number of pointed observations about big-city life. As well as its location-shot New Wave feel, *La Grande vie* presents Berlin in both a joyous and a melancholic light. In an audition at the theatre, the director tells Doris 'faites voir vos jambes' ('show off your legs'). Whereas Bardot's character in *La Femme et le pantin* flaunted her body in ways that reinforced her agency, Doris is part of a more retrograde environment in which women must 'perform' various acts of femininity in order to succeed. Duvivier undercuts allegations of misogyny by presenting this dilemma in comic terms – Doris wears safety pins in her bra to be used as a potential weapon against over-eager suitors.

After working with one of Italy's biggest stars, Duvivier turned to a different star for his next film, *Boulevard* (1960). Jean-Pierre Léaud had burst onto the scene a year earlier as Antoine Doinel in François Truffaut's *Les 400 coups*. Doinel is a young boy, unloved by his parents, who runs away from home and turns to a life of petty crime. Léaud would play a similar character to Doinel in *Boulevard*. The film marks the actor's only credited role in between his breakthrough performance and the next entry in the 'Antoine Doinel' cycle, *Antoine et Colette*, in 1962. Léaud's acting style has been described as 'histrionic and naturalistic, transparent and opaque, pliable and inflexible' (Hawker 2000), qualities all on display in Duvivier's film.

Adapted from Robert Sabatier's 1956 novel, *Boulevard* tells the story of Georges, also known as 'Jojo' (Léaud), a rebellious teenager who lives alone in a cramped Pigalle apartment. He has run away from home to avoid his vicious stepmother (Anne Béquet) and survives by selling newspapers on the street. Jojo is in love with Jenny (Magali Noël), but, when she rejects him for ex-boxer Dicky (Pierre Mondy), Jojo focuses his attentions on Marietta (Monique Brienne). At the end of the film, having been bullied by Dicky and seeing Marietta in the arms of another man, Jojo tries to kill himself by jumping from his apartment block. His father (Julien Verdier) comes to his rescue, reconciling his son with the news that he has left his stepmother.

Recurring Duvivier themes are replayed: the abusive 'mother', the uneasy relationship with the father, male violence, the redemptive then elusive possibility of love, and suicide as a last resort. The triangular relationship between Dicky, Jenny, and Jojo has strong Oedipal overtones because both men are in love with the same woman. Dicky and Jenny also act as Jojo's surrogate parents (his real father is absent for much of the film). This set-up is further complicated in a later scene, when Jojo's screams 'tocard! tocard! tocard!' ('loser') at Dicky. Dicky responds by threatening to kill Jojo, but Jojo continues to bait him until Dicky throws a knife and just misses Jojo's head. It is another version of the 'death drive' that animates so many characters in Duvivier's films, from *Poil de carotte* to *Anna Karenina*. Jojo frequently takes refuge on the roof of his apartment, and at one point he takes Marietta there to show her the sights of the city laid out in front of her. When he tells her that he would like to live there forever, she says 'on ne peut pas vivre dans les nuages' ('you can't live in up the clouds'). He replies 'pourquoi pas?' ('why not?'). Like Bastien and Ségard in *Le Paquebot Tenacity*, or Pépé, Jojo seeks an escape to an 'elsewhere' to insulate himself from his bleak everyday reality. When Jojo smashes the neon signs on the apartment roof, shouting 'salauds' ('bastards') to the passers-by below, memories of Jean Gabin at the end of *Le Jour se lève* are invoked.

The relationship between father and son is restored at the close of the film. As with *Poil de carotte*, the paternal figure returns to save the son's life. In *Boulevard*, this reconciliation between father and son can only take place once the wicked stepmother has been cast aside. Earlier, Jojo comes to his father's café to ask for some money. Duvivier captures the role the stepmother plays in both their lives in a single shot: behind her till, she resembles Germaine Kerjean in *Voici le temps des assassins*, another vengeful, spiteful misandrist. She tells her husband that, if he gives Jojo money, she will leave him. She asks him 'Est-ce que tu es un homme ou une mauviette?'[25] Once again, patriarchal authority is challenged and the role of the paterfamilias called into question by a dominant woman. Later, when Jojo learns that his father has shown his stepmother the door, he laughs uncontrollably. It is another example of the Duvivier paroxysm, but inverted. There is no cathartic violence; rather an ecstatic reaction, shot in close-up, to the banishment of the abject mother. Jojo laughs once more when his father tells him that he gave the stepmother 'une belle paire de baffes' ('a couple of good slaps'). It is an uneasy end to the film, whereby violence to the female is framed as an uplifting gesture of male reconciliation. In Léaud's previous film, Truffaut had famously ended with a freeze-frame on his face; here Duvivier also privileges the face, but this time it is a laughing, open, mobile one. Both Doinel and Jojo face uncertain futures. In Duvivier's world, 'salauds' exist everywhere. The restorative 'happy ending' of *Boulevard* will be temporary.

Boulevard is late Duvivier but glimpses of his earlier style remain. Like Jean-Pierre Melville, who had already filmed on location in Pigalle for *Bob le flambeur* (1956) and captured its sleazy cosmopolitanism,

25 'Are you a man or a mouse?'

Duvivier anchors his story here. He films on location on the streets of Pigalle and Montmartre, inspecting the richness of this milieu with an ethnographer's eye. Scenes take place in boxing halls, cafés, streets, and squares, and are often underscored with a modern jazz soundtrack. Interesting camera effects, such as Jojo's drunken point-of-view shots as he climbs a staircase, a long tracking shot down a Paris street as he runs from a police officer, and a series of rapid cuts in the boxing hall, are neat modern inflections. Duvivier's slice of social realism was not a success, receiving box-office admissions of just 800,000 (the second lowest of any post-war Duvivier film) and generally negative reviews. Yet *Boulevard* remains a forgotten film and is of interest for the way it interfaces with certain aesthetic and formal norms of the New Wave and expands continuities with Duvivier's earlier work.

Le Diable et les dix commandements (1962)

Breaking chronology slightly, *Le Diable et les dix commandements*, released in 1962, was another interesting formal experiment by Duvivier. Shot in between *La Chambre ardente* and *Chair de poule*, in *Le Diable et les dix commandements*, Duvivier turned away from the sustained *noir* and *fantastique* sensibilities of those films towards a lighter late style. It saw him return to the format that made his name in the 1930s: the sketch film. The script, by Duvivier, Barjavel, and Maurice Bessy (with extra dialogue from Jeanson and Michel Audiard), consists of seven episodes that show what happens when one of the Ten Commandments is broken.[26] Like the multi-directed *Les Sept péchés capitaux* (1962), another sketch film that deals with religious subject matter (the seven deadly sins), *Le Diable et les dix commandements* features a galaxy of French stars, many of whom had worked with Duvivier before, such as Michel Simon, Marcel Dalio, Charles Aznavour, Lino Ventura, Fernandel, Alain Delon, Danielle Darrieux, Jean-Claude Brialy, and Louis de Funès.[27] At the very start,

---

26 Two of the sketches feature more than one of the Commandments.
27 Despite this impressive list, *Le Diable et les dix commandements* proved only to be a modest commercial success. With over 1.8 million spectators, it scored the fourteenth best box-office results for the 1962–63 season.

the Devil – incarnated in a snake – emerges from the mouth of a gargoyle. With a voiceover by Claude Rich, the snake links each of the stories together, finishing each one with an unexpected twist. After the darker strains of Duvivier's previous *films à sketch*, such as *Un Carnet de bal*, *Flesh and Fantasy*, and *Sous le ciel de Paris*, *Le Diable et les dix commandements* is more episodic, alternating between farce and frivolous boulevard comedy. In 'Tu ne jureras point' ('Thou shalt not take the Lord's name in vain'), Michel Simon plays a handyman in a convent who loses his job after an outburst of blasphemy in scenes reminiscent of the gentle anti-clericalism of the Don Camillo series. 'Tu ne déroberas point' ('Thou shalt not steal') stars Jean-Claude Brialy and Louis de Funès as a bank clerk and a thief who team up to split the loot from a robbery, and features an amusing moment in which a suspicious police officer helps Brialy tie up his briefcase, which is about to open and reveal the stolen money. There's even an acerbic taunt at the pretentions of the New Wave by the snake: 'J'aime la Nouvelle Vague, moi. Tous ces gaillards qui pensent que la vie est un voyage et qu'il vaut mieux le faire en première classe, qui louchent un peu sur l'argent du voisin.'[28]

Other stories are darker. In 'Tu ne tueras point' ('Thou shalt not kill'), the tone drastically lurches towards the existential nihilism of *Voici le temps des assassins*. Charles Aznavour plays a priest who seeks to avenge his sister's suicide after her fall into prostitution and drug addiction at the hands of Lino Ventura. In an ingenious twist, Aznavour provokes Ventura into killing him, moments before the prearranged arrival of the police. In 'Tes père et mère honoreras' ('Honour thy father and mother') and 'Tu ne mentiras point' ('Thou shalt not lie'), a young man (Alain Delon) learns that his mother (Madeleine Robinson) is in fact his stepmother. He tracks down his real mother, Clarisse Ardant (Danielle Darrieux), to Paris, where she is a famous stage actress. Like Christine in *Un Carnet de bal*, Clarisse is a self-absorbed narcissist who initially mistakes Delon's inquiries for a romantic interest. She preens in front of mirrors, gazing at her own image, and admits she cannot remember who his real father was. Delon returns home, disillusioned. Typical Duvivier themes of revenge and family dysfunction resonate throughout.

28 'I love the New Wave. All those con-men who think that life is like a journey and it's best to travel in first class and lust after their neighbour's money.'

These two bookend 'Un seul Dieu tu adoreras' ('Thou shalt have no other Gods before me'), the entry that best reflects Duvivier's worldview. A man (Fernandel) claiming to be God visits a child and her grandparents at an Alpine cottage. The family has lost their faith, and the woman (Germaine Kerjean) berates 'God' for her miserable existence. She demands a miracle, so 'God' makes her crippled husband (Gaston Modot) walk again. The old woman dies. 'God' leaves and is picked up at the side of the road by two men who drive him back to a psychiatric hospital. This unexpected ending completely undercuts the intensity of the dying woman's complaints and criticisms against God; she had earlier outlined her view of the world: 'C'est pareil partout [...] partout ça brûle, ça crie, ça saigne; non, vous n'êtes pas ce que vous dites, Y'a pas de bon Dieu'.[29] Even the 'miracle' is revealed to be a sham. The old man is no cripple but chooses paralysis as a means to avoid work. Once more, dissimulation and deception are key undertones, especially within the family unit.

'But leave it to Mr. Duvivier': a trio of noir

It is a great shame that critics have dismissed Duvivier's late work, because the trio of *La Chambre ardente* (1962), *Chair de poule* (1963), and *Diaboliquement vôtre* (1967) contains arguably some of his most compelling work from a visual, formal, and thematic perspective. The first, *La Chambre ardente*, is an adaptation by Duvivier and Charles Spaak of *The Burning Court*, written in 1937 by the American John Dickson Carr, best known for his impossible-crime puzzles with gothic and supernatural overtones. *La Chambre ardente* was a French–German co-production, which accounts for the geographical shift (the action is transposed from rural Philadelphia to the Black Forest) and the casting of German actor Walter Giller and Austrian actress Nadja Tiller alongside New Wave acolytes Jean-Claude Brialy and Claude Rich, and Georges Franju's muse Édith Scob (*Les Yeux sans visage* [1960] and *Judex* [1963]). As he had done with *Marianne de ma jeunesse* (1955) and *L'Affaire Maurizius* (1954) – and even further back, with *L'Ouragan sur la montagne* (1922), Duvivier decamped

---

29 'It's the same everywhere [...] everywhere you go, people are burning, screaming and bleeding; no, you are not who you say you are; there is no just God.'

to Germany for two months, shooting in Bavaria with a largely German crew.

The title refers to a court in the seventeenth century where famous poisoners – such as the Marquise de Brinvilliers – were interrogated and tortured. The byzantine plot includes witchcraft and poison; nephews squabbling over an inheritance; secret love affairs; a mysterious figure who administers a fatal glass of eggnog, walks straight through a wall, and disappears into the darkness; and a corpse that disappears from its coffin. Duvivier and Spaak reproduce Carr's two central enigmas faithfully; namely, how did a woman apparently walk through a wall, and how did Desgrez's body disappear from its coffin. Throughout *La Chambre ardente*, Duvivier interlaces the *policier* and the supernatural and generates suspense from the way the assassin avoids suspicion. In the vein of the best 'locked-room' mysteries, the screenplay casts suspicion on each of the main characters. Mathias Desgrez (Frédéric Duvallès) and Marie (Scob) are descendants of the Marquise de Brinvilliers and three family members (Brialy, Rich, Perrette Pradier) greedily covet an ailing uncle's fortune. A police inspector (sardonically played by Claude Piéplu) is summoned to solve the mystery, but he, like the detective in Carr's novel, is peripheral to the action. This is because Duvivier chooses, in a narrative tactic reminiscent of *La Tête d'un homme*, to reveal the killer's identity early on (it is Desgrez's nurse, Myra [Tiller]) rather than unveiling her at the end. For Duvivier, *La Chambre ardente* demonstrates the extent to which people will go to fund an exorbitant lifestyle. The focus on rapaciousness and 'veulerie' (spinelessness) that we saw in *La Tête d'un homme*, *Voici le temps des assassins* and above all *Panique* resurfaces once more, in the guise of a supernatural *fait divers*. Amid the uncanny events stands Giller's bewildered Boissard, the surrogate spectator who seeks a rational explanation to the unfolding chaos.

Duvivier and Spaak replicate the supernatural elements in Carr's novel. Since *Le Reflet de Claude Mercœur*, via *Flesh and Fantasy* and *Marianne de ma jeunesse*, the *fantastique* has rarely been far from the surface in Duvivier's world. Here, the German forest setting, the crypts and mausoleums, and the sounds of screws tightened into position in a coffin lid are all examples of Duvivier's foray into the uncanny. Early on, Marie describes the Black Forest as 'moitié merveilleux, moitié sinistre' ('half marvellous, half sinister'), a rather fitting description of the tone and visual style of *La Chambre ardente* as well as of Duvivier's own belief system. Part of this ambivalence is generated by Roger Fellous' cinematography. His camera is forever gliding through the house, filming the comings and goings of the guests and the servants with fluid tracking shots. Multiple close-up shots of faces reveal emotions of surprise, sadness, or shock. Once again, Bosley Crowther (1963) at the *New York Times* praised Duvivier, this time for the way his camera 'casts a glacial spell, like a patient, evil eye'. These unsettling images are bolstered by Georges Auric's melodramatic, portentous music. Like Mario Bava's *giallo* films, or Franju's *Pleins feux sur l'assassin* (1961), another film that traded in the uncanny, recounting a centuries-old legend against the backdrop of a country house, *La Chambre ardente* is an exercise in rococo style.

Duvivier clearly revelled in the black, cynical humour introduced by Spaak. There are some trademark visual embellishments, such as when Marie reaches for some pills and Duvivier focuses on a second bottle on the shelf above, labelled with a skull and crossbones. This Hitchcockian touch readies the spectator for a potential narrative twist (and, read retrospectively, is an example of the dramatic principle of 'Chekhov's gun'). In a scene that calls to mind Hitchcock's *Suspicion* (1941), a translucent glass of medicine is carried up the staircase to the aged Desgrez. We see a pair of black velvet gloved hands but not the person carrying the glass. Later, in two brief but striking scenes, Marie sees a fly land on Desgrez's dead face and then crawl across his eyes and nose as the lid of the coffin descends. When Boissard first informs Marie of Desgrez's death, Duvivier cuts back to a static tableau of the dead man, eyes wide and mouth agape. Then, as Desgrez's body is exhumed for the autopsy, Duvivier deploys the tropes of classic gothic horror: out of the mist come the sounds of wolves and owls, a close-up of Scob's ghostly face, and an opened coffin with no body.

The real *coup de théâtre* in *La Chambre ardente* is the funeral scene, in which Desgrez's body is laid out for viewing while the assembled mourners are invited to waltz around the coffin as Strauss' 'Emperor Waltz' plays on the soundtrack. The scene is a pure fabrication by Duvivier and Spaak; it is both morbidly comic and deeply unsettling to see a series of point-of-view shots as characters look at the corpse as they dance. This tonal disjointedness is further underlined by the fact that the waltz is being played by a full orchestra, and yet the only musicians we see in the scene are a small group of string players on a balcony. Nearly a quarter of a century after *The Great Waltz*, Strauss is recuperated once more, absorbed into one of Duvivier's most exuberant sequences. His Hollywood treatment of the composer had featured swirling cameras, and those same movements are copied here as the camera spins around the coffin. The delirium does not end there. Duvivier prolongs the scene by having the mourners accompanied to the crypt by a brass band playing an up-tempo military march.

This being a Duvivier and Spaak film, *La Chambre ardente* also targets the interplay between the protagonists, laying bare their weaknesses, ambiguities, and fears. Like their previous partnerships (most notably *La Belle équipe* and *La Fin du jour*), Duvivier and Spaak show what happens to a group when it is put under pressure, both internally (from their own double-crossing) and externally (from a series of unnerving incursions). Marc (Brialy) is having an affair with Myra, and their relationship is characteristically lop-sided. She sows seeds of doubt in Marc's mind, convincing him that his uncle's killer must be his brother or his wife. Coincidentally, Myra is putting on her stockings during this scene, using her body, like Gina did with Jean in *La Belle équipe*, as a way of tipping the power balance in her favour. The film's climax culminates with a paroxysm. Marc tries to strangle Myra, chases her into the woods, and forces her head under a nearby river, drowning her. Once again, Duvivier punishes the female transgressor in a particularly graphic way. For Crowther (1963), *La Chambre ardente* epitomised the director's late style: 'But leave it to Mr. Duvivier [...] he has evoked a hypnotic fusion of mood, setting and mounting tension with a glittering, cold precision perfectly suited to his bloodless characters.' Even in his twilight years, Duvivier's cool, detached method was an apt match for such pulp source material.

Chair de poule, released in 1963, saw Duvivier return to the work of James Hadley Chase, this time to adapt, with René Barjavel, *Come Easy, Go Easy* (1960). Whereas Duvivier's previous Chase adaptation, *L'Homme à l'impérmeable*, had a balanced comic and dramatic register (due in large part to Fernandel's physical and vocal dexterity), *Chair de poule* is far bleaker in its depiction of a distrustful, treacherous world that is dominated by money and the thwarted promises of escape. Throughout the film, set in and around a small mountainside service station (filmed on location at the Col de Vence in the Alpes-Maritimes), Duvivier interfaces with the American and the French *noir* traditions, in terms of the film's visual style, its representation of the *femme fatale*, and its cynical, pessimistic view of human relations. The recourse to venality in *Chair de poule* by several of its characters, plus its sadistic elements – hot oil thrown in the face of two men – make the film a companion piece to both *Voici le temps des assassins* and *La Chambre ardente*.

Daniel (Robert Hossein) is a safe-breaker who goes on the run from Paris after a botched heist leads to murder. Changing his name to Pierre, he takes refuge at an isolated petrol station in the south of France, working for Thomas (Georges Wilson). Thomas' wife Maria (Catherine Rouvel) coerces Daniel into stealing money from her husband's safe. Thomas is killed, but the safe remains locked until Daniel's accomplice Paul (Jean Sorel) reappears. Maria then plays the two friends off against each other; the film ends with Maria and Paul dead, Daniel bleeding to death as the police arrive, and ten million francs burning up in the back of an exploded truck.

Chair de poule is one of Duvivier's most underrated films and one of the best French *noirs* of the early 1960s. Part of what makes the film so pleasurable is Duvivier's systematic deployment of a raft of familiar *noir* techniques. Firstly, there are numerous allusions to both American and French *noir*. The isolated garage setting is a clear homage to James M. Cain's classic 1934 *noir The Postman Always Rings Twice* (and Tay Garnett's 1946 film version); the bored housewife who conspires to murder her husband inevitably recalls the antagonist of Billy Wilder's *Double Indemnity* (1944); while the shift from urban to rural setting for the playing out of the cat-and-mouse game with the *femme fatale* is a nod to Jacques Tourneur's *Out of the Past* (1947). Closer to home, the safe-cracking scene would have reminded audiences of the celebrated scene in Jules Dassin's *Du rififi chez les hommes* (1955), a film in which Robert Hossein had also starred. In *Chair de poule*, Duvivier and Barjavel fashion a similar cynical, stifling world. The iconography of *noir* dominates the opening minutes of the heist. It is raining hard in a nocturnal Paris, and Duvivier and cinematographer Léonce-Henri Burel (reuniting after *Marianne de ma jeunesse*) throw a huge shadow of a pursuing policeman onto the street walls as the policeman shoots Daniel in the back. The action then shifts to the Col de Vence, and Burel's cinematography resorts to high-key lighting to underpin the stifling sense of claustrophobia. This rocky, barren terrain is hot and sticky. It is a place where everyone seems to sweat and the sound of cicadas and crickets fills the air. Raymond Chirat (1968: 52) notes how Duvivier films the characters with a detached, unemotional objectivity, as if they were 'de sales insectes vus à la loupe' ('dirty insects seen under a magnifying glass'). An explicitly existentialist undercurrent courses through the film, articulated most notably by Maria, who tells Daniel, after they have killed Thomas, that 'on est condamné à vivre ensemble' ('we are condemned to live together').

These *noir* rhythms are enhanced by Rouvel's startling performance. She epitomises the *femme fatale*: jet-black hair and eyes, provocatively dressed, forever smoking. Her marriage to Thomas, the 'old husband', is a *noir* mainstay; she manipulates his desire for her for financial betterment. She conveys carnality, autonomy, and phallic power (one of her first actions is to torture a fly with the tip of a scissor blade; later, she draws a gun). When Thomas discovers that Daniel is trying to steal from him, Maria switches her allegiance and tries to convince her husband that Daniel is a thief and a killer. When Paul arrives at the col and Maria realises that he can open the safe instead of Daniel, she transfers her loyalty to him, taking his hand and suggesting they go dancing. In this sense, Maria follows a long line of Duvivier female archetypes, from Gina in *La Belle équipe* and Catherine in *Voici le temps des assassins*, via Alice in *Panique*, setting men against each other and threatening the integrity of their friendship.

Indeed, this importance of male friendship summons up a familiar Duvivier dynamic. Daniel is given a prison sentence in part because he does not provide the police with the name of his accomplice. Thomas wants Daniel to stay and work with him at the garage because 'un homme, ce qu'il lui faut, c'est des copains'.[30] Several crime films from this period, most notably *Touchez pas au grisbi* (1954), suggest that the prospect of male solidarity and mateship is far more gratifying than romantic love. Duvivier, as he had already done in *La Belle équipe*, *La Fin du jour*, and *The Impostor*, offers the consolation of camaraderie. It is surely no accident that the most touching scene in the film is when Daniel and Thomas meet for the first time on the col road. They talk about racing cars, and Daniel fixes Thomas' broken-down truck. They share cigarettes and Thomas invites Daniel to spend a few days at his house. A hyper-romantic

30 'what a man needs around him is his pals'.

score underscores this four-minute sequence, in which a male friendship develops before our eyes.

There is one extended Duvivier flourish in *Chair de poule*. Maria and Daniel are putting groceries away. Via a high-angle shot, we see Maria unroll a newspaper containing some meat. Duvivier then rapidly dollies towards the newspaper, revealing Daniel's face on the front cover and the headline 'Daniel Boisset s'evade' ('Daniel Boisset escapes'). Duvivier then cuts back to the original high-angle shot, and Daniel and Maria continue to talk and move around the kitchen. Neither of them 'see' the newspaper, and the scene ends with Daniel leaving the kitchen and Maria throwing the newspaper away. The postscript to this sequence is that Duvivier then cuts back to the kitchen, where Maria picks up the newspaper to hold her potato peelings and sees the picture of Daniel. The close-up of her face suggests a gradual realisation that she is now in control and can begin to plot her way out of her domestic situation. When Daniel returns to the kitchen, Maria has undergone a complete transformation. She sings and offers him vermouth; she is more confident now that she can start to manipulate Daniel, and Thomas. She asks Daniel to peel some potatoes. While he has been outside with Thomas, Maria has arranged several potatoes on the front page of the newspaper, artfully covering the incriminating photograph and headline. As Daniel peels the potatoes, his face is gradually revealed, and he eventually realises that he is incriminating himself. In a delightful piece of direction by Duvivier, Daniel drags his chair a few inches sideways so as to put his back to Maria, and in doing so draws the potatoes back over the evidence. He does not realise – but the audience does – that Maria has already uncovered his secret. Duvivier also intercuts two close-up shots of Maria looking at Daniel as he looks at the newspaper (and not at her). It is only when Maria then addresses him as 'Daniel', and not as Pierre, that he realises she has unearthed the truth. This is masterful storytelling by Duvivier. Clear and uncluttered, nothing has been wasted in this five-minute sequence: dialogue, camera movement, editing, and music all work together to trigger the film's 'complicating action'.

The early parts of *Chair de poule* quite self-consciously incorporate elements of the New Wave into their visual and aural fabric. The film is, along with *Boulevard*, the most 'modern' of Duvivier's post-war films. For instance, the score, which oscillates between the plaintive and the bombastic, is by Georges Delerue, Truffaut's regular composer.³¹ As Paul and his girlfriend Simone (Nicole Berger) return to their flat in the suburbs, they start a conversation as they walk down a Paris street and continue it – via a jump cut – on a bus. Once in the *banlieue*, Duvivier paints a bleak portrait of the monotony of the new modern France. Amid the large concrete apartment blocks behind Paul and Simone, diegetic sound emanates from all corners – car horns, street bustle, radio announcements, an unseen accordion, and a crying baby. Paul talks about the monotony of their life in a way that foreshadows Godard's *Deux ou trois choses que je sais d'elle* (1967): 'le boulot, le HLM, le HLM, le boulot' ('work, home, home, work'). Other New Wave ideas incorporated by Duvivier include the final close-up shot of Daniel laughing uncontrollably like Gérard Blain in the final moments of Claude Chabrol's *Le Beau Serge* (1958).

Bonnefille (2002: 200) ranks *Chair de poule* 'parmi les films les plus mineurs de Duvivier',³² while, Desrichard (2001: 84), who describes it as 'un petit polar sans ambition',³³ devotes only two short paragraphs to it. Both make unfavourable comparisons with *The Postman Always Rings Twice*. This is partly due to James Hadley Chase's own prose style, which involved inflecting his British version of *noir* with an excessive American tinge. Jacques de Baroncelli (1963) noted in his review that Chase resorted to 'un cocktail de violence, de sadisme et d'érotisme' to such a repetitive extent that his work now resembles 'des romans blafards'.³⁴ Other critics damned Duvivier with faint praise. Claude Garson (1963) wrote that all Duvivier has to do to make a film nowadays is 'mettre en images une histoire bien construite'.³⁵ The implicit criticism is that Duvivier was too old (he was sixty-seven when shooting began) to direct this kind of material. Michel Aubriant (1963) wrote in *Paris-Presse* that 'il [eût] fallu un Aldrich, [et que] c'est le gentil Julien Duvivier qui opère'.³⁶

Diaboliquement vôtre (1967), Duvivier's final film, is a microcosm of his universe: it is an adaptation of a thriller,³⁷ it has a co-written

---

31 Delerue's score for *Chair de poule* came in between Jean-Luc Godard's *Le Mépris* (1963) and Truffaut's *La Peau douce* (1964).
32 'among Duvivier's most minor films'.
33 'an insignificant crime film that lacks ambition'.
34 'a cocktail of violence, sadism, and eroticism'; 'pallid novels'.
35 'put into images a well-constructed story'.
36 'it needed a [Robert] Aldrich; instead we got nice old Julien Duvivier'.
37 *Manie de la persecution* (1962), by Louis C. Thomas.

screenplay (with Roland Giraurd), it cast a star actor as the lead (Alain Delon), and it incorporates favoured themes of confinement and fractured identity. Yet Duvivier's final film is also the most atypical of his entire career: it is shot in colour, drips with psycho-sexual undertones, and is profoundly modern in its use of *mise en scène* and character perspective.

Delon is Georges Campo, who, in the opening moments of the film, is involved in a car crash. He awakens from a three-week coma with amnesia, knowing little about himself or who he was before the crash. He returns to his country estate with his wife, Christiane (Senta Berger), and quickly settles into the luxury of – for him – these new surroundings. He is unable to remember previously living there, but tries to convince himself that he is not amnesic. The mystery increases when Georges (who has been unknowingly drugged) begins hearing voices that seek to implant particular memories of a previous existence in Hong Kong. Georges is nearly killed, first by a falling chandelier, then a vicious dog, and suffers hallucinations of combat in the Algerian war. Everything is revealed to be a plot by a friend, Freddie (Sergio Fantoni), who has killed the 'real' Georges, buried him, and replaced him with the Delon-Georges, a returning war veteran. Christiane has pretended all along to be his wife, and she and Freddie have used hypnopaedia (the power of suggestion through a hidden tape recorder) to brainwash Delon-Georges. Christiane kills the butler (Peter Mosbacher) and tries to frame Freddie. Delon provides an alibi for his 'wife', but, in the final shot of the film, a tape recorder is brought to the police chief, who plays it and hears Freddie's hypnotic voiceovers, which ultimately incriminate his 'wife'.

Duvivier brings some startlingly modern touches to the film's opening section. After the impact of the crash, he abruptly cuts to a hospital ward corridor and then, via a series of woozy dissolves, cuts back to the road down which Delon was driving, then back to the hospital corridor, then to a close-up of a nurse in a surgical facemask, then back to the road, then to an overhead theatre lamp and a series of surgical implements. The contrasts in time and space are reinforced through a sound design that alternates between the austere silence of the operating theatre and Delon's revving car engine followed by the screech of tyres. Duvivier then films a close-up of Delon's bandaged face as the bandages are slowly removed, gradually revealing his face and his star image. He was already a star in 1962 when Duvivier cast him in *Le Diable et les dix commandements* thanks to his career-defining roles in *Rocco and His Brothers* (1960) and *L'Eclisse* (1962), and, by 1967, he had worked with Visconti again in *The Leopard* (1963). *Diaboliquement vôtre* was Delon's first film after *Le Samourai*, in which he played contract killer Jef Costello.

It seems fitting that the opening sequence of the car travelling at high speed through the French countryside is shot from the perspective of the driver. This point of view does not alter for the remainder of the film, for the events that follow are primarily seen through the eyes of Delon's character. The early part of the film is Hitchcockian. We, like Georges, only incrementally realise that there is a conspiracy against him and that he is trapped in the house, unaware of the forces that control him or why they are doing so. Each piece of evidence is analysed both by Georges and the spectator. When he almost falls through the barn's trap door onto a combine harvester, we begin to suspect, as does he, that Christiane led him there deliberately. When he tells Kim that he has never drunk so much green tea in his life, we ask ourselves whether this is how he is being drugged. So far, so Boileau-Narcejac. Throughout the film, Georges becomes increasingly suspicious of everyone around him and the situation in which he finds himself. The initial pleasures of his confinement – a mansion, a beautiful wife – become progressively more imprisoning. He walks with a cane; his 'wife' is sexually unavailable; there is a large gate at the border of the property, guarded by a dog; and he is subjected to disturbing nightmares. Even the drugs he is given to ease his amnesia serve to confuse him. The missing body of the real Georges in the garden returns us to the major narrative twist in *La Chambre ardente*. Once more, the (dis)appearance of a corpse is emblematic of a protagonist's physical and psychological entrapment.

The film's stylish modern sheen is aided by François de Roubaix's jazzy, syncopated soundtrack and Henri Decaë's lush cinematography. Decaë was already strongly associated with directors who were part of the New Wave (he shot *Les Amants* [1958] and *Les 400 coups*) and had worked with Jean-Pierre Melville on multiple occasions. He had already filmed Alain Delon in René Clément's *Plein Soleil* (1960) and *Les Félins* (1964), and both Decaë and Delon arrived on the set of *Diaboliquement vôtre* after having just wrapped Melville's *Le Samourai*. While *Le Samourai* deployed a minimalist colour scheme of blues and greys (Melville famously referred to it as 'un film en couleur en noir et blanc')[38], Decaë floods the visual palette of *Diaboliquement vôtre* with bold slabs of primary colours. Aided by the superior quality of the Eastman colour process, the cinematography exploits the psychedelic and fantastical excesses of Thomas' original novel. In one scene, a red lampshade, green towel, blue pyjamas, and white night robe appear in the same shot.

The reference to the war in Algeria is a typical Duvivier touch. Not only does it remind us of his previous incursions into the French colonial space (*Maman Colibri, Les Cinq gentlemen maudits, Pépé le Moko*) but it also underlines how his films often chimed with socio-political contemporary events. Georges is continually haunted by Algeria. The return of these repressed memories is heralded by a jump cut, the sound of machine guns, and an overexposed screen in which a series of images (the Casbah, belly-dancers, music, a night club) are filmed as garish, psychedelic red and green flashes by Decaë. Such flourishes are typical of French cinema's reluctance to deal with the Algerian war face on; here, the blaze of primary colours creates a particularly unrealistic *mise en scène* that sanctions only an oblique engagement with the conflict. Like Jacques Demy's *Les Parapluies de Cherbourg* (1964) and Claude Chabrol's *Le Boucher* (1969), *Diaboliquement vôtre* positions the war firmly in the background.

As with *La Chambre ardente* and *Voici le temps des assassins*, Duvivier makes the woman the chief antagonist. Berger's Christiane, like Delorme's Catherine and Rouvel's Maria, begins the film as a kind of *faux-naive*, but by the end she has murdered and doublecrossed her male partner. Christiane manufactures the plot, like Myra in *La Chambre ardente*. Duvivier includes a particularly unsettling dynamic in *Diaboliquement vôtre* that plays on the power relations between Christiane and the male characters. The mansion is tended by a Chinese servant named Kim (played by the German actor Mosbacher) who devotes himself to Christiane. He cooks and cleans, sews Christiane's clothes, styles her hair, and puts her stockings on. He is well-muscled and always impeccably dressed, spending much of the film topless. At one point, he massages Christiane – she is naked, save for a green towel – with a mixture of ferocity and tenderness. These fetishising gestures partly remind us of the devotion

---

38 'a black-and-white film in colour'.

shown by Erich von Stroheim's butler to Gloria Swanson's waning star in *Sunset Boulevard* (1950) and serve to reinforce the dominance Christiane has over Kim, and other men.

In the final moments of *Diaboliquement vôtre*, during the police interrogation of Christiane, Pierre tries to save her by pretending to be 'Georges', telling the police officer that he is the owner of the estate and laying the blame on Freddie. This strange, dream-like film, and Duvivier's career, concludes with a condensed version of the director's recurring themes and core concerns: the fluidity of identity, the liminal space between truth and illusion, the split double, the 'bad' wife, entrapment, memory, and duplicity. Even at the last, Duvivier's sureness of touch and strict thematic consistency did not desert him.

Conclusion

The box-office numbers towards the end of Duvivier's career make particularly disheartening reading – *Boulevard*: 802,000 tickets sold; *La Chambre ardente*: 834,000; *Chair de poule*: 794,000; and *Diaboliquement vôtre*: 836,000. These figures, coupled with the critical neglect of Duvivier later films, suggest that he had fallen out of favour.

In turn, they bring into sharp focus Duvivier's wider disenchantment with the French film industry in the mid-1960s. His response to a questionnaire in 1965 from *Cahiers du cinéma* was bitter:

> En France, le producteur est assujetti au distributeur [...] le distributeur n'attache de valeur qu'au succès du moment [...] Résultat: voyez le tableau des films français en préparation ou en cours de tournage. Abandon de toute ambition, vulgarité, bassesse. Pas un seul grand projet en vue [...] J'ai lutté pour tenter de réaliser des films dignes d'intérêt au stade du projet. Je n'ai, pour ainsi dire, jamais pu réaliser un film qui m'était cher. Depuis ces dernières années notamment, je n'ai pu résoudre qu'à tourner des sujets imposés (Je dis imposés parce que c'était eux ou rien).[39] (Duvivier 1965: 31)

---

39 'In France, the producer is subservient to the distributor [...] the distributor is only interested in immediate success [...] Result: just look at the list of French films presently being shot or about to be made. They are bereft of ambition, vulgar, contemptible. Not a single important subject in sight [...]

Duvivier is talking about the likes of *La Femme et le pantin* and *La Chambre ardente* here. Perhaps he is being canny, blaming his decline on risk-averse producers who commission safe projects and 'impose' particular casting choices. Duvivier clearly felt out of place in French 1960s film culture, a fact made even starker by the number of film projects that he was unable to get off the ground at this time (see Bonnefille 2002: 232–49). For a director who had never been out of work for more than a few months at a time since *Haceldama* in 1919, the four-year lull between *Chair de poule* and *Diaboliquement vôtre* was a time of disappointment and industry neglect.[40]

Nevertheless, there is much to admire in Duvivier's late style. There is the skilful recycling of American tropes within the French *noir* system in *L'Homme à l'imperméable* and *Chair de poule*, the engagement with French youth culture in *La Femme et le pantin* and *Boulevard*, and the continued exploration of gender politics in *Pot-Bouille* and *La Chambre ardente*. Repressed historical events resurge from the past in *Marie-Octobre* and *Diaboliquement vôtre* (despite Duvivier's political agnosticism, both films say a great deal about the Occupation and the Algerian war at a time when French cinema scrupulously ignored the traumatic aftermath of these conflicts).

Many of these films feature the biggest French stars of the day, and Duvivier oftens twists the stardom of Bardot, Darrieux, Delon, Fernandel, and Philipe to conform to his own particular thematic concerns. In *La Femme et le pantin*, Duvivier does not seem interested in the Bardot myth. He does not wish to duplicate the sexual frankness of *Et Dieu…créa la femme*, but revels instead in the gradual decline and humiliation of Diaz (as triggered by Bardot). Likewise, the normally virile and dominant Delon is bed-ridden in *Diaboliquement vôtre*, tangled up in a plot over which he has no control. Such choices show how Duvivier sought to critique and contravene notions of stardom and agency.

François Truffaut (1954: 26) wrote in 'Une certaine tendance' that '[J]e ne puis croire à la coexistence pacifique de la Tradition de la

> I have struggled to make films that are worthy of interest from the outset. But I have not managed to make a film that was important to me. Particularly over recent years, I have only been able to shoot subjects imposed upon me (I say imposed, because it was these films or nothing).'

40 For more information on Duvivier's unfinished and unrealised projects between 1963 and 1967, see Bonnefille (2002b: 205–9).

Qualité et d'un cinéma d'auteurs.'[41] What I have suggested in this chapter, and indeed throughout this book, is that Duvivier *was* able to bridge the seemingly yawning chasm between auteur and tradition-of-quality cinema, between deeply personal, thematically consistent films and commercially motivated, audience-pleasing output.

References

Aubriant, M. (1963), '*Chair de poule*', *Paris-Presse*, 16 November, np.
Bardot, B. (1996), *Initiales B.B.*, Paris, Grasset and Fasquelle.
Bean, R. (1961), '*Boulevard*', *Films and Filming*, 7:10, p. 27.
Bonnefille, E. (2002), *Julien Duvivier: Le Mal aimant du cinéma français*, vol. 2, Paris, Harmattan.
Borger, L. (1998), 'Genius Is Just a Word', *Sight and Sound*, September, pp. 28–31.
Burch, N. and G. Sellier (1996), *La Drôle de guerre des sexes du cinéma français (1930–1956)*, Paris, Nathan.
Caussou, J.-L. (1957), '*L'Homme à l'imperméable*', *Cinéma*, 57, 17 April, np.
Chirat, R. (1968), *Julien Duvivier*, Lyon, Premier Plan.
Cousins, R. F. (1989), 'Recasting *Zola*: Gérard Philippe's Influence on Duvivier's Adaptation of *Pot-Bouille*', *Literature/Film Quarterly*, 17:3, pp. 142–8.
Crowther, B. (1958), '*Pot Bouille*', *New York Times*, 28 October, available at http://www.nytimes.com/movie/review?res=9B0DE4DB173BE43BBC40 51DFB6678383649EDE, accessed 16 September 2016.
Crowther, B. (1963), '*The Burning Court* [i.e. *La Chambre ardente*]', *New York Times*, 1 August, available at http://www.nytimes.com/movie/review?res= 9805E0D6133DE63BBC4953DFBE668388679EDE&pagewanted=print, accessed 16 September 2016.
de Baroncelli, J. (1963), '*Chair de poule*', *Le Monde*, 20 November, np.
Desrichard, Y. (2001), *Julien Duvivier: Cinquante ans de noirs destins*, Paris, BiFi/Durante.
Doniol-Valcroze, J. (1957), '*L'Homme à l'impermeable*', *France-observateur*, 10 March, np.
Driskell, J. (2012), *Marcel Carné*, Manchester and New York, Manchester University Press.
Duvivier, J. (1957), 'Pourquoi j'ai trahi Zola', *Les Lettres françaises*, 694, 31 October, p. 8.
Duvivier, J. (1965), 'Qui?, Pourquoi?, Comment?: Questionnaire', *Cahiers du cinéma*, 161:2, pp. 31–2.
Duvivier, J. (1996), 'Lettre à François Truffaut', *Positif*, 429, November, p. 96.

41 'I do not believe in the peaceful co-existence of the tradition of quality and an auteur cinema.'

Epstein, M. (1958), 'Comment ils travaillent? Julien Duvivier, *Marie-Octobre*', *La Technique cinématographique*, 189, July, pp. 327–8.
Esposito, M. (2001), '*Jean de Florette*: Patrimoine, the Rural Idyll and the 1980s', in *France on Film: Reflections on Popular French Cinema*, eds. L. Mazdon, London, Wallflower, pp. 11–26.
Garnier, P. (1996), 'La fête à Duvivier de Florence à Paris', *Libération*, 11 November, available at http://next.liberation.fr/culture/1996/11/14/la-fete-a-duvivier-de-florence-a-paris-a-l-occasion-de-plusieurs-retrospectives-et-publications-reev_188577, accessed 12 March 2015.
Garson, C. (1963), '*Chair de poule*', *L'Aurore*, 15 November, np.
Hawker, P. (2000), 'Jean-Pierre Léaud: Unbearable Lightness', *Senses of Cinema*, 8, available at http://sensesofcinema.com/2000/jean-pierre-leaud/lightness, accessed 12 March 2015.
Jeander (1959), '*La Femme et le le pantin*', *Libération*, 19 February, np.
Langlois, H. (2014), *Ecrits de cinéma*, Paris, Flammarion.
Leahy, S. (2002), 'Bardot and Dance: Representing the Real?', *French Cultural Studies* 13:37, pp. 49–64.
Leenhardt, R. (1935), '*Encore Le Mouchard et La Bandera*', *Esprit*, November, pp. 331–2.
Leprohon, P. (1968), *Julien Duvivier*, Paris, Avant-Scene/Collection Anthologie du Cinéma.
Lorcey, J. (1990), *Fernandel*, Paris, Ramsay.
Marcorelles, L. (1959), '*Pure essence* [review of *La Femme et le pantin*]', *Cahiers du cinéma*, 94, April, pp. 56–7.
Marquet, J.-P. (1952), 'D'un Duvivier à Jean Vigo', *Positif*, 2, p. 57.
Monod, M. (1957), '*Pot Bouille*: Zola sans Zola', *Les Lettres françaises*, 693, 24–30, p. 6.
Pillard, T. (2015), 'Questioning a Switch in Genres: Fernandel's Dramatic Films in the 1950s', *Contemporary French and Francophone Studies*, 19:1, pp. 76–89.
Ross, K. (1995), *Fast Cars, Clean Bodies: Decolonization and the Ordering of French Culture*, Cambridge, Mass., and London, MIT Press.
Sanders, G. (1960), *Memoirs of a Professional Cad*, London, G. P. Putnam's Sons.
Schilt, T. (2011), *François Ozon*, Urbana, University of Illinois Press.
Truffaut, F. (1957a), '*L'Homme à l'imperméable*', *Arts*, 13 March, np.
Truffaut, F. (1957b), '*Une parodie de Gervaise* [review of *Pot-Bouille*]', *Cahiers du cinéma*, 77, December, p. 58.
Truffaut, F. (1975), *Les Films de ma vie*, Paris, Flammarion.
Truffaut, F. (1954), 'Une certaine tendance du cinéma français', *Cahiers du cinéma*, 31 January, pp. 15–28.
Vincendeau, G. (2013), *Brigitte Bardot*, London, BFI/Palgrave.
Vinneuil, F. (1935), '*La Bandera*', *Action française*, 26 September, p. 332.
Zola, E. (1961), *Pot-Bouille*, Lausanne, Éditions Rencontre.

Conclusion

Julien Duvivier died on 29 October 1967, four weeks after shooting ended on *Diaboliquement vôtre*. Driving to his home in the sixteenth arrondissement of Paris, he suffered a heart attack behind the wheel, clipped an oncoming car, and smashed into a tree. He died instantly.

It is impossible to watch *Diaboliquement vôtre* now, with its car-accident opening and screeching tyres, without considering Duvivier's final moments. Like most films in the second half of Duvivier's career, the film garnered a lukewarm response from the press; many noted that it would be soon forgotten. Others criticised its rushed, uncertain ending (not realising that Duvivier was still editing the film when he died). The film was eventually finished by other hands; *Diaboliquement vôtre* remains the most 'impure' Duvivier film for that reason. Soon, numerous industry colleagues began to pen heartfelt obituaries and personal memories for newspapers and trade journals. Maurice Bessy (1967: 4) wrote in *Le Film français* that 'tu étais un visuel, un chercheur, un merveilleux conteur d'histoires'.[42] While many obituaries reprinted Henri Jeanson's appraisal of Duvivier from back in 1937 ('il apprenait son métier "comme un mécano"') (3),[43] Jean Renoir (1967: 2) reminded people that 'ce grand technicien, ce rigoriste, était un poète'.[44] The headline in *La Tribune de Genève* on 31 October read 'Julien Duvivier: le plus

---

42 'you had vision, you sought things out, you were a marvellous story-teller'.
43 'he learnt his trade like a mechanic would'.
44 'this rigorous technician was also a poet'.

américain des cinéastes français'.⁴⁵ *Le Figaro* (Anon. 1967) contained perhaps the best appraisal of the man and his style:

> A l'heure où le goût de la qualité semble considéré comme vertu mineure, où l'ignorance de la 'manière de faire' se cache derrière une pseudo-'vérité', le Syndicat des techniciens de la production cinématographique et sa section 'réalisateurs' saluent avec déférence le très grand maître technicien du cinéma mondial que fut Julien Duvivier.⁴⁶

And so we return, once more, at the end of the Duvivier story, to a familiar set of dichotomies – poetry and technique, visual flourish and narrative rigour, an 'American' in France and a European in Hollywood, and quality and truthfulness. These are all appropriate descriptions for an auteur who combined technical know-how with a balanced, consistent storytelling style. Some of those skills were honed in Hollywood, but that *savoir-faire* had been there all along, from *Haceldama* to *L'Homme à l'Hispano* to *Le Paquebot Tenacity*, before Duvivier had even set foot on the MGM lot. When he came back from America, Duvivier was proud to be a *mécano*, often achieving art without deliberately seeking it.

Duvivier's reputation continues to improve. He embodies the professionalism, versatility, and 'keep on working' philosophy to which many filmmakers around the world continue to aspire. And he lives on still. He has influenced Stephen Sondheim – 'I love Duvivier's stuff; it's always one inch short of opera [...] it's romantic melodrama' (Swayne 2005: 163). He is there in the list of people the 'director wishes to thank' on the end credits of *Blancanieves*, a 2012 Spanish black-and-white, silent version of Snow White. He is invoked by the singer Morrissey, who recalled in an interview how affected he was by the poetry of *Boulevard* (Gobbo 2015). In 2015, sixty-nine years after rejecting the chance to show the film in competition, the Cannes Film Festival re-released a new 2K digital print of *Panique*.

The purpose of this book has been to argue that Duvivier is a giant of classic French cinema with a career spanning key moments

---

45 'Julien Duvivier: the most American of French directors'.
46 'At a time when an appreciation of quality is considered a somewhat minor virtue, and when an ignorance of "doing things right" hides behind a sort of pseudo-truth, the Directors branch of the Film Production Technicians Union would like to respectfully pay tribute to Julien Duvivier, the great technical master of world cinema.'

of French film history. There are many impressive aspects of this story: its sheer longevity (1919 to 1967); its serendipitous dovetailing with the profound technological, cultural, and artistic leaps that were taking place in French cinema during that period (the conversion from silent to sound film in 1929–30; the development of the poetic realist aesthetic in the mid-to late-1930s; the industry exodus to Hollywood in the 1940s; the return to France and a much-changed film landscape in the 1950s and 1960s; and the transition to colour); its internationalism (working with the studio systems of Germany, Italy, Spain, England, and Czechoslovakia, and filming on location in such far-flung places as Quebec, Algeria, Majorca, and the Alps); and the wealth of actors he was able to call upon (from Baur to Bardot, via Darrieux and Delon, Fernandel and Fonda).

While Duvivier did not engage directly with the seismic transformations of French society, we should not confuse the apolitical with the apathetic. His films hummed rather than loudhailed their political allegiances, and were sensitive to historical and social change. *Marie-Octobre*, for instance, skewed a state-endorsed discourse of a largely consensual collective memory of the war and the abiding stranglehold of the glorious Resistance myth, while Duvivier's forays into costume drama (*Anna Karenina*, *Pot-Bouille*) allowed contemporary discussions about marriage and the position of women in post-war France to be refracted through its Second Empire settings. *Boulevard* and *Chair de poule* featured young Parisian working-class men seemingly being left behind by the economic prosperity of the *trente glorieuses*; thirty years earlier, Duvivier had injected his populist films (such as *Le Paqubot Tenacity* and *La Belle équipe*) with similar 'types'. Thus, the book has engaged with key debates in French film studies, notably auteurism, stardom, genre, and questions of the national and international, and as well as Duvivier's historical range and political inflections.

Duvivier's existential pessimism and misanthropy manifested thematically across many of his films. His is a paranoiac cinema – fear of crowds, fear of women, fear of the group, fear of the unknown. He returned again and again to the notion of the crowd dynamic and to individuals being threatened, humiliated, or overrun by the group. This is most evident in his 1930s work, but it is a central aspect of films as diverse as *Panique*, *Marie-Octobre*, and *Diaboliquement vôtre*. Also fundamental to Duvivier's body of work is the idea that the male individual or the bonded male group could often be undone by a scheming or meddling woman. In the early part of Duvivier's career, such women were caricatured as grasping and unloving (both versions of *Poil de carotte*, *David Golder* and *Les Cinq gentlemen maudits*), but they became progressively more destructive (Romance in *La Belle équipe* and *Panique*, and Delorme in *Voici le temps des assassins*). Duvivier complicated his gender politics even further in *Au royaume des cieux* and *La Chambre ardente* by having supposedly nurturing and maternal figures (school director, nurse) play cruel, heartless antagonists. This is why Duvivier's cinema is pessimistic, bleak, dark, and misanthropic – the individual is not only prone to attack from faceless external forces (*La Divine croisière*, *La Bandera*, *The Impostor*) but also more often than not is susceptible to ruthless assaults from people closest to them.

What I have been arguing throughout this book is that Duvivier's auteur status is secure, and definitive. Andrew Sarris (1996: 39) once wrote that the three premises of the auteur theory 'may be visualised as three concentric circles: the outer circle as technique, the middle circle as personal style, and the inner circle as interior meaning'. Technique, personal style, and interior meaning appear as recurring principles across Duvivier's cinema, from *Au bonheur des dames* to *Pot-Bouille*, from *La Tête d'un homme* to *Tales of Manhattan*. That is why I have sought to drive a wedge between Duvivier and the 1930s, to unmoor him from the restrictive anchor points of *Pépé le Moko* and *La Belle équipe*, and to open his career up for inspection. Films such as *Voici le temps des assassins*, *La Chambre ardente*, and *Chair de poule* are delirious genre films, still pyrite-flecked with surprises and shocks. All of the above are visually distinctive films that tell us a great deal about fin-de-siècle Paris, or cast a foreigner's eye on the class and race iniquities of America, or signpost how the *policier* was slowly mutating into poetic realism and psychological *noir*.

Duvivier's auteur credentials are buttressed by a technical and visual prowess. Plot points, character archetypes, sonic design, and *mise en scène* all gel. We need only to watch the 'unhappy' ending of *La Belle équipe* or notice how his camera circles Catherine Rouvel's ruthless Maria in *Chair de poule* to see that this was a director in total control of his craft. From the use of double exposure in *Le Tourbillon de Paris* to express the tension between the inner thoughts and outward appearances of Lil Dagover's tortured opera singer to the 'shaky-cam' bar brawl scene in *Boulevard*, when Jean-Pierre Léaud staggers from one side of the room to the other in an out-of-focus point-of-view shot, Duvivier was always innovating, pushing at the limits of what cinema could achieve.

Finally, then, this is Duvivier talking about *Le Petit monde de Don Camillo*, but he might just as well have been talking about his whole career: 'On s'est demandé souvent la recette de Julien Duvivier. Elle est là: d'être disponible. De réaliser chaque fois le film que l'on attend de lui. D'être sensible au grands courants de son époque [...] De ne pas se démoder. De ne pas vieillir' (Aubriant 1952: 12).[47] I hope I have shown that Duvivier and his films are all of these things: open, adept, professional, sensitive, relevant, and, above all, alive.

References

Anon. (1967), 'Julien Duvivier', *Le Figaro*, 7 November, np.

Aubriant, M. (1952), 'Julien Duvivier veut tuer Don Camillo', *Cinémonde*, 956, 28 November, p. 12.

Bessy, M. (1967), 'Julien Duvivier', *Le Film français*, 1216, 3 November, p. 4.

Gobbo, S. (2015), 'Morrissey, éternel "charming man"', *L'Hebdo*, 1 October, available at http://www.hebdo.ch/hebdo/culture/detail/morrissey-%C3%A9ternel-%C2%ABcharming-man%C2%BB, accessed 1 November 2015.

Jeanson, H. (1937), 'Julien Duvivier d'Antoine au *Carnet de bal*', *Pour vous*, 441, 29 April, p. 3.

Renoir, J. (1967), 'Duvivier, ce professionnel', *Le Figaro littéraire*, 6 November, p. 2.

Sarris, A. (1996), *The American Cinema: Directors and Directions 1929–1968*, New York, Da Capo Press.

Swayne, S. (2005), *How Sondheim Found His Sound*, Ann Arbor, University of Michigan Press.

---

47 'People have often asked what the Julien Duvivier formula is. Here it is: to be open. To direct the film that is expected of you each time. To be sensitive to the main trends of the period [...] To not go out of fashion. To not get old.'

Filmography

Direction is by Julien Duvivier unless otherwise indicated and only completed, major projects are included. English-language titles of French films are in brackets. Length for silent films is approximate. All films are in black and white except for *La Femme et le pantin* and *Diaboliquement vôtre*.

Silent films

Haceldama ou le prix du sang (1919)
    75 min.
    Production: Julien Duvivier for Burdigala Film.
    Screenplay: Julien Duvivier.
    Photography: Gaston Aron, Julien Duvivier.
    Editor: Julien Duvivier.
    Principal actors: Séverin Mars, Camille Bert, Suzy Milé, Yvonne Brionne.

Les Roquevillard (1921–2)
    95 min.
    Production: Julien Duvivier for Célor Films, Société Régionale de Cinématographie, Films Julien Duvivier.
    Screenplay: Julien Duvivier.
    Adaptation: Based on the novel *Les Roquevillard* by Henri Bordeaux (1906).
    Photography: Paul Castanet, Albert Cohendy.
    Principal actors: Jeanne Desclos, Maxime Desjardins, Georges Melchior, Edmond van Daële.

L'Ouragan sur la montagne (The Hurricane on the Mountain) (1922)
90 min.
Production: Geneva Films (Zurich), Célor Films, Société Régionale de Cinématographie.
Screenplay: Julien Duvivier, Philippe Amiguet.
Photography: Gaston Haon.
Principal actors: Gaston Jacquet, Camille Beuve, Lotte Loring, Marie Pillar.

Le Reflet de Claude Mercœur (The Reflection of Claude Mercœur) (1923)
92 min.
Production: Julien Duvivier for Films Julien Duvivier, Célor Films, Pathé Consortium.
Screenplay: Julien Duvivier.
Adaptation: Based on the novel *Le Reflet de Claude Mercœur* by Frédéric Boutet (1921).
Photography: Paul Thomas Parguel.
Set: Gaston David.
Principal actors: Gaston Jacquet, Maud Richard, Camille Beuve, Jean Prévost.

Cœurs farouches (1923)
92 min.
Production: Julien Duvivier for Célor Films.
Screenplay: Julien Duvivier with the collaboration of Asté Esbarbès.
Principal actors: Desdemona Mazza, Gaston Jacquet, Rolla Norman, Jean Lorette.

Credo ou la tragédie de Lourdes (1924)
97 min.
Production: Julien Duvivier for Films Julien Duvivier, Célor Films.
Screenplay: Julien Duvivier.
Adaptation: Based on an idea of Georges d'Esparbes.
Photography: Paul Thomas.
Set: Gaston David.
Principal actors: Henry Krauss, Gaston Jacquet, Rolla Normand, Angele Decori.

La Machine à refaire la vie (A Machine for Recreating Life) (1924)
180 min.
Screenplay: Julien Duvivier with Henri Lepage.

L'Œuvre immortelle (1924)
  Production: Hippolyte de Kenpeneer pour Belga Films (Belgium).
  Screenplay: Julien Duvivier, Maurice Widy.
  Adaptation: Julien Duvivier, from a short story, *L'Horrible Expérience*, by Maurice Widy.
  Photography: Henri Barreyre.
  Principal actors: Suzanne Christy, Yvonne Willy, Jacques van Hoven, Jimmy O'Kelly.

L'Abbé Constantin (1925)
  97 min.
  Assistant director: Raoul Kofler.
  Production: Marcel Vandal and Charles Delac for Le Film d'Art.
  Screenplay: Julien Duvivier.
  Adaptation: Based on a novel by Ludovic Halévy (1882) and a play by Pierre Decourcelle and Hector Crémieux (1887).
  Photography: Fanzli Walter, André Dantan.
  Set: Fernand Delattre.
  Principal actors: Jean Coquelin, Georges Lannes, Geneviève Cargèse, Pierre Stephen.

Poil de carotte (The Red Head) (1925)
  108 min.
  Assistant director: Henri Lepage.
  Production: Marcel Vandal and Charles Delac for Le Film d'Art, Majestic Films, Films Legrand.
  Screenplay: Julien Duvivier, Jacques Feyder.
  Adaptation: Based on a novel by Jules Renard (1894).
  Photography: Ganzli Walter, André Dantan.
  Set: Fernand Delattre.
  Principal actors: Henry Krauss, André Heuzé, Fabien Haziza, Charlotte Barbier-Krauss.

L'Homme à l'Hispano (1926)
  145 min.
  Production: Marcel Vandal and Charles Delac for Le Film d'Art.
  Screenplay: René Hervil.
  Adaptation: Based on a novel by Pierre Frondaie (1925).
  Photography: Armand Thirard, Émile Pierre.
  Set: Fernand Delattre.
  Principal actors: Huguette Duflos, Georges Galli, Acho Chakatouny, Madeleine Rodrigue.

L'Agonie de Jérusalem (1927)
  97 min.
  Production: Marcel Vandal and Charles Delac for Le Film d'Art.
  Screenplay: Julien Duvivier.
  Photography: René Guichard, Émile Pierre, Armand Thirard.
  Set: Fernand Delattre.
  Principal actors: Edmond van Daël, Maurice Schutz, Marguerite Madys, Gaston Jacquet.

Le Mariage de Mademoiselle Beulemans (The Marriage of Mademoiselle Beulemans) (1927)
  87 min.
  Production: Marcel Vandal and Charles Delac for Le Film d'Art.
  Screenplay: Julien Duvivier.
  Adaptation: Based on a play by Jean-François (Frantz) Fonson and Fernand Wicheler (1908).
  Photography: René Guychard, Armand Thirard.
  Set: Fernand Delattre.
  Principal actors: Andrée Brabant, Jean Dehelly, Gustave Libeau, Suzanne Christy.

Le Mystère de la Tour Eiffel (1927)
  129 min.
  Production: Marcel Vandal and Charles Delac for Le Film d'Art.
  Screenplay: Julien Duvivier, Alfred Machard.
  Photography: René Guychard, Armand Thirard.
  Set: Fernand Delattre.
  Principal actors: Félicien Tramel, Gaston Jacquet, Régine Bouet, Jean Diener.

Le Tourbillon de Paris (The Maelstrom of Paris) (1928)
  87 min.
  Assistant director: André Berthomieu.
  Production: Marcel Vandal and Charles Delac for Le Film d'Art, Wengeroff Films.
  Screenplay: Julien Duvivier.
  Adaptation: Based on the novel *La Sarrazine* by Germaine Acremant (1926).
  Photography: André Dantan, René Guychard.
  Set: Fernand Delattre.
  Editor: Marthe Poncin.
  Principal actors: Lil Dagover, Gaston Jacquet, Léon Bary, Hubert Daix.

La Divine croisière (The Divine Voyage) (1929)
136 min.
Assistant director: Michel Bernheim.
Production: Marcel Vandal and Charles Delac for Le Film d'Art.
Screenplay: Julien Duvivier.
Photography: André Dantan, René Guychard, Armand Thirard.
Set: Christian-Jaque.
Principal actors: Line Noro, Henry Krauss, Suzanne Christy, Jean Murat.

La Vie miraculeuse de Thérèse Martin (The Miraculous Life of Teresa of Lisieux) (1929)
124 min.
Production: Marcel Vandal and Charles Delac for Le Films d'Art.
Screenplay: Julien Duvivier.
Adaptation: Inspired by *L'Histoire d'une âme de Thérèse de Lisieux* (1895).
Photography: René Guychard, Armand Thirard.
Set: Christian-Jaque.
Principal actors: Simone Bourday, André Marnay, François Viguier, Janine Borelli.

Maman Colibri (Mother Hummingbird) (1929)
89 min.
Production: Marcel Vandal and Charles Delac for Le Films d'Art, UFA.
Screenplay: Noël Renard, Julien Duvivier.
Adaptation: Based on a play by Henri Bataille (1904).
Photography: Gaston Aron, René Guychard, Armand Thirard.
Set: Christian-Jaque.
Principal actors: Maria Jacobini, Jean Dax, Jean-Paul de Baëre, Frank Lederer.

Au Bonheur des dames (1930)
112 min.
Production: Marcel Vandal and Charles Delac for Le Films d'Art, UFA.
Screenplay: Noël Renard, Julien Duvivier.
Adaptation: Based on a novel by Émile Zola (1883).
Photography: René Guychard, Armand Thirard, Émile Pierre, André Dantan.
Set: Christian-Jaque, Fernand Delattre, Percy Day.
Principal actors: Dita Parlo, Pierre de Guinguand, Armand Bour, Adolphe Candé.

Sound films

David Golder (1930)
 86 min.
 Production: Marcel Vandal and Charles Delac for Le Film d'Art, La Société Générale de Cinématographie.
 Screenplay: Julien Duvivier.
 Adaptation: Based on a novel by Irène Némirovsky (1929).
 Photography: Georges Périnal, Armand Thirard, Ganzli Walter.
 Set: Lazare Meerson.
 Editor: Jean Feyte.
 Principal actors: Harry Baur, Paule Andral, Jackie Monnier, Gaston Jacquet.

Les Cinq gentlemen maudits (The Five Accursed Gentlemen) (1931)
 85 min.
 Production: Marcel Vandal and Charles Delac for Le Film d'Art, La Société Générale de Cinématographie.
 Screenplay: Julien Duvivier.
 Adaptation: Based on a novel by André Reuzé (1931).
 Photography: Armand Thirard, René Moreau.
 Set: Lazare Meerson.
 Editors: Marthe Poncin, Lily Jumel.
 Principal actors: Harry Baur, René Lefèvre, Robert Le Vigan, Georges Péclet.

Allô Berlin? Ici Paris! (Hello Berlin, Here's Paris) (1932)
 89 min.
 Production: Frank Clifford.
 Adaptation: Based on a novel by Rolf E. Vanloo (1931).
 Photography: Reimar Kuntze, Heinrich Balasch, Max Brinck.
 Set: Eric Czerwonsky.
 Principal actors: Germaine Aussey, Josette Day, Wolfgang Klein, Charles Redgie.

Poil de carotte (The Red Head) (1932)
 80 min.
 Production: Marcel Vandal and Charles Delac for Le Film d'Art.
 Screenplay: Julien Duvivier.
 Adaptation: Based on the novel (1894) and the play *La Bigote* (1909), by Jules Renard.
 Photography: Armand Thirard, Émile Monniot.

Set: Lucien Aguettant, Lucien Carré.
Editors: Marthe Poncin, Jean Feyte, Jean-Paul Le Chanois.
Principal actors: Harry Baur, Robert Lynen, Catherine Fonteney, Christiane Dor.

La Tête d'un homme (A Man's Neck) (1932)
102 min.
Assistant directors: Gilbert de Knyff, Pierre Calmann.
Production: Marcel Vandal and Charles Delac for Le Film d'Art.
Screenplay: Louis Delaprée, Julien Duvivier, Pierre Calmann.
Adaptation: Based on a novel by Georges Simenon (1931).
Photography: Armand Thirard, Émile Pierre.
Set: Georges Wakhévitch.
Editor: Marthe Bassi [Marthe Poncin].
Principal actors: Harry Baur, Gina Manès, Valery Inkijinoff, Gaston Jacquet.

Le Petit roi (The Little King) (1933)
90 min.
Production: Marcel Vandal and Charles Delac for Le Film d'Art.
Screenplay: Julien Duvivier.
Adaptation: Based on a novel by André Lichtenberger (1910).
Photography: Armand Thirard, Joseph Barth.
Set: Lucien Aguettand.
Editor: Marthe Poncin.
Principal actors: Robert Lynen, Arlette Marchal, Béatrice Bretty, Paul Andrale.

Le Paquebot Tenacity (The SS *Tenacity*) (1934)
85 min.
Production: Marcel Vandal and Charles Delac for Le Film d'Art.
Screenplay: Charles Vildrac, Julien Duvivier.
Adaptation: Based on a play by Charles Vildrac (1920).
Photography: Nicholas Hayer, Armand Thirard, Christian Matras, Willy.
Set: Jacques Krauss.
Editor: Marthe Poncin.
Principal actors: Marie Glory, Albert Préjean, Hubert Prélier, Pierre Laurel.

Maria Chapdelaine (The Naked Heart) (1934)
75 min.

Production: René Pignières, Léon Beytout, Alex Nalpas (for La Société Nouvelle de Cinématographie).
Screenplay: Julien Duvivier.
Adaptation: Based on the novel of the same name by Louis Hémon (1913).
Photography: Jules Krüger, Armand Thirard, Georges Périnal.
Set: Jacques Krauss.
Editors: Marthe Poncin, Claude Ibéria.
Principal actors: Madeleine Renaud, Jean Gabin, Jean-Pierre Aumont, Suzanne Desprès.

Golgotha (Behold the Man) (1935)
96 min.
Production: Ayres d'Aguiar for Ichtys Films Union (Krikorian).
Screenplay: Julien Duvivier and Joseph Reymond.
Adaptation: Based on a book by Joseph Reymond (1934).
Photography: Jules Krüger.
Set: Jean Perrier.
Editor: Marthe Poncin.
Principal actors: Robert Le Vigan, Harry Baur, Jean Gabin, Edwige Feuillère.

La Bandera (Escape from Yesterday) (1935)
102 min.
Production: René Pignières, Léon Beytout, André Gargour (for La Société Nouvelle de Cinématographie).
Screenplay: Charles Spaak, Julien Duvivier.
Adaptation: Based on a novel by Pierre Mac Orlan (1931).
Photography: Jules Krüger.
Set: Jacques Krauss.
Editor: Marthe Poncin.
Principal actors: Jean Gabin, Annabella, Viviane Romance, Robert Le Vigan.

Le Golem (The Golem; The Legend of Prague; The Man of Stone) (1936)
102 min.
Production: Charles Philipp, Frank Kassler (for A-B Films), Barrandov, Metropolis.
Screenplay: Julien Duvivier, André-Paul Antoine, Josef Kodicek.
Adaptation: Based on a novel by Gustav Meyrink (1914).
Photography: Jan Stallich, Vaclav Vich.

Set: André Andreiev, Stepan Kopecky.
Editor: Jiri Slavicek.
Principal actors: Harry Baur, Ferdinand Hart, Germaine Aussey, Roger Karl.

La Belle équipe (They Were Five) (1936)
94 min.
Production: Arys Nissotti (for Ciné-Arys Productions).
Screenplay: Charles Spaak, Julien Duvivier.
Photography: Jules Krüger.
Set: Jacques Krauss.
Editor: Marthe Poncin.
Principal actors: Jean Gabin, Viviane Romance, Charles Vanel, Aimos.

L'Homme du jour (The Man of the Hour) (1936)
94 min.
Production: Julien Duvivier (for Les Films Maurice).
Screenplay: Charles Spaak, Julien Duvivier, Charles Vildrac.
Photography: Roger Hubert.
Set: Jacques Krauss.
Editor: Marthe Poncin.
Principal actors: Maurice Chevalier, Elvire Popesco, Robert Lynen, Josette Day.

Pépé le Moko (1937)
88 min.
Production: Robert and Raymond Hakim (for Paris Film Production).
Screenplay: Ashelbé [Henry La Barthe], Julien Duvivier, Jacques Constant.
Adaptation: Based on a novel by Ashelbé (1931).
Photography: Jules Krüger.
Set: Jacques Krauss.
Editor: Marguerite Beaugé.
Principal actors: Jean Gabin, Mireille Balin, Lucas Gridoux, Line Noro.

Un Carnet de bal (Life Dances On; Dance Program; Dance of Life) (1937)
102 min.
Production: Jean Lévy-Strauss (for Production Sigma Films), Pierre Frogerais.
Screenplay: Julien Duvivier.

Adaptation: Based on the play *Le Pêcheur d'ombre* by Jean Sarment (1921).
Photography: Michel Kelber.
Set: Serge Pimenoff, Jean Douarinou.
Editor: André Versein.
Principal actors: Marie Bell, Harry Baur, Pierre Blanchar, Raimu.

Marie Antoinette (1938) (uncredited direction)
160 min.
Production: MGM.
Screenplay: Claudine West, Donald Ogden Stewart, Ernest Vajda, Julien Duvivier, Francis Scott Fitzgerald.
Adaptation: Based on a book by Stefan Zweig (1932).
Photography: William Daniels.
Set: Cédric Gibbons.
Editor: Slvako Vorkapitch.
Principal actors: Norma Shearer, Tyrone Power, John Barrymore, Robert Morley.

The Great Waltz (French title: *Toute la ville danse*) (1938)
103 min.
Production: MGM.
Screenplay: Walter Reisch, Samuel Hoffenstein, Gottfried Reinhardt, Vicky Baum.
Adaptation: Based on an original story by Gottfried Reinhardt (1934) and a musical comedy by Oscar Hammerstein II (1934).
Photography: Joseph Ruttenberg.
Set: Cedric Gibbons.
Editor: Tom Held.
Principal actors: Fernand Gravey, Luise Rainer, Miliza Korjus, Lionel Atwill.

La Fin du jour (The End of the Day) (1939)
114 min.
Production: Arys Nissotti, Régina, Francinex.
Screenplay: Charles Spaak, Julien Duvivier.
Photography: Christian Matras, Armand Thirard, Robert Juillard, Ernest Bourreaud.
Set: Jacques Krauss.
Editor: Marthe Poncin.
Principal actors: Michel Simon, Victor Francen, Louis Jouvet, Madeleine Ozeray.

La Charrette fantôme (The Phantom Wagon) (1939)
109 min.
 Production: Paul Graetz (for Transcontinental Films), Columbia Pictures.
 Screenplay: Julien Duvivier.
 Adaptation: Based on the novel *Körkarlen* (a.k.a. *Le Charretier de la mort*), by Selma Lagerlöf (1912).
 Photography: Jules Krüger.
 Set: Jacques Krauss.
 Editor: Jean Feyte.
 Principal actors: Pierre Fresnay, Marie Bell, Micheline Francey, Louis Jouvet.

Untel père et fils (The Heart of a Nation) (1940)
111 min.
 Production: Julien Duvivier, Paul Graetz (for Transcontinental Films).
 Screenplay: Charles Spaak, Marcel Achard, Julien Duvivier.
 Photography: Jules Krüger.
 Set: Guy de Gastyne, Paul Louis Boutié.
 Editor: Marthe Poncin.
 Principal actors: Lucien Nat, Raimu, Louis Jouvet, Michèle Morgan.

Lydia (1941)
91 min.
 Production: Alexander Korda.
 Screenplay: Ben Hecht, Samuel Hoffenstein, André De Toth.
 Photography: Lee Garmes.
 Set: Vincent Korda, Jack Okey.
 Editor: William Hornbeck.
 Principal actors: Merle Oberon, Joseph Cotten, Alan Marshal, Edna May Olivier.

Tales of Manhattan (French title: *Six destins*) (1942)
122 min.
 Production: Borris Morros, S. P. Eagle [Sam Spiegel], 20th Century Fox.
 Screenplay: Ben Hecht, David Ogden Smith, Alan Campbell.
 Photography: Joseph Walker.
 Set: Richard Day.
 Editor: Robert Bischoff.
 Principal actors: Charles Boyer, Rita Hayworth, Thomas Mitchell, Edward G. Robinson, Henry Fonda.

Flesh and Fantasy (French title: *Obsessions*) (1943)
  98 min.
  Production: Charles Boyer, Julien Duvivier for Universal.
  Screenplay: Ernest Pascal, Samuel Hoffenstein, Ellis Saint-Joseph, Laszlo Vadnay.
  Adaptation: Based on stories by Ellis Saint-Joseph (first episode, 1943), by Oscar Wilde (*Lord Arthur Saville's Crime*, 1891, second episode), and by Laszlo Vadnay (third episode, 1943).
  Photography: Paul Ivano, Stanley Cortez.
  Set: Robert Boyle.
  Editor: Arthur Hilton.
  Principal actors: Edward G. Robinson, Charles Boyer, Robert Benchley, David Hoffman.

Destiny (1944) (uncredited direction)
  65 min.
  Directors: Reginald Le Borg, Julien Duvivier (not credited).
  Production: Howard Benedict for Universal.
  Screenplay: Roy Chanslor, Ernest Pascal.
  Photography: Paul Ivano, George Robinson.
  Set: Victor Gangelin, Russel A. Gausman.
  Editor: Paul Landres.
  Principal actors: Gloria Jean, Alan Curtis, Frank Craven, Grace McDonald.

The Impostor (French title: *L'Imposteur*) (1944)
  87 min.
  Production: Julien Duvivier for Universal.
  Screenplay: Julien Duvivier.
  Photography: Paul Ivano.
  Set: Russel A. Gausman, Edward R. Robinson.
  Editor: Paul Landres.
  Principal actors: Jean Gabin, Richard Whorf, Allyn Joslyn, Ellen Drew.

Panique (Panic) (1946)
  102 min.
  Production: Pierre O'Connell for Filmsonor.
  Screenplay: Julien Duvivier, Charles Spaak.
  Adaptation: Based on the novel *Les Fiançailles de M. Hire* by Georges Simenon (1933).
  Photography: Nicolas Hayer.
  Set: Serge Piménoff.

Editor: Marthe Poncin.
Principal actors: Michel Simon, Viviane Romance, Paul Bernard, Charles Dorat.

Anna Karenina (1948)
139 min.
Production: Alexander Korda.
Screenplay: Jean Anouilh, Julien Duvivier, Guy Morgan.
Adaptation: Based on the novel *Anna Karenina* (1875–7) by Leo Tolstoy.
Photography: Henri Alekan.
Set: André Andreiev, William Shingleton.
Editor: Russel Lloyd.
Principal actors: Vivien Leigh, Ralph Richardson, Kieron Moore, Sally Ann Howes.

Au royaume des cieux (The Sinners; Woman Hunt) (1949)
108 min.
Production: Arys Nissoti, Julien Duvivier, Pierre O'Connell.
Screenplay: Julien Duvivier.
Photography: Victor Arménise.
Set: René Moulaert.
Editor: Marthe Poncin.
Principal actors: Serge Reggiani, Suzanne Cloutier, Suzy Prim, Liliane Maigné.

Black Jack (Captain Black Jack) (1950)
113 min.
Production: Julien Duvivier, Alexander Salkind.
Screenplay: Charles Spaak, Julien Duvivier.
Adaptation: Based on a novel by Robert Gaillard (1949).
Photography: André Thomas.
Set: Sigfrido Burman, Jean André.
Editors: Margarita de Ochoa, Marthe Poncin.
Principal actors: George Sanders, Herbert Marshall, Patricia Roc, Howard Vernon.

Sous le ciel de Paris (Under the Sky of Paris) (1951)
111 min.
Production: Pierre O'Connell, Arys Nissoti.
Screenplay: Julien Duvivier, René Lefèvre.
Photography: Nicolas Hayer.

Set: René Moulaert.
Editor: André Gaudier.
Principal actors: Brigitte Auber, Christiane Lénier, Jean Brochard, Daniel Ivernel.

Le Petit monde de Don Camillo (The Little World of Don Camillo) (1952)
106 min.
Production: Giuseppe d'Amato for Produzione Giuseppe Amato, Rizzoli Films (Rome), Francinex (Paris).
Screenplay: Julien Duvivier, René Barjavel.
Adaptation: Based on the stories of Giovanni Guareschi (1950).
Photography: Nicolas Hayer.
Set: Virgilio Marchi.
Editor: Maria Rosada.
Principal actors: Fernandel, Gino Cervi, Sylvie, Vera Talchi.

La Fête à Henriette (Holiday for Henrietta) (1952)
120 min.
Production: Georges Lourau, Arys Nissoti, Pierre O'Connell.
Screenplay: Julien Duvivier, Henri Jeanson.
Photography: Roger Hubert.
Set: Jean d'Eaubonne.
Editor: Marthe Poncin.
Principal actors: Dany Robin, Michel Auclair, Hildegarde Kneff, Henri Crémieux.

Le Retour de Don Camillo (The Return of Don Camillo) (1953)
110 min.
Production: Robert Chabert for Francinex-Filmsonor-Ariane (Paris), Guiseppe Amato for Rizzoli Films (Rome).
Screenplay: Julien Duvivier, René Barjavel.
Adaptation: Based on the stories of Giovanni Guareschi (1950).
Photography: Anchise Brizzi.
Set: Virgilio Marchi.
Editor: Marthe Poncin.
Principal actors: Fernandel, Gino Cervi, Paolo Stoppa, Édouard Delmont.

L'Affaire Maurizius (On Trial) (1954)
109 min.
Production: Henry Deutschmeister for Franco-London Film (Paris), Arrigo Colombo for Jolly Films (Rome).

Screenplay: Julien Duvivier.
Adaptation: Based on the novel *Der Fall Maurizius* (1928) by Jacob Wasserman.
Photography: Robert Lefebvre.
Set: Max Douy.
Editor: Marthe Poncin.
Principal actors: Madeleine Robinson, Daniel Gélin, Eleonora Rossi-Drago, Anton Walbrook.

Marianne de ma jeunesse (Marianne of My Youth) (1955)
109 min.
Production: André Daven, Georges Lourau, Pierre O'Connell for Filmsonor, Francinex, Régina, Alfram Films (Paris), Royal Films (Munich).
Screenplay: Julien Duvivier.
Adaptation: Based on the novel *Douloureuse Arcadie* by Peter de Mendelssohn (1935).
Photography: Léonce-Henri Burel.
Set: Jean d'Eaubonne.
Editor: Marthe Poncin.
Principal actors: Marianne Hold, Pierre Vaneck, Isabelle Pia, Gil Vidal.

Voici le temps des assassins (Deadlier than the Male) (1956)
113 min.
Production: René Bézard, Raymond Borderie, Pierre Cabaud, Georges Agiman (no credit).
Screenplay: Julien Duvivier, Maurice Bessy, Charles Dorat.
Photography: Armand Thirard.
Set: Robert Gys.
Editor: Marthe Poncin.
Principal actors: Jean Gabin, Danièle Delorme, Lucienne Bogaert, Gérard Blain.

L'Homme à l'imperméable (The Man in the Raincoat) (1957)
113 min.
Production: Jacques Bar for Cité Films, CTI, CIPRA, Théâtre et Cinéma – Abbey Films (Paris), Monica Films (Rome).
Screenplay: Julien Duvivier, René Barjavel.
Adaptation: Based on the novel *Tiger by the Tail* (1954) by James Hadley Chase.
Photography: Roger Hubert.
Set: Robert Clavel.

Editor: Marthe Poncin.
Principal actors: Fernandel, Jean Rigaux, Judith Magre, Bernard Blier.

Pot-Bouille (Lovers of Paris; The House of Lovers) (1957)
118 min.
Production: Robert and Raymond Hakim for Paris Films Production (Paris).
Screenplay: Julien Duvivier, Léo Joannon, Henri Jeanson.
Adaptation: Based on the novel of the same name by Emile Zola (1882–3).
Photography: Michel Kelber.
Set: Léon Barsacq.
Editor: Madeleine Gug.
Principal actors: Gérard Philipe, Danielle Darrieux, Dany Carrel, Jacques Duby.

La Femme et le pantin (A Woman Like Satan) (1959)
116 min.
Production: Christine Gouze-Rénal for La Société Nouvelle Pathé Cinéma, Gray Films (Paris), Dear Film (Rome).
Screenplay: Jean Aurenche, Albert Valentin, Julien Duvivier.
Adaptation: Based on the novel of the same name by Pierre Loüys (1898).
Photography: Roger Hubert.
Set: Georges Wakhévitch.
Editor: Jacqueline Sadoul.
Principal actors: Brigitte Bardot, Antonio Vilar, Espanita Cortez, Michel Roux.

Marie-Octobre (Secret Meeting) (1959)
102 min.
Production: Lucien Viard for Orex Films, Abbey Films, Doxa Films, Société Française Théâtre et Cinéma.
Screenplay: Julien Duvivier, Jacques Robert.
Adaptation: Based on the novel of the same name by Jacques Robert (1948).
Photography: Robert Lefebvre.
Set: Georges Wakhévitch.
Editor: Marthe Poncin.
Principal actors: Danielle Darrieux, Bernard Blier, Robert Dalban, Paul Frankeur.

La Grande vie (The High Life) (1960)
104 min.
> Production: Kurt Ulrich (Berlin), Alf Teich for Capitole Films, SN Pathé Cinéma (Paris), Novella Films (Rome).
> Screenplay: Richard A. Stemmle, René Barjavel, Julien Duvivier.
> Adaptation: Based on the novel *Das Kunstseine Mädchen: La Jeune Fille en soie artificielle* (1932) by Irmgard Keun.
> Photography: Goran Strindberg.
> Set: Rolf Zehetbauer, Gabriel Pellon, Peter Röhrig.
> Editor: Klaus Eckstein.
> Principal actors: Guiletta Masina, Hanns Messemer, Gert Frobe, Alfred Balthof.

Boulevard (1960)
95 min.
> Production: Lucien Viard for Orex Films.
> Screenplay: Julien Duvivier, René Barjavel.
> Adaptation: Based on the novel of the same name by Robert Sabatier (1956).
> Photography: Roger Dormoy.
> Set: Robert Bouladoux.
> Editor: Paul Cayatte.
> Principal actors: Jean-Pierre Léaud, Magali Noël, Pierre Mondy, Jacques Duby.

La Chambre ardente (The Burning Court) (1962)
109 min.
> Production: Comacico, Mondex Films, UFA (Paris), Laura Cinematografica, Taurus Cinematografica (Rome).
> Screenplay: Julien Duvivier, Charles Spaak.
> Adaptation: Based on the novel *The Burning Court* (1937) by John Dickson Carr.
> Photography: Roger Fellous.
> Set: Will Schatz.
> Editors: Paul Cayatte, Nicole Colombier.
> Principal actors: Nadja Tiller, Jean-Claude Brialy, Claude Rich, Pierrette Pradier.

Le Diable et les dix commandements (The Devil and the Ten Commandments) (1962)
135 min.
> Production: Claude Jaeger, Robert Amon.

Screenplay: Julien Duvivier, René Barjavel.
Adaptation: René Barjavel, Pascal Jardin.
Photography: Roger Fellous.
Set: François de Lamothe.
Editor: Paul Cayatte.
Principal actors: Fernandel, Danielle Darrieux, Louis de Funès

Chair de poule (Highway Pickup) (1963)
109 min.
Production: Robert and Raymond Hakim.
Screenplay: Julien Duvivier, René Barjavel.
Adaptation: Based on the novel *Tirez sur la chevillette/ Come Easy, Go Easy* (1960) by James Hadley Chase.
Photography: Léonce-Henri Burel.
Set: François de Lamothe.
Editor: Suzanne de Troye.
Principal actors: Robert Hossein, Catherine Rouvel, Jean Sorel, Georges Wilson.

Diaboliquement vôtre (Diabolically Yours) (1967)
96 min.
Production: Raymond Danon for Les Films Copernic, Comacico, Lira Films, SNC (Paris), Igor Films (Rome), Pegaso (Milan, Rome), R. Eichberg Film (Munich).
Screenplay: Julien Duvivier.
Adaptation: Based on the novel *Manie de la persécution* (1962) by Louis Thomas.
Photography: Henri Decaë.
Set: Léon Barsacq.
Editor: Paul Cayatte.
Principal actors: Alain Delon, Santa Berger, Sergio Fantoni, Peter Mosbacher.

Select bibliography

Bonnefille, Eric (2002), *Julien Duvivier: Le Mal aimant du cinéma français*, 2 volumes (vol. 1: *1896–1940*; vol. 2: *1940–1967*), Paris, Harmattan.

A comprehensive film-by-film account of Duvivier's career that offers rich historical and cultural contextualisation. Volume 1 starts with *Haceldama* and ends with *Untel père et fils*; Volume 2 runs from *Lydia* to *Diaboliquement vôtre*.

Borger, Lenny (1998), 'Genius Is Just a Word', *Sight and Sound*, September, pp. 28–31.

One of the few English-language overviews of Duvivier's career; it briefly touches on several of his themes and approaches.

Chirat, Raymond (1968), *Julien Duvivier*, Lyon, Premier Plan.

This two-part study offers a chronological appraisal of Duvivier's career, then close readings of each of his films.

Desrichard, Yves (2001), *Julien Duvivier: Cinquante ans de noirs destins*, Paris, BiFi/Durante.

An excellent study of Duvivier's films that also contains extensive reviews of his films and samples of his writings on cinema.

Leprohon, Pierre (1968), *Julien Duvivier*, Paris, Avant-Scène/Collection Anthologie du Cinéma.

A clear, early study. The first in-depth analysis of Duvivier's films, published a year after his death.

Niogret, Hubert (2010), *Julien Duvivier: 50 ans de cinéma*, Paris, Bazaar and Co.

A marvellous synthesis of film analysis, biography, thematic consistency, and interviews with Duvivier's many colleagues.

Vincendeau, Ginette (1998), *Pépé le Moko*, London, BFI.

To date, the only book-length monograph in English on Duvivier, wonderfully analysing his most famous film. A lively, comprehensive account of the film's multiple influences, both historical and visual.

Index

Abel, Richard 35, 42, 46, 66
Allo Berlin? Ici Paris! (1932) 60–2, 68, 97, 205
Andrew, Dudley 1, 3, 82, 87
Anna Karenina (1948) 14, 19–20, 151–4, 157, 159, 173, 176, 195, 206, 227
anti-Semitism 4, 56–7, 146
Antoine, André 10–11, 18, 28, 33, 43, 66
arrival of sound in French cinema 34, 51, 54–5, 61
Au bonheur des dames (1930) 20–2, 26, 40, 42–6, 66, 145, 161, 194, 200n.21, 228
Au royaume des cieux (1949) 19, 21, 147, 155–6, 160, 186, 228
authorship 5, 15–18, 86, 114, 124, 137, 151, 171, 177, 183, 186–7, 189, 197, 223, 226–8

Bandera, La (1935) 6, 19, 22, 42, 75, 79–82, 84, 86, 91, 97, 130–2, 134, 191, 228
Bardot, Brigitte 9, 13–14, 187, 197–200, 203, 205, 222, 227

Barjavel, René 2, 16, 168, 190, 204–5, 208, 213–14
Baur, Harry 2, 31, 55–6, 58, 62, 67, 73–5, 87–9, 227
Bazin, André 133, 135, 138
Belle équipe, La (1936) 2, 4, 6, 13, 16, 19, 21, 23, 33, 69, 77, 79–80, 82–3, 86, 91, 95, 97, 124, 126, 145, 147, 161, 164, 170, 172, 179, 213, 215, 227–8
Bergstrom, Janet 118–19, 130–1, 135
Bessy, Maurice 1, 9, 12, 93, 117, 149, 178, 208, 225
Black Jack (1950) 21, 29, 156–9, 176, 198
Borger, Lenny 15, 26, 28, 186
Boulevard (1960) 138n.42, 186–7, 206–8, 216, 221–2, 226–7, 229
box-office figures, Duvivier's 86, 127n.26, 148, 170–1, 176, 182, 190, 197, 199, 208n.27, 221
Boyer, Charles 86, 94–5, 113n.8, 119n.19, 123–4, 127–9
Breen, Joseph 122

Burch, Noël, and Sellier, Geneviève 19, 56–7, 83, 147, 179, 204
Butler, Margaret 145, 155, 161, 175

Cahiers du cinéma 2, 8, 11–13, 151, 166, 189, 197–8, 221
Carné, Marcel 3, 10–11, 16, 36, 54, 70, 79, 92–3, 123, 132–3, 143, 145, 148–9, 155, 162, 164, 174, 189, 194, 202
Carnet de bal, Un (1937) 1, 6, 17, 19, 22–3, 86–90, 92–4, 97, 111, 118, 120, 122–3, 133–5, 143, 155, 159, 165, 173, 189–90, 202, 209
Cayatte, André 4, 172
Chair de poule (1963) 18, 187, 190, 208, 210, 213–17, 221–3, 227–8
Chambre ardente, La (1962) 21–2, 33, 75, 93, 128n.28, 158, 173, 187, 208, 210–14, 219–22, 228
Charrette fantôme, La (1939) 21, 31, 89–90, 92–4, 97, 128, 175
Chase, James Hadley 190, 192, 213, 217
Chevalier, Maurice 23, 76–8, 160
Chirat, Raymond 113, 215
Christian-Jaque 16, 45n.22, 145, 189, 194
Cinq gentlemen maudits, Les (1931) 11, 20, 58–60, 71, 84, 160, 175, 198, 220, 228
Clair, René 3, 10, 12, 26, 31, 46, 60, 77, 82, 92, 119, 128, 143, 148n.11, 149, 160, 162, 164

Classical Hollywood cinema 124, 126, 137
claustrophobia 5, 18, 20, 41, 81, 202
Clouzot, Henri-Georges 144, 162, 193, 201
Cœurs farouches (1924) 33–4
colonial cinema 59–60, 84–5
Cooke, Alistair 1, 22, 82
Credo ou la tragédie de Lourdes (1924) 33, 46–7, 49, 59, 198
Crisp, Colin 21, 54–5, 57, 70, 86, 148

Darrieux, Danielle 13–14, 187, 194, 197, 200–3, 208–9, 222, 227
David Golder (1930) 22, 29, 36, 46, 51, 55–8, 60, 68n.18, 69, 76, 82, 97, 173, 195, 205, 228
Delac, Charles 59, 62
Delon, Alain 187, 208–9, 218–19, 222, 227
Delorme, Danièle 15, 18, 177, 220, 228
Diable et les dix commandements, Le (1962) 208–9, 219
Diaboliquement vôtre (1967) 9, 22, 31, 186–7, 189, 210, 217–21
Divine croisière, La (1929) 40–1, 46
double, figure of the 32–3, 38, 57–8, 60, 62, 78, 129, 131, 147, 221
Du rififi chez les hommes (1955) 190, 214
Duvivier, Christian 66, 119, 125n.23

fantastique 23, 28, 155, 174, 208
Femme et le pantin, La (1959) 13, 158, 197–200, 204–5, 222
femme fatale 4–5, 57–8, 198, 214–15
Fernandel 2, 13, 87–9, 121, 124, 167–70, 190–4, 203, 208, 210, 213, 222, 227
Fête à Henriette, La (1952) 5, 17, 33, 78, 163–6, 169, 171–3, 176, 186
Feyder, Jacques 3, 12, 26, 34, 59, 113, 117, 119n.19
film criticism, Duvivier's 29–30, 149–51
Fin du jour, La (1939) 2, 9, 20–1, 34, 89–92, 97, 116, 161, 213, 215
Flesh and Fantasy (1943) 31, 75, 122, 127–9, 133, 135, 175, 209, 211
Frank, Nino 51, 63
Fünf verfluchten Gentlemen, Die (1931) 58

Gabin, Jean 2–3, 6, 13, 16, 20, 23, 31, 33, 68n.17, 71–2, 75, 79–86, 90, 97, 119n.19, 130–3, 149, 177–9, 181–2, 191, 196, 203, 207
garce, figure of the 19, 83, 97, 124, 147, 177, 179
gender 4, 19–20, 42, 97, 147, 153, 186–7, 191, 222, 228
Godard, Jean-Luc 3, 8, 165, 217
Golem, Le (1936) 75–6, 93, 128
Golgotha (1935) 1, 40, 72–6, 81–2, 147

Grande vie, La (1960) 11, 19, 151, 187, 200, 204–6
Great Waltz, The (1938) 1, 21, 89, 110, 114–19, 123–4, 128, 136, 138, 189, 213
Greene, Graham 1, 18, 77
group dynamics 5, 20, 77–8, 82, 91, 153, 162, 186, 196, 201–2, 213, 227–8

Haceldama ou le prix du sang (1919) 11, 21, 24, 26–30, 37, 55, 71, 73, 222, 226

Impostor, The (1944) 19–21, 31, 33, 42, 78, 113, 130–6, 176n.46, 215, 228
insolite 32, 93, 128n.28, 129

Jacquet, Gaston 31–2, 47, 62
Jeanson, Henri 2, 14, 16–17, 55, 69, 75, 81, 84–7, 149, 155, 160, 163–5, 194, 197, 200n.21, 201–2, 208, 225
Jouvet, Louis 15, 87–8, 90, 92–4

Korda, Alexander 120, 151–2, 154–5
Krauss, Jacques 55, 84–5
Kristeva, Julia 180

L'Abbé Constantin (1925) 34
L'Affaire Maurizius (1954) 58n.5, 144, 171–6, 186, 195, 210
L'Agonie de Jérusalem (1927) 46–8, 173
L'Homme à l'Hispano (1926) 35–7, 42, 226

L'Homme à l'imperméable (1957) 37, 124, 186, 190–5, 213, 222
L'Homme du jour (1937) 23, 37, 76–9, 161
L'Œuvre immortelle (1924) 34
L'Ouragan sur la montagne (1922) 29, 31, 38, 210
Le Vigan, Robert 14, 58, 72–4, 80, 94, 132
Léaud, Jean-Pierre 68, 138n.42, 187, 204, 206–7, 229
Leenhardt, Roger 12–13, 16–17, 188
Leigh, Vivien 9, 151–2, 154
Leprohon, Pierre 8, 13, 21, 51, 137, 159, 197, 200
Logis de l'horreur, Le (1922), 29n.5
Lydia (1941) 19, 113, 119–22, 134–5, 143, 202
Lynen, Robert 67–8

Machine à refaire la vie, La (1924) 34–5
Maman Colibri (1929) 41–2, 51, 58, 84, 121, 199, 220
Maria Chapdelaine (1934) 19, 71–2, 79, 97
Mariage de Mademoiselle Beulemans, Le (1927) 10, 20, 37–8, 59
Marianne de ma jeunesse (1955) 12, 23, 93, 173–6, 210–11, 214
Marianne, meine Jugendliebe (1955) 175–6
Marie-Octobre (1959) 17, 20, 33, 187, 200–4, 222, 227
Mayer, Louis B. 87, 111, 113

Melville, Jean-Pierre 14, 94n.39, 162, 207, 219–20
Metro-Goldwyn-Mayer (MGM) 87, 111–18, 128, 226
misogyny 4, 19, 57, 66, 83, 97, 147, 180
Mitchell, Thomas 127
Mystère de la Tour Eiffel, Le (1927) 38–9

noir 1, 5, 8, 13, 19, 26, 33, 58, 63, 84, 97, 124, 129, 146, 149–50, 163, 166, 174, 178, 187, 190–95, 198, 208, 214–15, 217, 222, 228

Ophüls, Max 138, 176

Panique (1946) 3, 13, 17, 22, 40, 74, 77, 96, 143–50, 156, 160, 162, 173, 176–7, 178n.50, 181, 186, 188, 191, 196, 199, 211, 215, 226–8
Paquebot Tenacity, Le (1934) 20, 29, 54, 69–73, 77, 97, 207, 226
paroxysm / paroxystic display 18, 88, 91, 93, 180, 207, 213
patriarchy 83, 180–2, 199, 207
Pépé le Moko (1937) 1–2, 6, 8, 15, 17–21, 23, 29, 42, 60, 71, 75, 77, 79–81, 84–6, 97, 113n.8, 115, 125, 131–2, 150, 154, 157–8, 165, 178, 188n.3, 191, 194, 220, 228
Petit monde de Don Camillo, Le (1952) 162n.28, 164, 167–71, 189, 229

Petit roi, Le (1933) 68, 72
Petrie, Graham 137–8
Philipe, Gérard 194–7, 203, 222
poetic realism 1, 39, 55, 63, 69–70, 79–80, 84, 92, 97, 115, 145, 148–50, 173, 227–8
Poil de carotte (1925) 65–7, 173, 228
Poil de carotte (1932) 1, 20, 65, 67–8, 96–7, 134, 173, 196, 206–7, 228
Popular Front 79–80, 82, 90, 126, 179
Positif 2, 189
Pot-Bouille (1957) 1, 6, 21, 31, 187, 194–7, 222, 227–8

Raimu 87, 94–5
Reflet de Claude Mercœur, Le (1923) 31–3, 38, 47, 51, 78, 93, 211
Reggiani, Serge 155, 200, 204
Réincarnation de Serge Renaudier, La (1920), 29n.5
religion 44, 46–50, 171
Renoir, Jean 1, 3–4, 11, 13–14, 26, 43, 54, 62, 64, 67, 79, 82, 92, 119, 127, 129, 132, 135, 143, 157, 186, 225
Retour de Don Camillo, Le (1953) 170–1
Rivette, Jacques 3, 9, 189
Robeson, Paul 125–6
Robinson, Edward G. 123, 125, 127, 129
Rohdie, Sam 5, 21

Roquevillard, Les (1922) 29–31
Ross, Kristin 193

Sarris, Andrew 228
Schatz, Thomas 118
Selznick, David O. 117
Simenon, Georges 55, 62–3, 65, 146
Simon, Michel 9, 19–20, 90, 144, 149–50, 208–9
Société Cinématographique des Auteurs et Gens de Lettres (SCAGL) 10, 66
song 20, 23, 39–40, 61–2, 64–5, 70, 78, 82, 115, 160
Sous le ciel de Paris (1951) 12, 21, 94, 144, 159–63, 166, 169, 173, 176, 186, 191, 209
Spaak, Charles 2, 13, 16–17, 55, 80, 83, 91, 144, 146, 148, 157, 159, 210–13
stardom 39, 77, 79, 97, 120, 168, 176, 183, 194–8, 206, 218–19, 222, 227
Strauss II, Johann 114–16, 212–13

Tales of Manhattan (1942) 1, 77–8, 122–30, 134–5, 147, 159, 171, 228
Tête d'un homme, La (1932) 23, 60, 62–5, 67–9, 72, 81–2, 97, 161, 172, 178, 181, 191, 211, 228
Touchez pas au grisbi (1954) 178, 190, 215
Tourbillon de Paris, Le (1928) 39–40, 42, 46, 51, 77, 121, 124, 228

tradition of quality 187, 189, 194, 222–3
Truffaut, François 11–12, 183, 187–8, 197, 206, 222–3

Untel père et fils (1945) 1, 94–6, 161, 176n.46

Vandal, Marcel 59, 62
Vanel, Charles 82, 172–3
Vie miraculeuse de Thérèse Martin, La (1929) 46, 48–50

Vincendeau, Ginette 15, 54, 79–80, 84–5, 131–2, 198
Voici le temps des assassins (1956) 1, 11, 18–19, 23, 58, 144, 148, 156, 173–4, 176–83, 186–8, 190, 199, 207, 209, 211, 214–15, 220, 228

Wyler, William 2, 136

Zola, Emile 10, 13, 26–7, 42–5, 194–7

EU authorised representative for GPSR:
Easy Access System Europe, Mustamäe tee 50,
10621 Tallinn, Estonia
gpsr.requests@easproject.com

www.ingramcontent.com/pod-product-compliance
Lightning Source LLC
Chambersburg PA
CBHW050136240426
43673CB00043B/1691